BERLITZ

SWEDISH

for travellers

By the staff of Berlitz Guides

How best to use this phrase book

● We suggest that you start with the **Guide to pronunciation** (pp. 6–9), then go on to **Some basic expressions** (pp. 10–15). This gives you not only a minimum vocabulary, but also helps you get used to pronouncing the language. The phonetic transcription throughout the book enables you to pronounce every word correctly.

● Consult the **Contents** pages (3–5) for the section you need. In each chapter you'll find travel facts, hints and useful information. Simple phrases are followed by a list of words applicable to the situation.

● Separate, detailed contents lists are included at the beginning of the extensive **Eating out** and **Shopping guide** sections (Menus, p. 39, Shops and services, p. 97).

● If you want to find out how to say something in Swedish, your fastest look-up is via the **Dictionary** section (pp. 164–189). This not only gives you the word, but is also cross-referenced to its use in a phrase on a specific page.

● If you wish to learn more about constructing sentences, check the **Basic grammar** (pp. 159–163).

● Note the **colour margins** are indexed in Swedish and English to help both listener and speaker. And, in addition, there is also an **index in Swedish** for the use of your listener.

● Throughout the book, this symbol ☛ suggests phrases your listener can use to answer you. If you still can't understand, hand this phrase book to the Swedish-speaker to encourage pointing to an appropriate answer. The English translation for you is just alongside the Swedish.

Library of Congress Catalog Card No. 88-64116.

Second revised edition—2nd printing 1989
Printed in Switzerland

Contents

Travelling around 65

Sightseeing 80

Relaxing 86

Making friends 92

Shopping guide 97

Acknowledgments

We are particularly grateful to Christina Sonesson for her help in the preparation of this book, and to Dr. T.J.A. Bennett who devised the phonetic transcription.

Guide to pronunciation

You'll find the pronunciation of the Swedish letters and sounds explained below, as well as the symbols we use in the transcriptions. The imitated pronunciation should be read as if it were English, with exceptions as indicated below. It is based on Standard British pronunciation, though we have tried to take into account General American pronunciation as well. If you follow the instructions carefully you'll have no difficulty in reading our transcriptions so as to make yourself understood.

Swedish uses intonation (or more correctly "tones"), sometimes to distinguish between words. Without considerable training, a foreigner can't differentiate between the tones, much less use them correctly. Swedes don't expect foreigners to use intonation. Thus we haven't shown the tones in our transcriptions.

In the phonetic transcription of this book you will notice that some letters are placed in parentheses e.g. **mew**ker(t). In daily conversation, these letters are rarely pronounced by Swedes, although it is certainly not incorrect to do so. Syllables printed in **bold type** should be stressed. A bar over a vowel symbol (e.g., sh$\overline{ay}$f) indicates a long vowel.

Consonants

Letter	Approximate pronunciation	Symbol	Example	
b, c, d, f, h, l, m, n, p, v, w, x	as in English			
ch	at the beginning of words borrowed from French, like **sh** in **sh**ut	sh	**chef**	sh$\overline{ay}$f
g	1) before stressed **i, e, y, ä, ö,** and sometimes after **l** or **r**, like **y** in **y**et	y	**ge**	y$\overline{ay}$

	2) before **e** and **i** in many words of French origin, like **sh** in **sh**ut	sh	**geni**	sha̅y̅**nee**
	3) elsewhere, generally like **g** in **g**o	g	**gaffel**	**gah**ferl
j, dj, gj, lj, hj	at the beginning of words always like **y** in **y**et	y	**ja** **ljus**	yaa ye̅w̅ss
k	1) before stressed **i, e, y, ä, ö,** generally like **ch** in Scottish lo**ch**, but pronounced in the front of the mouth	kh	**köpa**	**khu̅r̅**pah
	2) elsewhere, like **k** in **k**it	k	**klippa**	**klip**pah
kj	like **ch** in Scottish lo**ch**, but pronounced in the front of the mouth	kh	**kjol**	kho̅o̅l
qu	like **k** in **k**it followed by **v** in **v**at	kv	**Lindquist**	**lin(d)**kvist
r	slightly rolled near the front of the mouth	r	**ryka**	**re̅w̅**kah
s	1) in the ending **-sion** like **sh** in **sh**ut	sh	**mission**	mi**sho̅o̅n**
	2) elsewhere, like **s** in **s**o	s/ss	**ses**	sa̅y̅ss
	3) the groups **sch, skj, sj, stj** are pronounced like **sh** in **sh**ut	sh	**schema**	**sha̅y̅**mah
sk	1) before stressed **e, i, y, ä, ö,** like **sh** in **sh**ut	sh	**skänk**	shehnk
	2) elsewhere, like **sk** in **sk**ip	sk	**skola**	**sko̅o̅**la
t	1) in the ending **-tion** like **sh** in **sh**ut or like **ch** in **ch**at	sh tsh	**station** **nation**	stah**sho̅o̅n** nah**tsho̅o̅n**
	2) elsewhere, like **t** in **t**op	t	**tid**	teed
tj	like **ch** in Scottish lo**ch**, but pronounced in the front of the mouth; sometimes with a **t**-sound at the beginning	kh	**tjäna**	**khai**nah
z	like **s** in **s**o	s	**zenit**	**sa̅y̅**nit

N.B. The consonants **d, l, n, s, t,** if preceded by **r,** are generally pronounced with the tip of the tongue turned up well behind the front teeth. The **r** then ceases to be pronounced. We indicate this pronunciation of **d, l, n, s** or **t** by printing a small **r** above the line, e.g. *svart* is pronounced svah[r]t.

Vowels

A vowel is generally long in stressed syllables when it's the final letter or followed by only one consonant. If followed by two or more consonants or in unstressed syllables, the vowel is generally short.

a	1) when long, like **a** in car	aa	**dag**	daa(g)
	2) when short, between **a** in cat and **u** in cut	ah	**tack**	tahk
e	1) when long, like **ay** in **say**, but a *pure* vowel, not a diphthong	a̅y̅	**sen**	sa̅y̅n
	2) when followed by **r**, like **a** in man; long or short	æ̅	**erfara**	**æ̅r**faarah
	3) when short, like **e** in get	eh	**beck**	behk
	4) when unstressed, like **a** in about	er*	**betala**	ber**taa**lah
ej	like **a** in mate	ay	**nej**	nay
i	1) when long, like **ee** in bee	ee	**vit**	veet
	2) when short, between **ee** in meet and **i** in hit	i	**hinna**	**hi**nnah
	3) in a few words, e.g. in the personal pronoun **mig,** like **a** in mate	ay	**mig**	may
o	1) when long, often like **oo** in **soon**, but with the lips more tightly rounded, and with a puff of breath at the end	o̅o̅	**sko**	sko̅o̅
	2) the same sound can be short	oo	**solid**	soo**leed**
	3) when long, sometimes like **aw** in r**aw**, but with the tongue a little higher in the mouth and the lips closely rounded	aw	**son**	sawn
	4) when short, sometimes like **o** in hot	o	**korrekt**	ko**rrehkt**
u	1) when long, like Swedish **y**, but with the tongue a little lower in the mouth, and with a puff of breath at the end; you'll find it very hard to distinguish from Swedish **y**, so we'll use the same symbol for both	e̅w̅	**hus**	he̅w̅ss

* The **r** should not be pronounced when reading this transcription.

	2) when short, a little more like the **u** of p**u**t; a very difficult sound	ew	**full**	fewl
y	like German **ü** in **ü**ber, or French **u** in **u**ne; round your lips and try to say **ee** as in b**ee**; long or short	$\overline{\text{ew}}$ ew	**vy** **syster**	v$\overline{\text{ew}}$ **sew**sterr
å	1) when long, like **aw** in r**aw**, but with the tongue a little higher in the mouth and the lips closely rounded	aw	**gå**	gaw
	2) when short, like **o** in h**o**t	o	**sång**	song
ä	1) when followed by **r**, like **a** in m**a**n, long or short	$\overline{\text{æ}}$ æ	**ära** **värka**	$\overline{\text{æ}}$rah **vær**kah
	2) elsewhere, like **e** in g**e**t; long or short	ai eh	**läsa** **bäst**	**lai**ssah behst
ö	like **ur** in f**ur**, but with the lips rounded and without any **r**-sound; long or short; when followed by **r**, it is pronounced with the mouth a little more open	$\overline{\text{ur}}$ ur	**röd** **köld** **öra**	r$\overline{\text{ur}}$d khurld $\overline{\text{ur}}$rah

Pronunciation of the Swedish alphabet

A	aa	**H**	haw	**O**	$\overline{\text{oo}}$	**V**	v$\overline{\text{ay}}$
B	b$\overline{\text{ay}}$	**I**	ee	**P**	p$\overline{\text{ay}}$	**X**	ehkss
C	s$\overline{\text{ay}}$	**J**	y	**Q**	k$\overline{\text{ew}}$	**Y**	$\overline{\text{ew}}$
D	d$\overline{\text{ay}}$	**K**	kaw	**R**	ær	**Z**	s$\overline{\text{æ}}$tah
E	$\overline{\text{ay}}$	**L**	ehl	**S**	ehss	**Å**	aw
F	ehf	**M**	ehm	**T**	t$\overline{\text{ay}}$	**Ä**	$\overline{\text{æ}}$
G	g$\overline{\text{ay}}$	**N**	ehn	**U**	$\overline{\text{ew}}$	**Ö**	$\overline{\text{ur}}$

The letter **w** occurs only in names, foreign words and their derivatives, as well as in certain abbreviations.

Some basic expressions

Yes.	**Ja.**	yaa
No.	**Nej.**	nay
Please.	**Var snäll och .../ ..., tack.**	vaar snehl ok/ ... tahk
Thank you.	**Tack.**	tahk
Thank you very much.	**Tack så mycket.**	tahk saw **mew**ker(t)
That's all right/ You're welcome.	**Ingen orsak.**	**ing**ern ooʳsaak

Greetings *Hälsningsfraser*

Generally people say "Goddag" or "Hej" and shake hands when introduced. The terms Mr., Mrs. and Miss (*herr*—hehr, *fru*—frew, *fröken*—**frur**kern) are very rarely used. People are introduced by their full name. *Hej* (hay) is an informal expression you'll hear all the time, similar to "Hallo" ("Hi!"). When speaking to someone use *ni,* the polite form for "you", until you have been introduced. From then on you can use the more informal *du.* Younger people always call each other *du.*

Good morning.	**God morgon.**	goo(d) **mor**ron
Good afternoon.	**God middag.**	goo(d) **mid**dah(g)
Good evening.	**God afton.**	goo(d) **ahf**ton
Good night.	**God natt.**	goo(d) naht
Goodbye.	**Adjö.**	ahyur
See you later.	**Vi ses.**	vee sayss
How do you do? (Pleased to meet you.)	**Goddag.**	**god**daa(g)
How are you?	**Hur mår ni/du?**	hewr mawr nee/dew
Very well, thanks.	**Bara bra, tack.**	**baa**rah braa tahk
And you?	**Och ni/du?**	ok nee/dew

How's life?	**Hur står det till?**	hewr stawr day(t) til
Fine.	**Bra, tack.**	braa tahk
I beg your pardon?	**Förlåt?**	fur^{r}**lawt**
Excuse me. (May I get past?)	**Förlåt/Ursäkta.**	fur^{r}**lawt**/**ew**^{r}sehktah
Sorry!	**Förlåt!**	fur^{r}**lawt**

Questions *Frågor*

Where?	**Var?**	vaar
How?	**Hur?**	hewr
When?	**När?**	nær
What?	**Vad?**	vaad
Why?	**Varför?**	**vahr**furr
Who?	**Vem?**	vehm
Which?	**Vilken?**	**vil**kern
Where is ...?	**Var är/Var finns/ Var ligger ...?**	vaar ær/vaar finss/ vaar **lig**gerr
Where are ...?	**Var är/Var finns/ Var ligger ...?**	vaar ær/vaar finss/ vaar **lig**gerr
Where can I find ...?	**Var hittar jag ...?**	vaar **hit**tahr yaa(g)
Where can I get ...?	**Var kan jag få tag på ...?**	vaar kahn yaa(g) faw taag paw
How far?	**Hur långt?**	hewr longt
How long?	**Hur länge?**	hewr **lehng**er
How much?	**Hur mycket?**	hewr **mew**ker(t)
How many?	**Hur många?**	hewr **mong**ah
How much does this cost?	**Hur mycket kostar det här?**	hewr **mew**ker(t) **kos**tahr day(t) hær
When does ... open/ close?	**När öppnar/ stänger ...?**	nær **urp**nahr/ **stehng**err
What do you call this/that in Swedish?	**Vad heter det här/ det där på svenska?**	vaa(d) **hay**terr day(t) hær/ day(t) dær paw **svehn**skah
What does this/that mean?	**Vad betyder det här/ det där?**	vaa(d) ber**tew**derr day(t) hær/day(t) dær

Do you speak ...? *Talar ni ...?*

Do you speak English?	**Talar ni engelska?**	**taa**lahr nee **ehng**erlskah
Does anyone here speak English?	**Finns det någon här som talar engelska?**	finss da̅y̅(t) **naw**gon hæ̅r som **taa**lahr **ehng**erlskah
I don't speak (much) Swedish.	**Jag talar inte (så bra) svenska.**	yaa(g) **taa**lahr **in**ter (saw braa) **svehn**skah
Could you speak more slowly?	**Kan ni tala lite långsammare?**	kahn nee **taa**lah **li**ter **long**sahmahrer
Could you repeat that?	**Kan ni upprepa det där?**	kahn nee **ewp**ra̅y̅pah da̅y̅(t) dæ̅r
Could you spell it?	**Kan ni bokstavera det?**	kahn nee bookstah**va̅y̅**rah da̅y̅(t)
Could you write it down please?	**Skulle ni kunna skriva det?**	**skew**ler nee **kew**nah **skree**vah da̅y̅(t)
Can you translate this for me/us?	**Kan ni översätta det här för mig/oss?**	kahn nee **u̅r̅**ver^{r}sehtah da̅y̅(t) hæ̅r fu̅r̅r may/oss
Could you point to the ... in the book?	**Kan ni peka på ... i boken?**	kahn nee **pa̅y̅**kah paw ... ee **bo̅o̅**kern
word	**ordet***	**o̅o̅**^{r}dert
phrase	**uttrycket**	**e̅w̅**trewkert
sentence	**meningen**	**ma̅y̅**ningern
Just a moment.	**Ett ögonblick.**	eht **u̅r̅**gonblik
I'll see if I can find it in this book.	**Jag skall se om jag kan hitta det i den här boken.**	yaa(g) skah(l) sa̅y̅ om yaa(g) kahn **hi**ttah da̅y̅(t) ee dehn hæ̅r **bo̅o̅**kern
I understand.	**Jag förstår.**	yaa(g) fur^{r}**stawr**
I don't understand.	**Jag förstår inte.**	yaa(g) fur^{r}**stawr in**ter
Do you understand?	**Förstår ni?**	fur^{r}**stawr** nee

Can/May ...? *Kan ...?*

Can I have ...?	**Kan jag få ...?**	kahn yaa(g) faw
Can we have ...?	**Kan vi få ...?**	kahn vee faw
Can you show me ...?	**Kan ni visa mig ...?**	kahn nee **vee**ssah may

* For information on the definite article see grammar section page 159

I can't.	**Jag kan inte.**	yaa(g) kahn **in**ter
Can you tell me ...?	**Kan ni säga mig ...?**	kahn nee **seh**yah may
Can you help me?	**Kan ni hjälpa mig?**	kahn nee **yehl**pah may
Can I help you?	**Kan jag hjälpa er?**	kahn yaa(g) **yehl**pah a̅y̅r
Can you direct me to ...?	**Kan ni visa mig vägen till ...?**	kahn nee **vee**ssah may **vai**gern til

What do you want? *Vad önskar ni?*

I'd like to ...	**Jag skulle vilja/ Jag vill ...**	yaa(g) **skew**ler **vil**yah/ yaa(g) vil
We'd like to ...	**Vi skulle vilja/ Vi vill ...**	vee **skew**ler **vil**yah
I'd like a ...	**Jag skulle vilja ha en/ett ...**	yaa(g) **skew**ler **vil**yah haa ehn/eht
Could you bring/give me ...?	**Kan ni ge mig ...?**	kahn nee ya̅y̅ may
Could you show me ...?	**Kan ni visa mig ...?**	kahn nee **vee**ssah may
I'm looking for ...	**Jag letar efter ...**	yaa(g) **la̅y̅**tahr **ehf**terr
I'm hungry.	**Jag är hungrig.**	yaa(g) æ̅r **hewn**gri(g)
I'm thirsty.	**Jag är törstig.**	yaa(g) æ̅r **turr**sti(g)
I'm tired.	**Jag är trött.**	yaa(g) æ̅r trurt
I'm lost.	**Jag hittar inte.**	yaa(g) **hit**tahr **in**ter
It's important.	**Det är viktigt.**	day(t) æ̅r **vik**tit
It's urgent.	**Det är brådskande.**	day(t) æ̅r **bro**skahnder

It is/There is ... *Det är/Det finns ...*

It is ...	**Det är ...**	da̅y̅(t) æ̅r
Is it ...?	**Är det ...?**	æ̅r da̅y̅(t)
It isn't ...	**Det är inte ...**	da̅y̅(t) æ̅r **in**ter
Here it is.	**Här är det.**	hæ̅r æ̅r da̅y̅(t)
Here they are.	**Här är de.**	hæ̅r æ̅r dom
There it is.	**Där är det.**	dæ̅r æ̅r da̅y̅(t)

There they are.	**Där är de.**	dæ̅r æ̅r dom
There is/There are ...	**Det finns ...**	da̅y̅(t) finss
Is there/Are there ...?	**Finns det ...?**	finss da̅y̅(t)
There isn't/aren't ...	**Det finns inte ...**	da̅y̅(t) finss **in**ter
There isn't/aren't any.	**Det finns ingen/ inga.**	da̅y̅(t) finss **in**gern/ **in**gah

It's ... *Den är ...*

big/small	**stor/liten***	sto̅o̅r/**lee**tern
quick/slow	**snabb/långsam**	snahb/**long**sahm
hot/cold	**varm/kall**	vahrm/kahl
full/empty	**full/tom**	fewl/toom
easy/difficult	**lätt, enkel/svår**	leht **ehn**kerl/svawr
heavy/light	**tung/lätt**	tewng/leht
open/shut	**öppen/stängd**	**ur**pern/stehngd
right/wrong	**rätt/fel**	reht/fa̅y̅l
old/new	**gammal/ny**	**gah**mahl/ne̅w̅
old/young	**gammal/ung**	**gah**mahl/ewng
next/last	**nästa/sista**	**neh**stah/**sis**tah
beautiful/ugly	**vacker/ful**	**vah**kerr/fe̅w̅l
free (vacant)/ occupied	**ledig/upptagen**	**la̅y̅**di(g)/**ewp**taagern
good/bad	**bra/dålig**	braa/**daw**li(g)
better/worse	**bättre/sämre**	**beh**trer/**sehm**rer
early/late	**tidig/sen**	**tee**di(g)/sa̅y̅n
cheap/expensive	**billig/dyr**	**bil**li(g)/de̅w̅r
near/far	**nära/långt (bort)**	**næ̅**rah/longt (bo^{r}t)
here/there	**här/där**	hæ̅r/dæ̅r

Quantities *Kvantitet*

a little/a lot	**lite/mycket**	**lee**ter/**mew**ker(t)
few/a few	**få/några**	faw/**naw**grah
much/many	**mycket/många**	**mew**ker(t)/**mon**gah
more/less	**mer/mindre**	ma̅y̅r/**min**drer
more than/less than	**mer än/mindre än**	ma̅y̅r ehn/**min**drer ehn

* For neuter and plural forms, see grammar section page 160 (adjectives).

enough/too much	**tillräckligt/för mycket**	**til**rehkli(g)t/fu̅r̅r **mew**ker(t)
some/any	**några/inga**	**naw**grah/**ing**ah

A few more useful words *Några fler användbara ord*

at	**vid**	veed
on	**på**	paw
in	**i**	ee
to	**till**	til
after	**efter**	**ehf**terr
before (time)	**innan, före**	innahn, **fu̅r̅**rer
before (place)	**framför**	**frahm**furr
for	**för**	fu̅r̅r
from	**från**	frawn
with	**med**	ma̅y̅d
without	**utan**	**e̅w̅**tahn
through	**genom**	**ya̅y̅**nom
towards	**mot**	mo̅o̅t
until	**till**	til
during	**under**	**ewn**derr
next to	**bredvid**	bra̅y̅(d)**veed**
behind	**bakom**	**baa**kom
between	**mellan**	**meh**lahn
since	**sedan**	sehn
above	**ovanför**	**aw**vahnfu̅r̅r
below	**nedanför**	**na̅y̅**dahnfu̅r̅r
under	**under**	**ewn**derr
inside	**inne**	**in**ner
outside	**ute**	**e̅w̅**ter
up/upstairs	**upp/där uppe**	ewp/dær **ew**per
down/downstairs	**ner/där nere**	na̅y̅r/dær **na̅y̅**rer
and	**och**	ok
or	**eller**	**eh**lerr
not	**inte**	**in**ter
never	**aldrig**	**ahl**drig
nothing	**ingenting, inget**	**ing**ernting, **ing**ert
none	**ingen**	**ing**ern
very	**mycket**	**mew**ker(t)
too (also)	**också**	**ok**so
yet	**än**	ehn
soon	**snart**	snaa^{r}t
now	**nu**	ne̅w̅
then	**då, sedan**	daw, sehn
perhaps	**kanske**	**kahn**sher
only	**bara**	**baa**rah

Arrival

Passport control *Passkontroll*

Here's my passport.	**Här är mitt pass.**	hæ̅r æ̅r mit pahss
I'll be staying ...	**Jag tänker stanna ...**	yaa(g) **tehn**kerr **stah**nah
a few days	**några dagar**	**naw**grah **daa**(gah)r
a week	**en vecka**	ehn **veh**kah
a month	**en månad**	ehn **maw**nahd
I don't know yet.	**Jag vet inte än.**	yaa(g) va̅y̅t **in**ter ehn
I'm here on holiday.	**Jag är här på semester.**	yaa(g) æ̅r hæ̅r paw seh**mehs**terr
I'm here on business.	**Jag är här i affärer.**	yaa(g) æ̅r hæ̅r ee ah**fæ̅**rerr
I'm just passing through.	**Jag är bara på genomresa.**	yaa(g) æ̅r **baa**rah paw **ya̅y̅**nomra̅y̅ssah

If things become difficult:

I'm sorry, I don't understand.	**Förlåt, jag förstår inte.**	fur^{r}**lawt**, yaa(g) fur^{r}**stawr** **in**ter
Does anyone here speak English?	**Finns det någon här som talar engelska?**	finss da̅y̅(t) **naw**gon hæ̅r som **taa**lahr **ehng**erlskah

TULL
CUSTOMS

After collecting your baggage at the airport (*flygplatsen*—**fle̅w̅g**plahtsern) you have a choice: use the green exit if you have nothing to declare, or leave via the red exit if you have items to declare.

varor att förtulla
goods to declare

inget att förtulla
nothing to declare

The chart below shows you what you can bring in duty free (the allowances in parentheses are for non-European residents).*

 Cigarettes		 Cigars		 Tobacco	 Spirits		 Wine
200 (400)	or	50 (100)	or	250 g. (500 g.)	1 l. (1 l.)	and	1 l. (1 l.)

I have nothing to declare.	**Jag har inget att förtulla.**	yaa(g) haar **in**gert aht fur**ʳtew**lah
I have ...	**Jag har ...**	yaa(g) haar
a carton of cigarettes	**en limpa cigarretter**	ehn **lim**pah siggah**reh**terr
a bottle of whisky	**en flaska whisky**	ehn **flah**skah **wis**ki
It's for my personal use.	**Det är för mitt personliga bruk.**	da̅y̅(t) æ̅r fu̅r̅r mit pæʳ**sho̅o̅n**liggah bre̅w̅k
It's a gift.	**Det är en present.**	da̅y̅(t) æ̅r ehn preh**sehnt**

Passet, tack.	Your passport, please.
Har ni något att förtulla?	Do you have anything to declare?
Var snäll och öppna den här bagen.	Please open this bag.
Ni måste betala tull för det här.	You'll have to pay duty on this.
Har ni något mer bagage?	Do you have any more luggage?

* All allowances are subject to change.

Baggage—Porter *Bagage - Bärare*

In principle porters are not available at the airports, though if necessary you can book one in advance when you buy your plane ticket. But you'll always find luggage trolleys.

Please take this luggage.	**Var snäll och ta det här bagaget.**	vaar snehl ok taa da̅y̅(t) hær bah**gaa**shert
That's my suitcase/ travelling bag.	**Det där är min väska/bag.**	da̅y̅(t) dær ær min **veh**skah/"bag"
That's mine.	**Det där är mitt.**	da̅y̅(t) dær ær mit
Please take this to the ...	**Var snäll och ta det här till ...**	vaar snehl ok taa da̅y̅(t) hær til
bus	**bussen**	**bew**ssern
luggage lockers	**förvaringsboxarna**	furr**vaa**ringsboksahʳnah
taxi	**taxin**	**tah**ksin
How much is that?	**Vad kostar det?**	vaa(d) **kos**tahr da̅y̅(t)
There's one suit-case missing.	**Det fattas en väska.**	da̅y̅(t) **fah**tahss ehn **veh**skah
Where are the luggage trolleys (carts)?	**Var finns bagage-kärrorna?**	vaar finss bah**gaash**-khæroʳnah

Changing money *Växla pengar*

Where's the currency exchange office?	**Var ligger växel-kontoret?**	vaar **li**ggerr **veh**kserl-kont**o̅o̅**rert
Can you change these traveller's cheques (checks)?	**Kan ni lösa in de här resecheckerna?**	kahn nee **lu̅r̅**ssah in dom hær **ra̅y̅**sserkhehkeʳnah
I'd like to change some ...	**Jag skulle vilja växla några ...**	yaa(g) **skew**ler **vil**yah **veh**kslah **naw**grah
dollars	**dollar**	**do**llahr
pounds	**pund**	pewnd
Can you change this into Swedish crowns?	**Kan ni växla det här till svenska kronor?**	kahn nee **vehks**lah da̅y̅(t) hær til **svehn**skah **kro̅o̅**noor
What's the exchange rate?	**Vilken är växelkursen?**	**vil**kern ær **veh**kserlkewʳsern

BANK—CURRENCY, see page 129

Where ...? *Var ...?*

Where is the ...?	**Var är ...?**	vaar ær
booking office	**biljettkassan**	bil**yeht**kahssahn
duty-free shop	**tax-free-shopen**	**tahks**-free-shopern
newsstand	**tidningskiosken**	**tee(d)**ningskhioskern
restaurant	**restaurangen**	rehstor**rahng**ern
Where can I hire a car?	**Var kan jag hyra en bil?**	vaar kahn yaa(g) **hew**rah ehn beel
Where can I get a taxi?	**Var kan jag få tag på en taxi?**	vaar kahn yaa(g) faw taag paw ehn **tahk**si
How do I get to ...?	**Hur kommer jag till ...?**	hewr **kom**merr yaa(g) til
Is there a bus into town?	**Finns det någon buss in till stan?**	finss day(t) **naw**gon bewss in til staan

Hotel reservation *Hotellreservation*

Do you have a hotel guide?	**Har ni någon hotellguide?**	haar nee **naw**gon hotehl"guide"
Could you reserve a room for me?	**Kan ni beställa ett rum åt mig?**	kahn nee ber**steh**lah eht rewm awt may
in the centre	**i centrum**	ee **sehn**trewm
near the airport	**nära flygplatsen**	**næ**rah **flewg**plahtsern
near the railway station	**nära järnvägs-stationen**	**næ**rah **yæ**rnvaigs-stahshoonern
a single room	**ett enkelrum**	eht **ehn**kerlrewm
a double room	**ett dubbelrum**	eht **dew**berlrewm
not too expensive	**inte för dyrt**	inter furr dewrt
I'll be staying from ... to ...	**Jag tänker stanna från ... till ...**	jaa(g) **tehn**kerr stahna frawn ... til
Where is the hotel?	**Var ligger hotellet?**	vaar **lig**gerr ho**teh**lert
Can you recommend a guest house?	**Kan ni rekommendera något pensionat?**	kahn nee rehkommern**day**-rah **naw**got pahnshoo**naat**
Are there any flats (apartments) vacant?	**Finns det några lediga våningar?**	finss day(t) **naw**grah **lay**diggah **vaw**ningahr
Do you have a street map?	**Har ni någon karta över stan?**	haar nee **naw**gon **kaa**rtah **ur**verr staan

HOTEL/ACCOMMODATION, see page 22

Car hire (rental) *Biluthyrning*

To hire a car you must produce a valid driving licence, that you have held for at least one year, and your passport. Some firms set a minimum age of 21, others 25 depending on engine size. Most companies require a deposit, but this is waived if you present an accepted credit card.

I'd like to hire (rent) a car.	**Jag skulle vilja hyra en bil.**	yaa(g) **skew**ler **vil**yah **h$\overline{ew}$**rah ehn beel
small	**liten**	**lee**tern
medium-sized	**mellanstor**	**meh**lahnst$\overline{oo}$r
large	**stor**	st$\overline{oo}$r
automatic	**med automatlåda**	m$\overline{ay}$d aa(ew)too**maat**-lawdah
I'd like it for ...	**Jag vill ha den ...**	yaa(g) vil haa dehn
a day	**en dag**	ehn daa(g)
a week	**en vecka**	ehn **veh**kah
Are there any week-end arrangements?	**Har ni några speciella weekend-priser?**	haar nee **naw**grah spehssi**eh**lah "weekend"-**pree**sserr
Do you have any special rates?	**Har ni några specialpriser?**	haar nee **naw**grah spehssi**yaal**preesserr
What's the charge ...?	**Vad kostar det ...?**	vaad **kos**tahr d$\overline{ay}$(t)
per day	**per dag**	p$\overline{æ}$r daa(g)
per week	**per vecka**	p$\overline{æ}$r **veh**kah
Is mileage included?	**Är kilometer-kostnaden inräknad?**	$\overline{æ}$r khillom**m$\overline{ay}$terr**-kostnahdern **in**raiknahd
What's the charge per kilometre?	**Vad är kilometer-kostnaden?**	vaad $\overline{æ}$r khillom**m$\overline{ay}$**terr-**kost**nahdern
I'd like to leave the car in ...	**Jag vill lämna bilen i ...**	yaa(g) vil **lehm**nah **bee**lern ee
I'd like full insurance.	**Jag vill ha helförsäkring.**	yaa(g) vil haa **h$\overline{ay}$l**fur^{r}saikring
How much is the deposit?	**Hur stor är depo-neringsavgiften?**	h$\overline{ew}$r st$\overline{oo}$r $\overline{æ}$r dehpo-**nn$\overline{ay}$**ringsaavyiftern
I have a credit card.	**Jag har kreditkort.**	yaa(g) haar kreh**deet**koo^{r}t
Here's my driving licence.	**Här är mitt körkort.**	h$\overline{æ}$r $\overline{æ}$r mit **kh$\overline{ur}$r**koo^{r}t

CAR, see page 75

Taxi *Taxi*

Taxis are clearly marked and available in every town. All taxis are metered, but it's advisable to ask the approximate fare if travelling a long distance. After midnight and if you order the taxi in advance there is an extra charge. The tip is not included in the fare.

Where can I get a taxi?	**Var kan jag få tag på en taxi?**	vaar kahn yaa(g) faw taag paw ehn **tah**ksi
Where is the taxi stand?	**Var är taxi-stationen?**	vaar æ̅r **tah**ksi-stahsho̅o̅nern
Could you get me a taxi?	**Kan ni skaffa mig en taxi?**	kahn nee **skah**fah may ehn **tah**ksi
What's the fare to ...?	**Vad kostar det till ...?**	vaad **kos**tahr da̅y̅(t) til
How far is it to ...?	**Hur långt är det till ...?**	he̅w̅r longt æ̅r da̅y̅(t) til
Take me to ...	**Kör mig till ...**	khu̅r̅r may til
this address	**den här adressen**	dehn hæ̅r ah**drehs**sern
the airport	**flygplatsen**	**fle̅w̅g**plahtsern
the town centre	**(stads)centrum**	**(stahds)sehn**trewm
the ... Hotel	**hotell ...**	hot**ehl**
the railway station	**järnvägsstationen**	**yæ̅ʳn**vaigsstasho̅o̅nern
Turn ... at the next corner.	**Sväng till ...** **vid nästa gathörn.**	svehng til ... veed **neh**stah **gaat**hu̅r̅ʳn
left/right	**vänster/höger**	**vehn**sterr/**hu̅r̅**gerr
Go straight ahead.	**Kör rakt fram.**	khu̅r̅r raakt frahm
Please stop here.	**Var snäll och stanna här.**	vaar snehl ok **stah**nah hæ̅r
I'm in a hurry.	**Jag har bråttom.**	yaa(g) haar **brot**tom
Could you drive more slowly?	**Kan ni köra lite långsammare?**	kahn nee **khu̅r̅**rah **lee**ter **long**sahmahrer
Could you help me carry my luggage?	**Kan ni hjälpa mig att bära bagaget?**	kahn nee **yehl**pah may aht **bæ̅**rah bah**gaa**shert
Could you wait for me?	**Kan ni vänta på mig?**	kahn nee **vehn**tah paw may
I'll be back in 10 minutes.	**Jag är tillbaka om 10 minuter.**	yaa(g) æ̅r til**baa**kah om 10 min**e̅w̅**terr

TIPPING, see inside back-cover

Hotel—Other accommodation

Early reservation and confirmation are essential in most major tourist centres during the high season. Most towns and arrival points have a tourist information office (*turistbyrå*—te̅w̅**rist**be̅w̅raw) and that's the place to go to if you're stuck without a room. You can get an up-to-date price list for all Swedish hotels, called "Hotels in Sweden", from the Swedish tourist office in your country.

Although there is no official rating system, there are different classes of accommodation.

Hotell (ho**tehl**)	In the bigger towns you will find a number of first-class and some de-luxe hotels. Facilities—and prices—vary across a wide range, but standards are always high. Breakfast is almost always included.
Familjehotell (fah**mil**yerhotehl)	In summer a number of hotels, particularly in large cities, offer special rates for families with children in rooms with three to six beds.
Turisthotell/ Pensionat (te̅w̅**rist**hotehl)/ (pahnsho̅o̅**naat**)	Simple but clean and comfortable, many tourist hotels and guest houses are found in summer resorts and winter sports centres. As a rule, breakfast and dinner are included. Rates are usually based on a three-day stay.
Sommarhotell (**so**mmahrhotehl)	In Stockholm, Gothenburg and Lund, modern blocks of student flats are opened to tourists in the summer. These are rooms particularly suitable for groups.
Motell (moo**tehl**)	Accommodation for motorists, usually with restaurant and car-service facilities.
Privatrum (priv**vaa**trewm)	Local and regional tourist associations can recommend rooms in private homes.
Stugor (**ste̅w̅**goor)	Summer chalets, quite expensive, are let by the week. Booking in advance is advisable.
Vandrarhem (**vahn**drahrhehm)	The Swedish Touring Club (STF) operates these comfortable, cheap hostels all over Sweden.

Checking in—Reception *I receptionen*

My name is ...	**Mitt namn är ...**	mit nahmn ær
I have a reservation.	**Jag har beställt rum.**	yaa(g) haar ber**stehlt** rewm
We've reserved 2 rooms.	**Vi har beställt 2 rum.**	vee haar ber**stehlt** 2 rewm
Here's the confirmation.	**Här är bekräftelsen.**	hær ær ber**krehf**terlsern
Do you have any vacancies?	**Har ni några lediga rum?**	haar nee **naw**grah **la̅y̅**diggah rewm
I'd like a ...	**Jag skulle vilja ha ett ...**	yaa(g) **skew**ler **vil**yah haa eht
single room	**enkelrum**	**ehn**kerlrewm
double room	**dubbelrum**	**dew**berlrewm
We'd like a room ...	**Vi skulle vilja ha ett rum ...**	vee **skew**ler **vil**yah haa eht rewm
with twin beds	**med två sängar**	ma̅y̅d tvaw **sehng**ahr
with a double bed	**med dubbelsäng**	ma̅y̅d **dew**berlsehng
with a bath	**med bad**	ma̅y̅d baad
with a shower	**med dusch**	ma̅y̅d dewsh
with a balcony	**med balkong**	ma̅y̅d bahl**kong**
with a view	**med utsikt**	ma̅y̅d **e̅w̅**tsikt
at the front	**på framsidan**	paw **frahm**seedahn
at the back	**på baksidan**	paw **baak**seedahn
It must be quiet.	**Det måste vara tyst.**	da̅y̅(t) **mos**ter vaarah tewst
What floor is it on?	**Vilken våning ligger det på?**	**vil**kern **vaw**ning **lig**gerr da̅y̅(t) paw
Is there ...?	**Finns det ...?**	finss da̅y̅(t)
air conditioning	**luftkonditionering**	**lewft**kondishonna̅y̅ring
a conference room	**konferensrum**	konfeh**rahns**rewm
heating	**värme**	**vær**mer
hot water	**varmvatten**	**vahrm**vahtern
a laundry service	**tvättservice**	**tveht**"service"
room service	**rumsbetjäning**	**rewms**berkhaining
a radio/television in the room	**radio/TV på rummet**	**raa**dyo/**ta̅y̅**veh paw **rew**mert
running water	**rinnande vatten**	**rin**nahnder **vah**tern
a sauna	**bastu**	**bah**stew
a swimming pool	**swimmingpool**	"swimming pool"
a private toilet	**toalett på rummet**	tooah**leht** paw **rew**mert

CHECKING OUT, see page 31

Could you put an extra bed/a cot in the room?	**Kan ni ställa in en extra säng/barnsäng i rummet?**	kahn nee **steh**lah in ehn **ehks**trah sehng/**baa^{r}n**sehng ee **rew**mert

How much? *Hur mycket?*

How much does it cost ...?	**Vad kostar det ...?**	vaad **kos**tahr da̅y̅(t)
per night	**per natt**	pæ̅r̅ naht
per week	**per vecka**	pæ̅r̅ **veh**kah
for bed and breakfast	**för rum med frukost**	fu̅r̅r rewm ma̅y̅d **frew**kost
excluding meals	**utan måltider**	**e̅w̅**tahn **mawl**teederr
for full board (A.P.)	**för helpension**	fu̅r̅r **ha̅y̅l**pahnsho̅o̅n
for half board (M.A.P.)	**för halvpension**	fu̅r̅r **hahlv**pahnsho̅o̅n
Does the price include ...?	**Ingår ... i priset?**	**ing**gawr ... ee **prees**sert
breakfast	**frukost**	**frew**kost
service	**betjäningsavgift**	ber**khai**ningsaavyift
value-added tax (VAT)*	**moms**	moms
Is there any reduction for children?	**Ger ni någon rabatt för barn?**	ya̅y̅r nee **naw**gon rah**baht** fu̅r̅r baa^{r}n
Do you charge for the baby?	**Kostar det något för babyn?**	**kos**tahr da̅y̅(t) **naw**got fu̅r̅r **bai**bin
That's too expensive.	**Det är för dyrt.**	da̅y̅(t) æ̅r̅ fu̅r̅r de̅w̅^{r}t
Don't you have anything cheaper?	**Har ni inte något billigare?**	haar nee **in**ter **naw**got **bil**liggahrer

How long? *Hur länge?*

We'll be staying ...	**Vi tänker stanna ...**	vee **tehn**kerr **stah**nah
overnight only	**bara över natten**	**baa**rah **u̅r̅**verr **nah**tern
a few days	**några dagar**	**naw**grah **daa**(gah)r
a week (at least)	**en vecka (minst)**	ehn **veh**kah (minst)
I don't know yet.	**Jag vet inte än.**	yaa(g) va̅y̅t **in**ter ehn

---
* Americans note: a type of sales tax in Sweden

NUMBERS, see page 147

Decision *Beslut*

May I see the room?	**Kan jag få se på rummet?**	kahn yaa(g) faw sa͞y paw **rew**mert
That's fine. I'll take it.	**Det är bra. Jag tar det.**	da͞y(t) æ̅r braa. yaa(g) taar da͞y(t)
No. I don't like it.	**Nej. Jag tycker inte om det.**	nay. yaa(g) **tew**kerr **in**ter om da͞y(t)
It's too ...	**Det är för ...**	da͞y(t) æ̅r fu͞rr
cold/hot	**kallt/varmt**	kahlt/vahrmt
dark/small	**mörkt/litet**	murrkt/**lee**tert
I asked for a room with a bath.	**Jag bad om ett rum med bad.**	yaa(g) baa(d) om eht rewm ma͞yd baad
Do you have anything ...?	**Har ni något ...?**	haar nee **naw**got
better	**bättre**	**beh**trer
bigger	**större**	**stur**rer
cheaper	**billigare**	**bil**liggahrer
quieter	**tystare**	**tew**stahrer
Do you have a room with a (better) view?	**Har ni något rum med (bättre) utsikt?**	haar nee **naw**got rewm ma͞yd (**beh**trer) **e͞w**tsikt

Registration *Incheckning*

Upon arrival at a hotel or guest house you'll be asked to fill in a registration form (*inskrivningsblankett*—**in**skreevningsblahnkeht).

Efternamn/Förnamn	Name/First name
Hemort/Gata/Nummer	Home town/Street/Number
Hemland	Country of origin
Medborgare i .../Yrke	Citizen of .../Occupation
Födelsedatum/Födelseort	Date/Place of birth
Inrest ...	Arrived on ...
Passnummer	Passport number
Ort/Datum	Place/Date
Underskrift	Signature

What does this mean?	**Vad betyder det här?**	vaad ber**tew**derr day(t) hær

Kan jag få se passet, tack?	May I see your passport, please?
Skulle ni vilja fylla i den här blanketten?	Would you mind filling in this form?
Kan ni skriva under här?	Please sign here.
Hur länge tänker ni stanna?	How long will you be staying?

What's my room number?	**Vilket rumsnummer har jag?**	**vil**kert **rewms**newmerr haar yaa(g)
Will you have our luggage sent up?	**Kan ni skicka upp bagaget?**	kahn nee **shik**kah ewp bah**gaa**shert
Where can I park my car?	**Var kan jag parkera bilen?**	vaar kahn yaa(g) pahr**kay**rah **bee**lehn
Does the hotel have a garage?	**Har hotellet något garage?**	haar hot**eh**leht **naw**got gah**raash**
I'd like to leave this in the hotel safe.	**Jag skulle vilja lämna det här i kassaskåpet.**	yaa(g) **skew**ler **vil**yah **lehm**nah day(t) hær ee **kah**ssahskawpert

Hotel staff *Hotellpersonal*

hall porter	**portiern**	po^{r}tyay^{r}n
maid	**städerskan**	**staider**^{r}skahn
manager	**direktören**	dirrerk**tur**rern
page (bellboy)	**pickolon**	**pik**kolon
porter	**bäraren**	**bæ**rahrern
receptionist	**receptionisten**	rehsehpshoo**nis**tern
switchboard operator	**telefonisten**	tehlerfon**nis**tern
waiter	**kyparen/ servitören**	**khew**pahrern/ sehrvi**tur**rern
waitress	**servitrisen**	sehrvi**tree**ssern

To attract the attention of staff members say "Excuse me"—*Ursäkta* or *Förlåt*.

TELLING THE TIME, see page 153

General requirements *Allmänna förfrågningar*

The key to room ... please.	**Nyckeln till rum ..., tack.**	**new**ker(l)n til rewm ... tahk
Could you wake me at ..., please?	**Kan ni väcka mig klockan ... tack?**	kahn nee **veh**kah may **klo**kkahn ... tahk
May we have breakfast in our room, please?	**Skulle vi kunna få frukost på rummet?**	**skew**ler vee **kew**nah faw **frew**kost paw **rew**mert
Is there a bath on this floor?	**Finns det bad på den här våningen?**	finss da̅y̅(t) baad paw dehn hæ̅r **vaw**ningern
What's the voltage here?	**Vilken spänning är det?**	**vil**kern **speh**ning æ̅r da̅y̅(t)
Where's the shaver socket (outlet)?	**Var är uttaget för rakapparaten?**	vaar æ̅r **e̅w̅**ttaagert fu̅r̅r **raak**ahpahraatern
Can you find me a ...?	**Kan ni skaffa mig en ...?**	kahn nee **skah**fah may ehn
babysitter	**barnvakt**	**baa^{r}n**vahkt
secretary	**sekreterare**	sehkrer**ta̅y̅**rahrer
typewriter	**skrivmaskin**	**skreev**mahsheen
May I have a/an/ some ...?	**Skulle jag kunna få ...?**	**skew**ler yaa(g) **kew**nah faw
ashtray	**en askkopp**	ehn **ahs**kop
bath towel	**ett badlakan**	eht **baad**laakahn
(extra) blanket	**en (extra) filt**	ehn (**ehk**strah) filt
envelopes	**några kuvert**	**naw**grah kew**væ̅r**
(more) hangers	**(fler) hängare**	(fla̅y̅r) **hehng**ahrer
hot-water bottle	**en varmvattenflaska**	ehn **vahrm**vahternflahskah
ice cubes	**lite is**	**lee**ter ees
needle and thread	**nål och tråd**	nawl ok trawd
(extra) pillow	**en (extra) kudde**	ehn (**ehk**strah) **kew**der
reading lamp	**en läslampa**	ehn **lais**lahmpah
soap	**en tvål**	ehn tvawl
writing paper	**några brevpapper**	**naw**grah **bra̅y̅v**pahperr
Where's the ...?	**Var är ...?**	vaar æ̅r
bathroom	**badrummet**	**baad**rewmert
dining room	**matsalen**	**maat**saalern
emergency exit	**nödutgången**	**nu̅r̅d**e̅w̅tgawngern
hairdresser's	**frisersalongen**	fris**sa̅y̅^{r}**sahlongern
lift (elevator)	**hissen**	**his**sern
telephone	**telefonen**	tehler**fawn**ern
Where are the toilets?	**Var är toaletten?**	vaar æ̅r tooah**leh**tern

BREAKFAST, see page 38

Telephone—Post (mail) *Telefon – Post*

Can you get me Malmö 1234567?	**Kan ni ringa upp 1234567 i Malmö åt mig?**	kahn nee **ring**ah ewp 1234567 ee **mahl**mur awt may
Do you have any stamps?	**Har ni några frimärken?**	haar nee **naw**grah **free**mærkern
Would you post this for me, please?	**Kan ni posta det här åt mig, tack?**	kahn nee **pos**tah da̅y̅(t) hær awt may tahk
Are there any letters for me?	**Finns det några brev till mig?**	finss da̅y̅(t) **naw**grah bra̅y̅v til may
Are there any messages for me?	**Finns det något meddelande till mig?**	finss da̅y̅(t) **naw**got **ma̅y̅**da̅y̅lahnder til may
How much is my telephone bill?	**Hur stor är min telefonräkning?**	he̅w̅r sto̅o̅r ær min tehler**fawn**raikning

Difficulties *Svårigheter*

The ... doesn't work.	**... fungerar inte.**	... fewng**ga̅y̅**rahr **in**ter
air conditioning	**luftkonditioneringen**	**lewft**kondishonna̅y̅ringern
bidet	**bidén**	bee**da̅y̅n**
heating	**värmen**	**vær**mern
light	**ljuset**	**ye̅w̅**ssert
radio	**radion**	**raa**dyon
television	**TV:n**	**ta̅y̅**vehn
The tap (faucet) is dripping.	**Kranen droppar.**	**kraa**nern **drop**pahr
There's no hot water.	**Det finns inget varmvatten.**	da̅y̅(t) finss **ing**ert **vahrm**vahtern
The wash basin is blocked.	**Det är stopp i handfatet.**	da̅y̅(t) ær stop ee **hahn(d)**faatert
The window is jammed.	**Fönstret har fastnat.**	**furn**strert haar **fahs**naht
The curtains are stuck.	**Gardinerna har hakat upp sig.**	gahʳ**dee**nerʳnah haar **haa**kaht ewp say
The bulb is burned out.	**Glödlampan är trasig.**	**glu̅r̅d**lahmpahn ær **traa**ssig
My bed hasn't been made up.	**Min säng har inte blivit bäddad.**	min sehng haar **in**ter **blee**vit **beh**dahd

POST OFFICE AND TELEPHONE, see page 132

The ... is/are broken.	**... är trasig.**	... ær **traassig**
blind	**rullgardinen**	**rewl**gah^r**dee**nern
lamp	**lampan**	**lahm**pahn
plug	**stickkontakten**	**stik**kontahktern
switch	**strömbrytaren**	**strurm**bre̅w̅tahrern
venetian blinds	**persiennen**	peh^r**sieh**nern
Can you get it repaired?	**Kan ni laga den?**	kahn nee **laa**gah dehn

Laundry—Dry cleaner's *Tvätt – Kemtvätt*

I'd like these clothes ...	**Jag skulle vilja ha de här kläderna ...**	yaa(g) **skew**ler **vil**yah haa dom hær **klai**der^{r}nah
dry-cleaned	**kemtvättade**	**kha̅y̅m**tvehtahder
ironed	**strukna**	**stre̅w̅**knah
pressed	**pressade**	**preh**ssahder
washed	**tvättade**	**tveh**tahder
I need them ...	**Jag behöver dem ...**	yaa(g) ber**hu̅r̅**verr dom
today	**idag**	ee**daa(g)**
tonight	**i kväll**	ee **kvehl**
tomorrow	**i morgon**	ee **mor**ron
before Friday	**före fredag**	**fu̅r̅**rer **fra̅y̅**daa(g)
Can you ... this?	**Kan ni ... det här?**	kahn nee ... **da̅y̅(t)** hær
mend	**laga**	**laa**gah
stitch	**sy ihop**	**se̅w̅** ihoop
Can you sew on this button?	**Kan ni sy i den här knappen?**	kahn nee **se̅w̅** ee dehn hær **knah**pern
Can this be invisibly mended?	**Kan det här lagas så att det inte syns?**	kahn **da̅y̅(t)** hær **laa**gahss saw aht **da̅y̅(t)** **in**ter **sewnss**
Can you get this stain out?	**Kan ni få bort den här fläcken?**	kahn nee faw bo^{r}t dehn hær **fleh**kern
Is my laundry ready?	**Är min tvätt klar?**	ær min tveht klaar
This isn't mine.	**Det här är inte mitt.**	**da̅y̅(t)** hær ær **in**ter mit
There's something missing.	**Det fattas något.**	**da̅y̅(t)** **fah**tahss **naw**got
There's a hole in this.	**Det har gått hål på det här.**	**da̅y̅(t)** haar got hawl paw **da̅y̅(t)** hær

Hairdresser—Barber *Damfrisör – Herrfrisör*

Is there a ... in the hotel?	**Finns det någon ... på hotellet?**	finss da̅y̅(t) **naw**gon ... paw hote**hl**ert
hairdresser	**frisersalong**	friss**a̅y̅ʳ**sahlong
beauty salon	**skönhetssalong**	shu̅r̅n**ha̅y̅t**ssahlong
Can I make an appointment for Thursday?	**Kan jag få en tid på torsdag?**	kahn yaa(g) faw ehn teed paw **tooʳs**daa(g)
Could you ... my hair, please?	**Skulle ni kunna ... mitt hår?**	**skew**ler nee **kew**nah ... mit hawr
blow-dry	**föna**	**fu̅r̅**nah
cut	**klippa**	**klip**pah
dye	**färga**	**fær**yah
tint	**tona**	**to̅o̅**nah
with a fringe (bangs)	**med lugg**	ma̅y̅d lewg
I'd like a/some ...	**Jag skulle vilja ha ...**	yaa(g) **skew**ler **vil**yah haa
colour rinse	**en färgsköljning**	ehn **færy**shurlyning
face pack	**en ansiktsmask**	ehn **ahn**siktsmahsk
manicure	**manikyr**	mahnik**ke̅w̅r**
permanent wave	**en permanent**	ehn pehrmah**nehnt**
setting lotion	**en läggningsvätska**	ehn **lehg**ningsvehtskah
shampoo and set	**tvättning och läggning**	**tveht**ning ok **lehg**ning
I'd like a shampoo for ... hair.	**Jag vill ha ett schampo för ... hår.**	yaa(g) vil haa eht **shahm**poo fu̅r̅r ... hawr
normal/dry/ greasy (oily)	**normalt/torrt/ fett**	nor**maalt**/toʳt/ feht
Do you have a colour chart?	**Har ni en färgkarta?**	haar nee ehn **færy**kaaʳtah
I don't want any hairspray.	**Jag vill inte ha någon spray.**	yaa(g) vil **in**ter haa **naw**gon "spray"
I'd like a haircut, please.	**Klippning, tack.**	**klip**ning tahk
Don't cut it too short.	**Klipp inte för kort.**	klip **in**ter fu̅r̅r koʳt
A little more off the ...	**Ta lite mer ...**	taa **li**ter ma̅y̅r
back/top	**där bak/på hjässan**	dæ̅r̅ baak/paw **yeh**ssahn
neck/sides	**i nacken/på sidorna**	ee **nah**kern/paw **see**doʳnah

DAYS OF THE WEEK, see page 150

I'd like a shave.	**Rakning, tack.**	**raak**ning tahk
Would you trim my ..., please?	**Kan ni putsa ..., tack.**	kahn nee **pew**tsah ... tahk
beard	**skägget**	**sheh**gert
moustache	**mustaschen**	mew**staa**shern
sideboards (sideburns)	**polisongerna**	polissonger^{r}nah

Checking out *Avresa*

May I have my bill, please?	**Kan jag få räkningen, tack?**	kahn yaa(g) faw **raik**ningern tahk
I'm leaving early in the morning.	**Jag åker tidigt i morgon bitti.**	yaa(g) **aw**kerr **tee**di(g)t ee **mor**ron **bit**ti
Please have my bill ready.	**Kan ni ha räkningen klar?**	kahn nee haa **raik**ningern klaar
We'll be checking out around noon.	**Vi checkar ut vid tolvtiden.**	vee **kheh**kahr e̅w̅t veed **tolv**teedern
I must leave at once.	**Jag måste åka genast.**	yaa(g) **mos**ter **aw**kah **ya̅y̅**nahst
Is everything included?	**Är allt inkluderat?**	ær ahlt inklew**da̅y̅**raht
Can I pay by credit card?	**Kan jag betala med kreditkort?**	kahn yaa(g) ber**taa**lah ma̅y̅d kreh**deet**koo^{r}t
I think there's a mistake in the bill.	**Jag tror att det är ett fel på räkningen.**	yaa(g) tro̅o̅r aht da̅y̅(t) ær eht fa̅y̅l paw **raik**ningern
Can you get us a taxi?	**Kan ni skaffa oss en taxi?**	kahn nee **skah**fah oss ehn **tah**ksi
Would you send someone to bring down our luggage?	**Kan ni be någon ta ner bagaget?**	kahn nee ba̅y̅ **naw**gon taa na̅y̅r bah**gaa**shert
Here's the forwarding address.	**Här är eftersändningsadressen.**	hær ær **ehf**terr-sehn(d)ningsahdrehssern
You have my home address.	**Ni har min bostadsadress.**	nee haar min **bo̅o̅**staadsahdrehss
It's been a very enjoyable stay.	**Det har varit en mycket trevlig vistelse.**	da̅y̅(t) haar **vaa**rit ehn **mew**ker(t) **tra̅y̅**vli(g) **vis**terlser

TIPPING, see inside back-cover

Camping *Camping*

Camping is extremely popular and very well organized in Sweden. There are more than 700 sites, classified by one, two or three stars according to facilities offered. A camping carnet is needed except for holders of the "Camping International" card. If you camp on private property, ask the owner for permission.

Is there a camp site near here?	**Finns det någon campingplats i närheten?**	finss day(t) **naw**gon **kahm**pingplahtss ee **nær**haytern
Can we camp here?	**Kan vi campa här?**	kahn vee **kahm**pah hær
Do you have room for a ...?	**Har ni plats för ...?**	haar nee plahtss furr
tent	**ett tält**	eht tehlt
caravan (trailer)	**en husvagn**	ehn **hew**svahngn
What's the charge ...?	**Vad kostar det ...?**	vaa(d) **kos**tahr day(t)
per day	**per dag**	pær daa(g)
per person	**per person**	pær peh^{r}**shoon**
for a car	**för en bil**	furr ehn beel
for a tent	**för ett tält**	furr eht tehlt
for a caravan (trailer)	**för en husvagn**	furr ehn **hew**svahngn
Is there/Are there (a) ...?	**Finns det ...?**	finss day(t)
cooking facilities	**kokmöjligheter**	**kook**murylighayterr
drinking water	**dricksvatten**	**driks**vahtern
electricity	**elektricitet**	ehlehktrissi**tayt**
playground	**någon lekplats**	**naw**gon **layk**plahts
restaurant	**någon restaurang**	**naw**gon rehstor**rahng**
shopping facilities	**någon affär**	**naw**gon ah**fær**
sauna	**bastu**	**bah**stew
swimming pool	**någon swimmingpool**	**naw**gon "swimmingpool"
Where are the showers/toilets?	**Var är duscharna/ toaletterna?**	vaar ær **dew**shah^{r}nah/ tooah**leh**ter^{r}nah
Where can I get butane gas?	**Var kan jag få tag på butangas?**	vaar kahn yaa(g) faw taag paw bew**taan**gaass
Is there a youth hostel near here?	**Finns det något vandrarhem i närheten?**	finss day(t) **naw**got **vahn**drahrhehm ee **nær**haytern

CAMPING EQUIPMENT, see page 106

Eating out

Eating places in Sweden range from the ultra chic to the very quick. The following rundown will help you decide what to look for to suit your appetite and mood. Though if you want to have a drink, you'll have to wait till noon—the law is strict about licensing hours.

Cocktail bar ("cocktail bar") — Only in hotels in important towns. Sometimes snacks are served along with the drinks.

Dansrestaurang (**dahns**rehstorrahng) — For dancing and dining. Usually in big towns and hotels.

Fiskrestaurang (**fisk**rehstorrahng) — Fish and seafood specialities.

Gatukök (**gaa**tewkhu̅r̅k) — Typically Scandinavian "kitchen on the street" for a quick snack. Sausages or hamburgers with mashed potatoes or chips (French fries), meatballs or spring rolls, ice cream and soft drinks.

Grillbar (**gril**baar) — Self-service hamburgers, steaks, chips, etc., usually with beer or soft drinks only.

Gästgivargård (**yeh**shivvahrgaw^{r}d) — Old coaching inns in the countryside of southern Sweden (mainly Skåne) with rustic decor and often high culinary standards; many local specialities including *smörgåsbord* (see p. 41) which is usually served on Sundays and around Christmas.

Kafé (kah**fa̅y̅**) — Local coffee house that serves snacks (open sandwiches, buns, etc.). If called *Ölkafé* then beer and basic meals are served.

Konditori (konditto**ree**) — A coffee shop serving tea, coffee, soft drinks, pastries and ice cream. You may also find open sandwiches and other snacks.

Korvstånd (**korv**stond) — Swedish hot-dog stand.

Kvarterskrog (kvah^{r}**ta̅y̅**^{r}skro̅o̅g) — Small inexpensive neighbourhood restaurant. The food is generally good. Wine or beer may be served but no spirits.

Restaurang (rehsto**rrahng**)
Restaurants have no official rating system. You can take your meals in a variety of settings: classically elegant, modern or simply utilitarian. For something a little special, try dinner in a renovated medieval cellar, or on an old boat.

Most restaurants will serve international food, although you can get excellent Swedish specialities too.

Salladsbar (**sah**lahdssbaar)
Mostly self-service restaurants serving a variety of salads and vegetarian food.

Stekhus (**stay̅k**hew̅ss)
Steakhouse.

Värdshus (**vær(d)**shew̅ss)
Styled after old coaching inns, found on the outskirts of towns or in the country, some with high culinary standards. Many motels also call their restaurants *värdshus*.

Eating habits *Matvanor*

The Swedes have altered their eating habits to suit the modern way of life. Breakfast is usually a quick cup of tea or coffee with a sandwich, though cereals and yoghurt are also popular. Lunch used to be the most important meal of the day, but as lunch hours became shorter, people started to settle for a one-course meal. Dinner is served quite early—between 5 and 6 p.m. Hefty snacks bridge the gap between meals. The *smörgås* or open sandwich, is immensely popular, and fast food is on the up and up accompanied by the indispensable cup of coffee—black or with cream.

Meal times *När äter man?*

Breakfast (*frukost*—**frew**kost) is usually served from 7 to 10 a.m. and is generally included in the hotel arrangement.

Lunch (*lunch*—lewnsh) is normally served from 11.30 a.m. and dinner (*middag*—**mi**ddah(g)) from around 6 p.m.

Meal times are very flexible and many restaurants will serve a meal at any hour of the afternoon or evening.

Swedish cuisine *Det svenska köket*

Natural is the best way to describe the Swedish approach to food. A Swede can be lyrical at the thought of *färskpotatis,* new potatoes boiled with dill (one of the most commonly used herbs) and served simply with a pat of butter (always salted). Each season has its traditional specialities, and there is a number of genuine national dishes worth trying. Some may seem a bit strange to you, but if you have the chance to taste them you will probably be pleasantly surprised.

Dairy products have by tradition played an important part in the Swedish diet. Milk is the drink taken with everyday meals.

Nowadays Swedish cuisine is more cosmopolitan than it used to be, and the influence of French, Italian, Japanese and Chinese cuisine among others is apparent.

Vad önskar ni?	What would you like?
Jag rekommenderar det här.	I recommend this.
Vad önskas att dricka?	What would you like to drink?
Vi har inte ...	We don't have ...
Önskar ni ...?	Would you like ...?

Hungry? *Hungrig?*

I'm hungry/I'm thirsty.	**Jag är hungrig/ Jag är törstig.**	yaa(g) ǣr **hewng**ri(g)/ yaa(g) ǣr **turʳsti**(g)
Can you recommend a good restaurant?	**Kan ni föreslå en bra restaurang?**	kahn nee **fur**rerslaw ehn braa rehstor**rahng**
Are there any inexpensive restaurants around here?	**Finns det någon billig restaurang i närheten?**	finss da̅y̅(t) **naw**gon **bil**lig rehstor**rahng** ee **nǣr**ha̅y̅tern

If you want to be sure of getting a table in a well-known restaurant, it's better to book in advance.

I'd like to reserve a table for 4.	**Jag skulle vilja beställa ett bord för 4.**	yaa(g) **skew**ler **vil**yah ber**steh**lah eht boo(r)d fur 4
We'll come at 8.	**Vi kommer klockan 8.**	vee **kom**merr **klok**kahn 8
Could we have a ...?	**Skulle vi kunna få ett ...?**	**skew**ler vee **kew**nah faw eht
table in the corner	**hörnbord**	**hur(r)n**boo(r)d
table by the window	**fönsterbord**	**furn**sterrboo(r)d
table outside	**bord ute**	boo(r)d **ew**ter
table in a non-smoking area	**bord för icke rökare**	boo(r)d furr **ik**ker **rur**kahrer

Asking and ordering *Fråga och beställa*

Waiter/Waitress!	**Ursäkta.**	**ew(r)**sehktah
I'd like something to eat/drink.	**Jag skulle vilja ha något att äta/dricka.**	yaa(g) **skew**ler **vil**yah haa **naw**got aht **ai**tah/ **drik**kah
May I have the menu, please?	**Kan jag få matsedeln, tack?**	kahn yaa(g) faw **maatsay**derln tahk
Do you have a ...?	**Har ni någon ...?**	haar nee **naw**gon
set menu	**meny**	meh**new**
local speciality	**lokal specialitet**	loo**kaal** spehssiahli**tay(t)**
What do you recommend?	**Vad rekommenderar ni?**	vaad rehkommern**day**rahr nee
Could we have a/an ..., please?	**Kan vi få ... tack?**	kahn vee faw ... tahk
ashtray	**en askkopp**	ehn **ahs**kop
cup	**en kopp**	ehn kop
fork	**en gaffel**	ehn **gah**fehl
glass	**ett glas**	eht glaass
knife	**en kniv**	ehn kneev
napkin (serviette)	**en servett**	ehn sehr**veht**
plate	**en tallrik**	ehn **tahl**rik
spoon	**en sked**	ehn shayd
May I have some ...?	**Kan jag få lite ...?**	kahn yaa(g) faw **lee**ter
bread	**bröd**	brurd
butter	**smör**	smurr

lemon	**citron**	sitro͞on
oil	**olja**	**ol**yah
pepper	**peppar**	**peh**pahr
salt	**salt**	sahlt
seasoning	**kryddor**	**krew**door
sugar	**socker**	**sok**kerr
vinegar	**vinäger**	vinn**ai**gerr

Some useful expressions for those with special requirements:

I'm on a special diet.	**Jag håller diet.**	yaa(g) **hol**lerr dee**a͞yt**
I don't drink alcohol.	**Jag dricker inte alkohol.**	yaa(g) **drik**kerr **in**ter **ahl**kohawl
I mustn't eat food containing ...	**Jag får inte äta mat som innehåller ...**	yaa(g) fawr **in**ter **ai**tah maat som **in**nerhollerr
flour/fat	**mjöl/fett**	myu͞rl/feht
salt/sugar	**salt/socker**	sahlt/**sok**kerr
Do you have ... for diabetics?	**Har ni ... för diabetiker?**	haar nee ... fu͞rr deeah**ba͞y**tikkerr
cakes	**kakor**	**kaa**koor
fruit juice	**juice**	yo͞oss
a special menu	**en specialmeny**	ehn spehssi**yaal**mehne͞w
Do you have any vegetarian dishes?	**Har ni några vegetariska rätter?**	haar nee **naw**grah vehger**taa**riskah **reh**terr
Could I have ... instead of dessert?	**Kan jag få ... i stället för efterrätt?**	kahn yaa(g) faw ... ee **steh**leht fu͞rr **ehf**terreht
Can I have an artificial sweetener?	**Kan jag få sötningsmedel?**	kahn yaa(g) faw **su͞rt**ningsma͞yderl

And ...

I'd like some more.	**Jag skulle vilja ha lite mer.**	yaa(g) **skew**ler **vil**yah haa **lee**ter ma͞yr
Can I have more ... please?	**Kan jag få lite mer ..., tack?**	kahn yaa(g) faw **lee**ter ma͞yr ... tahk
Just a small portion.	**Bara en liten portion.**	**baa**rah ehn **lee**tern po^r**tsho͞on**
Nothing more, thanks.	**Tack, inte mer.**	tahk **in**ter ma͞yr
Where are the toilets?	**Var är toaletten?**	vaar ær tooah**leh**tern

Breakfast *Frukost*

Almost every hotel has a breakfast buffet consisting of a variety of breads (try *knäckebröd*—**kneh**kerbr̅u̅r̅d, crispbread), butter, cheese, ham, eggs, marmalade, juice, milk, tea and coffee. Try cornflakes with fermented milk (*filmjölk*—**feel**myurlk), a Swedish favourite.

I'd like breakfast, please.	**Jag skulle vilja ha frukost, tack.**	yaa(g) **skew**ler **vil**yah haa **frew**kost tahk
I'll have a/an/some ...	**Jag skall be att få ...**	yaa(g) skah(l) ba̅y̅ aht faw
bacon and eggs	**bacon och ägg**	"bacon" ok ehg
boiled egg	**ett kokt ägg**	eht kookt ehg
soft/hard	**löskokt/hårdkokt**	**l̅u̅r̅s**kookt/**haw^r^d**kookt
cereal	**flingor**	**fling**or
cheese	**ost**	oost
eggs	**ägg**	ehg
fried egg	**ett stekt ägg**	eht sta̅y̅kt ehg
scrambled eggs	**äggröra**	**ehg**r̅u̅r̅rah
fruit juice	**juice**	y̅o̅o̅ss
grapefruit	**grapefrukt-**	**"grape"**frewkt
orange	**apelsin-**	ahperl**seen**
ham and eggs	**skinka och ägg**	**shin**kah ok ehg
jam	**lite sylt**	**lee**ter sewlt
marmalade	**lite apelsin-marmelad**	**lee**ter ahperl**seen**-mahrmer**laad**
roll	**ett småfranska**	eht **smaw**frahnskah
toast	**lite rostat bröd**	**lee**ter **ros**taht br̅u̅r̅d
yoghurt	**en yoghurt**	ehn **yawg**(h)ew^r^t
May I have some ...?	**Kan jag få ...?**	kahn yaa(g) faw
bread	**lite bröd**	**lee**ter br̅u̅r̅d
butter	**lite smör**	**lee**ter sm̅u̅r̅r
(hot) chocolate	**(varm) choklad**	(vahrm) sho**klaa(d)**
coffee	**kaffe**	**kah**fer
decaffeinated	**koffeinfritt**	koffeh**een**frit
black	**utan grädde**	**e̅w̅**tahn **greh**der
with cream	**med grädde**	ma̅y̅d **greh**der
honey	**lite honung**	**lee**ter **haw**newng
(cold/hot) milk	**(kall/varm) mjölk**	(kahl/vahrm) myurlk
pepper	**lite peppar**	**lee**ter **peh**pahr
salt	**lite salt**	**lee**ter sahlt
tea	**te**	ta̅y̅
with milk/lemon	**med mjölk/citron**	ma̅y̅d myurlk/si**tr̅o̅o̅n**
(hot) water	**(varmt) vatten**	(vahrmt) **vah**tern

What's on the menu? *Vad står det på matsedeln?*

Restaurants now often display a menu *(matsedel)* outside. Besides ordering à la carte, you can usually order a fixed-price menu *(meny).* Some restaurants offer a dish of the day *(dagens rätt)* including bread, butter, drink (non-alcoholic) and coffee at quite a modest price.

Under the headings below you'll find alphabetical lists of dishes that might be offered on a Swedish menu, with their English equivalent. You can simply show the book to the waiter. If you want some cheese, for instance, let *him* point to what's available on the appropriate list. Use pages 36 and 37 for ordering in general.

Reading the menu *Att läsa matsedeln*

Meny	Set menu
Dagens rätt	Dish of the day
Barnmatsedel	Children's menu
Kökschefen rekommenderar ...	The chef proposes ...
Husets specialiteter	Specialities of the house
Veckans Grill	This week's grilled specialities
Valfria tillbehör	Choice of side-dishes
På beställning	Made on request
Mot extra kostnad	Extra charge
Två personer	For two
Serveringsavgift inräknad	Service charge included

bakverk	**baak**vehrk	pastries
drycker	**drew**kkerr	drinks
efterrätter	**ehf**terrehterr	desserts
fisk	fisk	fish
frukt	frewkt	fruit
från grillen	frawn **gril**lern	grilled (broiled)
fågel	**faw**gerl	poultry
förrätter	**fu̅r̅**rehterr	first course
glass	glahss	ice cream
grönsaker	**gru̅r̅n**saakerr	vegetables
huvudrätter	**he̅w̅**ve̅w̅drehterr	main course
kött	khurt	meat
ost	oost	cheese
pastarätter	**pah**stahrehterr	pasta
risrätter	**rees**rehterr	rice
sallader	**sah**lahderr	salads
skaldjur	**skaal**ye̅w̅r	seafood
soppor	**sop**poor	soups
smårätter	**smaw**rehterr	snacks
smörgåsar	**smurr**gawssahr	open sandwiches
smörgåsbord	**smurr**gawsbo̅o̅^{r}d	smörgåsbord
varmrätter	**vahrm**rehterr	main course
vilt	vilt	game
vinlista	**veen**listah	wine list
äggrätter	**ehg**rehterr	egg dishes

Smörgåsbord

The Swedish *smörgåsbord* (**smurr**gawsbōōʳd), of ancient origin, is well known abroad. It was originally intended as a large-scale hors d'œuvre but has become a kind of buffet meal. It is not usual to have both a *smörgåsbord* and a main course. These beautifully decorated tables, groaning under the weight of a multitude of hot and cold platters, used to be a common sight in homes and restaurants, especially around Christmas. Nowadays the *smörgåsbord* is usually only served in restaurants, especially *gästgivargårdar* and *värdshus* in the country.

You start at one end of the table, with a variety of herring, salmon, seafood, salads and other appetizers, serving yourself as many times as you like. Work your way through the cold meat, meatballs, small sausages and omelets. Then move on to the cheeses. If you still have room, you might manage a light dessert. The price is the same for big or small eaters alike. During the Christmas season the *smörgåsbord* becomes *julbord,* Yuletide table, even more lavish and served in almost all big restaurants every day of the week.

Aquavit and beer go especially well with this spread. It is rare to drink wine with *smörgåsbord.* Normally this is a lunchtime experience and it can take hours.

Are you serving smörgåsbord today?	**Serverar ni smörgåsbord idag?**	sehrvāyrahr nee **smurr**gawsbōōʳd ee**daa(g)**

gravad strömming i senapssås (**graa**vahd **strur**ming ee **sāy**nahpssawss) — marinated Baltic herring in mustard sauce, eaten with boiled potatoes sprinkled with dill (as are all herring dishes)

inkokt ål (**in**kookt awl) — jellied eel

inlagd sill (**in**lahgd sil) — herring marinated in vinegar, sugar and spices

Janssons frestelse (**yaan**sonss **frehs**terlser) — "Jansson's temptation"—layers of sliced potatoes, marinated sprats and onions, baked in cream

kalvsylta (**kahlv**sewltah)	jellied veal loaf (usually around Christmas)
kryddsill (**krewd**sil)	herring marinated in vinegar, sugar, allspice, mustard seeds and cloves
köttbullar (**khurt**bewlahr)	meatballs of minced beef and/or pork, flavoured with onion, salt, pepper and allspice
leverpastej (**la̅y̅**verrpahstay)	liver paté, usually of pork or veal liver
löjrom med lök och gräddfil (**lury**rom ma̅y̅d lu̅r̅k ok **grehd**feel)	bleak roe; served with raw, chopped onion and sour cream, and eaten on toast
matjessill med gräddfil och gräslök (**maht**yerssil ma̅y̅d **grehd**fil ok **grais**lu̅r̅k)	marinated herring with sour cream and chopped chives; often served with small boiled potatoes
revbensspjäll (**ra̅y̅v**ba̅y̅nsspyehl)	roasted spareribs (usually around Christmas)
rökt korv (ru̅r̅kt korv)	smoked sausage; variously flavoured according to region
rökt lax (ru̅r̅kt lahks)	smoked salmon; usually served with toast and wedges of lemon
rökt renstek (ru̅r̅kt **ra̅y̅n**sta̅y̅k)	smoked roast reindeer; sometimes served with horseradish cream
rökt ål (ru̅r̅kt awl)	smoked eel; often served with scrambled eggs
senapssill (**sa̅y̅**nahpssil)	salted herring in mustard sauce
sillsallad (**sil**sahlahd)	herring salad with pickled beetroot and gherkins, apples, potatoes, onions and whipped cream (usually served around Christmas)
solöga (**so̅o̅**lu̅r̅ga)	marinated sprats, chopped onions, capers and beetroot, with an egg yolk in the center
stekt prinskorv (sta̅y̅kt **prins**korv)	small fried sausages
ägg med kaviar (ehg ma̅y̅d **kahv**yahr)	hard-boiled eggs with red salted cod's roe or black salted lumpfish roe

Starters (Appetizers) *Förrätter*

It's by no means the rule to take a starter. Swedes are usually content with the main course, except on special occasions. Many dishes from the *smörgåsbord* are also served as starters.

I'd like a starter (an appetizer).	**Jag skulle vilja ha en förrätt.**	yaa(g) **skew**ler **vil**yah haa ehn **f̅u̅r**reht
grodlår	**grōōd**lawr	frog's legs
gåslever	**gaws**lāyverr	goose liver
hummer	**hew**merr	lobster
kaviar	**kahv**yahr	caviar
röd	rūrd	red (cod's roe, salted)
svart	svah^{r}t	black (lumpfish roe)
krabba	**krah**bah	crab
lax	lahks	salmon
gravad	**graa**vahd	marinated
rökt	rūrkt	smoked
löjrom	**lury**rom	bleak roe
musslor	**mew**sloor	mussels
ostron	**oo**stron	oysters
paté	pah**tāy**	paté
fisk-	fisk-	fish
grönsaks-	**grūrn**saaks-	vegetable
skaldjurs-	**skaal**yēw^{r}s-	seafood
vilt-	vilt-	game
räkcocktail	**raik**"cocktail"	prawn (shrimp) salad
sikrom	**seek**rom	whitefish roe
sniglar	**sneeg**lahr	snails

färska räkor (fæ^{r}skah **rai**koor) — unshelled prawns (shrimp), boiled while still on the trawler; generally served with toast and butter

sandwiches ("sandwiches") — 3 small open sandwiches, generally with salmon or shrimps, meat and cheese

sillbricka/silltallrik (**sil**brikkah/**sil**tahlrik) — a choice of almost every kind of herring available

smör, ost och sill (smūrr, oost ok sil) — butter, cheese and herring; small plate of herring with bread, butter and cheese often seen on menus in it's abbreviated form: S.O.S.

toast Skagen ("toast" **skaa**gern) — toast with chopped shrimps in mayonnaise, topped with bleak roe

Soups *Soppor*

I'd like some soup.	**Jag skulle vilja ha en soppa.**	yaa(g) **skew**ler **vil**yah haa ehn **sop**pah
What do you recommend?	**Vad föreslår ni?**	vaad **fu̅r̅**rerslawr nee

buljong	bew**lyong**	consommé
champinjonsoppa	shamhpin**yo̅o̅n**soppah	mushroom soup
fisksoppa	**fisk**soppah	fish soup
grönsakssoppa	**gru̅r̅n**saakssoppah	vegetable soup
hummersoppa	**hew**merrsoppah	lobster soup
kålsoppa	**kawl**soppah	cabbage soup
löksoppa	**lu̅r̅k**soppah	onion soup
nässelsoppa	**neh**sserlsoppah	nettle soup
oxvanssoppa	**ooks**svahnssoppah	oxtail soup
räksoppa	**raik**soppah	shrimp soup
sparrissoppa	**spah**rissoppah	asparagus soup
spenatsoppa	speh**naat**soppah	spinach soup
svartsoppa (**svah**^{r}tsoppah)	black soup made from goose blood and giblets; a southern Swedish speciality served in November, as a starter in a goose meal	
ärtsoppa (**æ**^{r}tsoppah)	yellow pea soup with lightly salted pork; traditionally served on Thursdays in winter as a main course, along with hot sweet Swedish *punsch,* and pancakes as dessert	
blåbärssoppa (**blaw**bæ̅^{r}ssoppah)	sweet bilberry soup; served as a dessert or as a vitamin-packed pick-me-up	

Salads *Sallader*

What salads do you have?	**Vad har ni för sallader?**	vaad haar nee fu̅r̅r **sah**lahderr

grönsallad (**gru̅r̅n**sahlahd)	lettuce, cucumber, tomatoes, parsley, dill, with oil and vinegar dressing; accompanies the main course
tonfisksallad (**to̅o̅n**fisksahlahd)	tuna fish salad—Swedish version of salad Niçoise
skaldjurssallad (**skaal**ye̅w̅^{r}ssahlahd)	assorted seafood salad (mostly mussels and shrimps)
västkustsallad (**vehst**kewstsahlahd)	assorted seafood salad with mushrooms, tomatoes, lettuce, cucumber, asparagus and dill

Egg dishes *Äggrätter*

crêpe	krehp	crepe
skaldjurs-	**skaal**ye̅w̅^{r}s-	seafood
förlorat ägg	fur^{r}**lo̅o̅**raht ehg	poached egg
omelett	omer**leht**	omelet
med ost	ma̅y̅d oost	with cheese
med skinka	ma̅y̅d **shin**kah	with ham
med svamp	ma̅y̅d svahmp	with mushrooms
pannkaka	**pahn**kaakah	pancake
stekt ägg	sta̅y̅kt ehg	fried egg
äggröra	**ehg**ru̅r̅rah	scrambled eggs

Fish and seafood *Fisk och skaldjur*

Sweden has a long coastline and many lakes, so it's not surprising that fish plays an important part in the country's diet. On the west coast the specialities are shellfish, fresh mackerel and cod. In the south and east, look for fresh herring, Baltic herring and whitefish. And in northern Sweden enjoy river trout and salmon as well as a distinctive red fish, char *(röding)*.

As for herring—the Swedish favourite—ask for *silltallrik* (**sil**tahlrik) and you'll get a sample of almost every variety available.

The crayfish season starts at midnight on the second Wednesday in August. It's taken quite seriously in Sweden, when the nights are long and the parties, floating on aquavit, flow into the early hours.

ansjovis	ahn**sho̅o̅**viss	marinated sprats
abborre	**ah**borrer	perch
bergtunga	**bæry**tewngah	type of dab
bläckfisk	**blehk**fisk	octopus
böckling	**bur**kling	smoked Baltic herring
flundra	**flewn**drah	flounder
forell	fo**rehl**	trout
gråsej	**graw**say	coley
gädda	**yeh**dah	pike
gös	yu̅r̅ss	pike-perch
havskräfta	**hahvs**krehftah	Dublin Bay prawn (saltwater crayfish)

hälleflundra	**heh**lerflewndrah	halibut
hummer	**hew**merr	lobster
kolja	**kol**yah	haddock
kräfta	**kreh**ftah	(freshwater) crayfish
krabba	**krah**bah	crab
kummel	**kew**merl	hake
lake	**laa**ker	burbot
lax	lahks	salmon
laxöring	**lahksur**ring	salmon trout
långa	**long**ah	ling
makrill	**mahk**ril	mackerel
marulk	**maa**rewlk	monkfish, anglerfish
multe	**mewl**ter	mullet
piggvar	**pig**vaar	turbot
räkor	**rai**koor	prawns (shrimp)
röding	**rur**ding	char
rödspätta	**rur(d)**spehtah	plaice
rödtunga	**rur(d)**tewngah	lemon sole
sardell	sah^r**dehl**	anchovy
sardin	sah^r**deen**	sardine
sik	seek	whitefish
sill	sil	herring
sjötunga	**shur**tewngah	sole
skarpsill	**skahrp**sil	sprats
slätvar	**slait**vaar	brill
stenbit	**stayn**beet	lump-fish
strömming	**strur**ming	Baltic herring
stör	sturr	sturgeon
tonfisk	**toon**fisk	tuna (tunny)
torsk	to^rsk	cod
vitling	**vit**ling	whiting
ål	awl	eel

baked	**ugnstekt**	**ewngn**stāykt
deep fried	**friterad**	fri**tay**rahd
fried	**stekt**	staykt
grilled	**halstrad, grillad**	**hahl**strahd, **gril**lahd
marinated	**marinerad, gravad**	mahri**nnay**rahd, **graa**vahd
poached	**pocherad**	po**shay**rahd
sautéed	**brynt**	brewnt
simmered	**kokt**	kookt
slightly salted	**rimmad**	**rim**mahd
smoked	**rökt**	rurkt
steamed	**ångkokt**	**ong**kookt

You'll probably come across some of the following fish and seafood dishes when eating out:

gravlax (**graav**lahks)	salmon marinated with salt, sugar (pepper) and dill; served with a sweet-sour mustard-vinegar-oil sauce with plenty of dill
gubbröra (**gewb**rūrrah)	marinated sprats, onions and hard-boiled eggs, fried in butter; served hot
inkokt lax (**in**kookt lahks)	simmered fresh salmon; served cold with mayonnaise or a hollandaise sauce
krabba (**krah**bah)	crab, available during the crab season (autumn); served with a mustard-dill sauce
kräftor (**krehf**toor)	freshwater crayfish simmered with dill, served cold; the season for this Swedish speciality starts on the second Wednesday in August
kräftströmming (**krehft**strurming)	Baltic herring baked with crushed tomatoes and lots of dill; served warm or cold with boiled potatoes
lutfisk (**lēwt**fisk)	dried ling, soaked in lye; simmered and served with a béchamel sauce, mustard or black pepper (traditional Christmas dish)
lättrökt lax (**leht**rūrkt lahks)	lightly smoked salmon, often served with creamed spinach, poached egg and lemon
rimmad lax med stuvad potatis (**rim**mad lahks māyd **stēw**vahd poo**taa**tiss)	lightly salted salmon with creamed potatoes and dill
sotare (**sōō**tahrer)	Baltic herring soaked in water and salt, grilled until black; served hot, often with dill butter
strömmingsflundror (**strur**mingsflewndror)	Baltic herrings, opened out and sandwiched in pairs with a parsley or dill filling, fried; served with mashed potatoes
stuvad abborre (**stēw**vahd **ah**borrer)	perch, poached with onion, parsley and lemon; served with boiled potatoes
surströmming (**sēw**ʳstrurming)	Baltic herring, specially processed, marinated and fermented (an autumnal northern Swedish speciality); served with small almond-shaped potatoes, chopped onions and unleavened barley bread; not for those with delicate noses

Meat *Kött*

What kind of meat is this?	**Vad för slags kött är det här?**	vaad fu̅r̅ slahgss khurt ǣr da̅y̅(t) hær
beef/lamb	**oxkött/lamm**	**ooks**khurt/lahm
pork/veal	**fläskkött/kalv**	**flehsk**khurt/kahlv
I'd like some ...	**Jag skulle vilja ha ...**	yaa(g) **skew**ler **vil**yah haa

biff	bif	beef steak
fläskfilé	**flehsk**filla̅y̅	fillet of pork
fläskkarré	**flehsk**kahra̅y̅	loin of pork
fläskkotlett	**flehsk**kotleht	pork chop
kalvbräss	**kahlv**brehss	sweetbread
kalvfilé	**kahlv**filla̅y̅	fillet of veal
kalvkotlett	**kahlv**kotleht	veal chop
kalvlever	**kahlv**la̅y̅verr	calf's liver
kalvstek	**kahlv**sta̅y̅k	roast veal
kalvsylta	**kahlv**sewlta	jellied veal loaf
kassler	**kah**slerr	lightly salted, smoked loin of pork
korv	korv	sausage
falukorv	**faa**lewkorv	lightly spiced sausage, fried in slices
fläskkorv	**flehsk**korv	spicy boiled pork sausage
isterband	**is**terrbahnd	fried sausage of pork, beef and barley grain
köttbullar	**khurt**bewlahr	meat balls
köttfärslimpa	**khurt**fæ^{r}slimpah	meat loaf
lammbog	**lahm**bo̅o̅g	shoulder of lamb
lammkotlett	**lahm**kotleht	lamb chop
lammsadel	**lahm**saaderl	saddle of lamb
lammstek	**lahm**sta̅y̅k	roast lamb
njure	**nye̅w̅**rer	kidney
oxbringa	**ooks**bringah	brisket of beef
oxfilé	**ooks**filla̅y̅	fillet of beef
oxrulader	**ooks**rewlaaderr	braised rolls of beef
pannbiff	**pahn**bif	hamburger
ragu	rah**ge̅w̅**	ragout
revbensspjäll	**ra̅y̅v**ba̅y̅nsspyehl	spareribs
rostbiff	**rost**bif	roast beef
råbiff	**raw**bif	steak tartare
skinka	**shin**kah	ham
kokt skinka	kookt **shin**kah	boiled ham
rökt skinka	ru̅r̅kt **shin**kah	smoked ham
tunga	**tew**ngah	tongue
wienerschnitzel	**vee**nerrshnitserl	breaded veal escalope

roast	**ugnstekt**	**ewngn**stāykt
boiled	**kokt**	kookt
braised	**bräserad**	brehs**sāy**rahd
fried	**stekt**	stāykt
grilled (broiled)	**grillad**	**gril**lahd
whole roasted	**helstekt**	**hāyl**stāykt
sautéed	**brynt**	brēwnt
smoked	**rökt**	rūrkt
underdone (rare)	**blodig**	**bloo**dig
medium	**medium**	**māy**deeyewm
well-done	**genomstekt**	**yāy**nomstāykt

biff à la Lindström (bif à la **lin(d)**strurm) — minced beef mixed with pickled beetroot, capers and onions, shaped into patties and fried

blodpudding med lingonsylt (**bloo(d)**pewding māyd **lin**gonsewlt) — black pudding (blood sausage), fried and served with cranberries; eaten as a main course

bruna bönor med fläsk (**brēw**nah **būr**noor māyd flehsk) — stewed brown beans flavoured with vinegar and golden syrup; served with thick slices of lightly salted pork

dillkött (**dil**khurt) — chunks of veal in a lemon and dill sauce

fläskpannkaka (**flehsk**pahnkaakah) — thick oven-baked pancake with bacon, served with cranberries

kåldolmar (**kawl**dolmahr) — cabbage rolls, stuffed with minced meat and rice; served with cream gravy

lövbiff (**lūrv**bif) — fried thinly sliced beef; served with fried onions

pepparrotskött (**peh**pahrrootskhurt) — boiled beef with horseradish sauce

pytt i panna (pewt ee **pah**nah) — Swedish hash; chunks of fried meat, sausages, onions and potatoes; served with a fried egg and pickled beetroot

sjömansbiff (**shūr**mahnsbif) — casserole with fried beef, onions and potatoes, braised in beer

slottsstek (**slots**stāyk) — pot roast with marinated sprats and golden syrup

Game and poultry *Vilt och fågel*

During the hunting season you'll find game on restaurant menus. Some varieties—woodland grouse, black grouse, ptarmigan and hazelhen—may be new to you. Try them!

Often game is marinated, for example with juniper berries, before being cooked, then served with an exceptionally rich sauce. Vegetables, cranberries and fruit jellies are also served with game. If you happen to be in southern Sweden on November 11; join in the celebration of *Mårten gås* and eat *svartsoppa,* black soup, and goose.

I'd like some game.	**Jag skulle vilja ha en vilträtt.**	yaa(g) **skew**ler **vil**yah haa ehn **vil**treht

anka	**ahn**kah	duck
björnstek	**byu̅r̅^{r}n**sta̅y̅k	roast bear
fasan	fah**saan**	pheasant
gås	gawss	goose
hare	**haa**rer	hare
hjort	yoo^{r}t	deer
järpe	**yær**per	hazelhen
kalkon	kahl**ko̅o̅n**	turkey
kyckling	**khew**kling	chicken
morkulla	**mo̅o̅r**kewlah	woodcock
orre	**or**rer	black grouse
rapphöna	**rahp**hu̅r̅nah	partridge
ren	ra̅y̅n	reindeer
renbog	**ra̅y̅n**bo̅o̅g	shoulder of reindeer
renfilé	**ra̅y̅n**filla̅y̅	fillet of reindeer
renskav	**ra̅y̅n**skaav	dried leg of reindeer, thinly sliced
renstek	**ra̅y̅n**sta̅y̅k	roast reindeer
rökt renstek	ru̅r̅kt **ra̅y̅n**sta̅y̅k	smoked roast reindeer
torkat renkött	torkaht **ra̅y̅n**khurt	dried fillet of reindeer
ripa	**ree**pah	ptarmigan
rådjur	**raw**ye̅w̅r	venison
rådjursfilé	**raw**ye̅w̅^{r}sfilla̅y̅	fillet of venison
rådjurssadel	**raw**ye̅w̅^{r}ssaaderl	saddle of venison
rådjursstek	**raw**ye̅w̅^{r}ssta̅y̅k	roast venison
tjäder	**khai**derr	woodland grouse
vildand	**vild**ahnd	wild duck
älg	ehly	elk
älgfilé	**ehly**filla̅y̅	fillet of elk
älgstek	**ehly**sta̅y̅k	roast elk

Vegetables *Grönsaker*

Could I have some vegetables?	**Skulle jag kunna få lite grönsaker?**	**skew**ler yaa(g) **kew**nah faw **lee**ter **grurn**saakerr
blomkål	**bloom**kawl	cauliflower
broccoli	**brok**koli	broccoli
brysselkål	**brew**sserlkawl	Brussels sprouts
bönor	**bur**noor	beans
endiv	ehn**deev**	chicory (endive)
fänkål	**fæn**kawl	fennel
grönkål	**grurn**kawl	kale
grönsallad	**grurn**sahlahd	lettuce
gurka	**gewr**kah	cucumber
haricots verts	ahrikko**vær**	French (green) beans
kronärtskocka	**kroo**nærtskokkah	artichoke
kålrot	**kawl**root	swede (rutabaga)
lök	lurk	onions
majs	mahyss	sweet corn (corn)
morötter	**moo**rurterr	carrots
paprika	**paa**prikkah	sweet pepper
grön/röd/gul	grurn/rurd/gewl	green/red/yellow
purjolök	**pewr**yoolurk	leeks
rädisor	**reh**dissoor	radishes
rödbetor	**rur(d)**baytoor	beetroots
rödkål	**rur(d)**kawl	red cabbage
saltgurka	**sahlt**gewrkah	salted gherkin
sparris	**spah**riss	asparagus
spenat	speh**naat**	spinach
svamp	svahmp	mushrooms
champinjoner	shahmpin**yoo**nerr	button mushrooms
kantareller	kahntah**reh**lerr	chanterelle mushrooms
tomater	too**maa**terr	tomatoes
vitkål	**veet**kawl	white cabbage
äggplanta	**ehg**plahntah	aubergine (eggplant)
ärtor	**ær**toor	peas
ättiksgurka	**eh**tiksgewrkah	pickled gherkin (pickle)

rotmos (**root**mooss) mashed swedes, potatoes and carrots; served with boiled, lightly salted pig's knuckle

boiled	**kokta**	**koo**ktah
creamed	**stuvade**	**stew**vahder
au gratin	**gratinerade**	grahti**nay**rahder
stuffed	**fyllda**	**fewl**dah

Potatoes, rice and noodles *Potatis, ris och pasta*

bakad potatis	**baa**kad poo**taa**tiss	baked potatoes
färskpotatis	**fær****skpoo**taatiss	new potatoes
kokt potatis	kookt poo**taa**tiss	boiled potatoes
pommes frites	pom frit	chips (French fries)
potatis	poo**taa**tiss	potato
-gratäng	-grah**tehng**	gratin
-kroketter	-kro**keh**terr	croquettes
-mos	-mooss	mashed
-puffar	-**pew**fahr	fritters
-sallad	-**sah**lahd	salad
ris	reess	rice
råstekt potatis	**raw**staykt poo**taa**tiss	fried potatoes
stekt potatis	staykt poo**taa**tiss	sautéed potatoes
stuvade makaroner	**stew**vahderr mahkah**roo**nerr	creamed macaroni

hasselbackspotatis (**hah**sserlbahks-pootaatiss) potatoes coated with melted butter, breadcrumbs and sometimes grated cheese, baked

kroppkakor (**krop**kaakoor) potato dumplings with a filling of minced bacon and onions; served with melted butter

raggmunk med fläsk (**rahg**mewnk mayd flaisk) potato pancake with lightly salted pork; served with cranberries

Sauces *Såser*

gräddfil	**grehd**fil	sour cream
kryddsmör	**krewd**smurr	herb butter
löksås	**lurk**sawss	onion sauce
persiljesmör	pehr**sil**yersmurr	parsley butter
skarpsås	**skahrp**sawss	sweet-sour mustard-cream sauce
sky	shew	gravy
vitlökssmör	**veet**lurkssmurr	garlic butter

hovmästarsås (**hawv**mehstahrsawss) sweet-sour mustard-vinegar-oil sauce with dill; served with fish and seafood

pepparotssås (**peh**pahrootssawss) béchamel sauce flavoured with horseradish

örtagårdssås (urtahgawrdssawss) mayonnaise mixed with sour cream, dill, parsley, chives, (garlic) and tarragon

... as for the herbs, *örter,* and spices, *kryddor:*

basilika	bahs**see**likkah	basil
dill	dil	dill
dragon	drah**go͞on**	tarragon
enbär	**a͞y**nbær	juniper berries
gräslök	**grais**lu͞rk	chives
ingefära	**in**gerfærah	ginger
kanel	kah**na͞yl**	cinnamon
kardemumma	kahʳder**mew**mah	cardamom
krasse	**krah**sser	cress
kryddpeppar	**krewd**pehpahr	allspice
kummin	**kew**min	caraway seeds
lagerblad	**laa**gerrblaad	bay leaf
mejram	**may**rahm	marjoram
muskot	**mew**skot	nutmeg
(krydd) nejlika	**(krewd) nay**likkah	clove
persilja	**peh**ʳsilyah	parsley
peppar	**peh**pahr	pepper
rosmarin	**raws**mahreen	rosemary
saffran	**sah**frahn	saffron
salvia	**sahl**veeah	sage
salt	sahlt	salt
vitlök	**veet**lu͞rk	garlic

Cheese *Ost*

Why not do like the Swedes and start the day with a slice or two on bread?

Grevé (**gra͞yva͞y**)	semi-hard cheese; a mixture between Gouda and Emmental
herrgårdsost (**hehr**gawʳdsoost)	very popular cheese; semi-hard with large holes. Nutty flavour; eaten young and mature
kryddost (**krewd**oost)	firm, strong, semi-dry cheese with caraway seeds
mesost (**ma͞y**ssoost)	amber coloured, sweet whey cheese; definitely an acquired taste
svecia (**sva͞y**ssiah)	popular semi-hard cheese; can be spiced depending on the region
Västerbotten (**veh**sterrbottern)	hard, pungent cheese from the north of Sweden
ädelost (**ai**derloost)	blue cheese; sharp taste

Fruit *Frukt*

Do you have (fresh) fruit?	**Har ni (färsk) frukt?**	haar nee (færsk) frewkt
I'd like a fruit salad.	**Jag skulle vilja ha fruktsallad.**	yaa(g) **skew**ler **vil**yah haa **frewkt**sahlahd

ananas	**ah**nahnahss	pineapple
apelsin	ahperl**seen**	orange
aprikos	ahpri**kkooss**	apricot
banan	bah**naan**	banana
bigarråer	biggah**raw**err	sweet cherries
björnbär	**byurrn**bær	blackberries
blåbär	**blaw**bær	bilberries (blueberries)
citron	si**troon**	lemon
dadlar	**dahd**lahr	dates
fikon	**fee**kon	figs
grapefrukt	**"grape"**frewkt	grapefruit
hallon	**hah**lon	raspberries
hasselnöt	**hah**sserlnurt	hazelnut
hjortron	**yoor**tron	Arctic cloudberries
jordgubbar	**yoord**gewbahr	strawberries
katrinplommon	kah**treen**ploomon	prunes
krusbär	**krews**bær	gooseberries
kvitten	**kvi**ttern	quince
körsbär	**khurs**bær	cherries
lingon	**ling**on	cranberries
mandel	**mahn**derl	almond
melon	meh**loon**	melon
persika	**pær**sikkah	peach
plommon	**ploo**mon	plums
päron	**pæ**ron	pear
rabarber	rah**bahr**berr	rhubarb
russin	**rew**ssin	raisins
rönnbär	**rurn**bær	rowanberries
smultron	**smewl**tron	wild strawberries
tranbär	**traan**bær	type of cranberries
valnöt	**vaal**nurt	walnut
vattenmelon	**vah**ternmehloon	watermelon
vinbär	**veen**bær	currants
röda	**rur**dah	red
svarta	**svahr**tah	black
vita	**vee**tah	white
vindruvor	**veen**drewvoor	grapes
blå	blaw	blue
gröna	**grur**nah	green
äpple	**eh**pler	apple

Dessert *Efterrätter*

I'd like a dessert, please.	**Jag skulle vilja ha en efterrätt.**	yaa(g) **skew**ler **vil**yah haa ehn **ehf**terreht
Something light, please.	**Någonting lätt, tack.**	**naw**gonting leht tahk
with/without ...	**med/utan ...**	mayd/**ew**tahn
cream	**grädde**	**greh**der
whipped cream	**vispgrädde**	**visp**grehder

chokladmousse	sho**klaa(d)**mooss	chocolate mousse
citronfromage	sit**roon**froomaash	lemon mousse
fläderblomssorbet	**flæ**derrbloomssorbay	elderflower sorbet
friterad camembert med hjortronsylt	fri**tay**rahd **kah**mahnbær mayd **yoo^{r}**tronsewlt	deep fried camembert with cloudberry jam
glass	glahss	ice cream
jordgubbs-	**yoo^{r}d**gewbs-	strawberry
vanilj-	vah**nily-**	vanilla
hjortron med glass	**yoo^{r}**tron mayd glahss	Arctic cloudberries with ice cream
jordgubbar med grädde	**yoo^{r}d**gewbahr mayd **greh**der	strawberries with cream
katrinplommonsufflé	kah**treen**ploomonsewflay	prune soufflé
lingonsorbet	**ling**onsorbay	cranberry sorbet
melon och hallon	meh**loon** ok **hah**lon	melon and raspberries
ris à la Malta	reess ah lah **mahl**tah	rice cream dessert with fruit juice
smultron med grädde	**smewl**tron mayd **greh**der	wild strawberries with cream
syltomelett	**sewlt**omerleht	sweet omelet with jam
våfflor med sylt	**vo**floor mayd sewlt	waffles with jam
äppelkaka med vaniljsås	**eh**perlkaakah mayd va**nily**sawss	apple cake with vanilla custard

marängsviss (mah**rehng**sviss) meringues with whipped cream and chocolate sauce

nyponsoppa (**new**ponsoppah) rose-hip soup; served with almond flakes and whipped cream

plättar (**pleh**tahr) small pancakes; eaten with sugar or jam, sometimes whipped cream

småländsk ostkaka (**smaw**lehnsk **oost**kaakah) curd cake from southern Sweden; served with jam

toscaäpplen (**tos**kahehplern) stewed apples covered with toffee sauce and almond flakes

Drinks *Alkoholhaltiga drycker*

High taxes make most alcohol expensive in Sweden. But if money is no object, you can get just about any drink you like. Note that alcohol is not served anywhere before noon.

Beer *Öl*

Beer is a very popular drink in Sweden. The stronger brew is called *starköl* (**stahrk**ūrl) and the weaker beer *lättöl* (**leht**ūrl).

I'd like a beer, please.	**Jag skulle vilja ha en öl, tack.**	yaa(g) **skew**ler **vil**yah haa ehn ūrl tahk
Do you have draught beer?	**Har ni fatöl?**	haar nee **faat**ūrl

Aquavit *Brännvin*

The national drink is served ice-cold in small glasses, to go with the *smörgåsbord* or appetizers. Aquavit, popularly known as *snaps* (snahps), contains about 40 per cent pure alcohol; it's often served with a beer chaser. Aquavit can be flavoured with various spices and herbs. In restaurants it is sold in measures of 2, 4, 6 or 8 centilitres (1 cl. = ⅓ oz.).

Bäska Droppar (**beh**skah **drop**pahr)	bitter-tasting aquavit, flavoured with wormwood
Herrgårds (Aquavit) (**hehr**gaw^{r}ds **ahk**vahveet)	flavoured with caraway seeds and whisky, matured in sherry barrels
O.P. (Anderson Aquavit) (oo pāy)	flavoured with aniseed, caraway seeds and fennel
Renat (Brännvin) (rāynaht)	colourless, unflavoured
Skåne (Akvavit) (**skaw**ner)	same as O.P. but with a weaker flavour
Svart-Vinbärs-Brännvin (svah^{r}t **veen**bæ^{r}s-brehnveen)	flavoured with blackcurrants

Glögg

Around Christmas the Swedes drink a sweet, hot punch called *glögg* (glurg). It is made of red wine, sugar, cloves, cinnamon, Seville orange peel and flavourless aquavit, and served with almonds and raisins.

Punsch

This popular after-dinner drink is a very sweet, power-packed liqueur made of arrak, sugar and pure alcohol. *Punsch* (pewnsh) is also served warm with the traditional Thursday pea soup.

Wine *Vin*

Sweden imports wine from France, Italy, Spain, Australia, California and elsewhere. You'll find excellent Bordeaux and Burgundy vintages in hotels and good restaurants, together with less expensive wines which can be ordered by the carafe or the glass.

May I have the wine list, please?	**Kan jag få vinlistan, tack?**	kahn yaa(g) faw **veen**listahn tahk
I'd like a ... of red wine.	**Jag skulle vilja ha ... rött vin.**	yaa(g) **skew**ler **vil**yah haa ... rurt veen
carafe	**en karaff**	ehn kah**rahf**
glass	**ett glas**	eht glaass
half bottle	**en halv flaska**	ehn hahlv **flahs**kah
A bottle of champagne, please.	**En flaska champagne, tack.**	ehn **flahs**kah shahm**pahny** tahk
Please bring me another ...	**Kan jag få en ... till, tack?**	kahn yaa(g) faw ehn ... til tahk
Where does this wine come from?	**Varifrån kommer det här vinet?**	**vaa**rifrawn **kom**mer dāy(t) hær **vee**nert

red/white/rosé	**rött/vitt/rosé**	rurt/vit/ross**a̅y̅**
dry	**torrt**	to^{r}t
light	**lätt**	leht
full-bodied	**fylligt**	**few**lit
sparkling	**mousserande**	moo**ssa̅y̅**rahnder
very dry	**mycket torrt**	**mew**ker(t) to^{r}t
sweet	**sött**	surt
chilled	**kylt**	khe̅w̅lt
at room temperature	**rumstempererat**	**rewm**stehmperr**a̅y̅**raht

Other alcoholic drinks *Andra alkoholhaltiga drycker*

In bars and restaurants you can get almost all the drinks you're used to at home. The customary international names are used and the drinks are mixed the same way.

I'd like ..., please.	**Jag skulle vilja ha ..., tack.**	yaa(g) **skew**ler **vil**yah haa ... tahk
aperitif	**en aperitif**	ehn ahperri**tif**
brandy	**en cognac**	ehn **kon**yahk
gin and tonic	**en gin och tonic**	ehn yin ok **ton**nik
liqueur	**ett glas likör**	eht glaass li**ku̅r̅r**
port	**ett glas portvin**	eht glaass **paw^{r}t**veen
rum	**rom**	rom
sherry	**ett glas sherry**	eht glaass **sheh**ri
vermouth	**ett glas vermouth**	eht glaass **vehr**mewt
vodka	**en vodka**	ehn **vod**kah
whisky	**en whisky**	ehn **vis**ki
neat (straight)	**ren**	ra̅y̅n
on the rocks	**med is**	ma̅y̅d ees
with water	**med vatten**	ma̅y̅d **vah**tern
with soda water	**med sodavatten**	ma̅y̅d **so̅o̅**dahvahtern

SKÅL!
(skawl)
CHEERS!

Nonalcoholic drinks *Alkoholfria drycker*

Of course you don't have to order wine or spirits in a bar. If you prefer, ask for a *juice* or *läsk* (soft drink):

I don't drink alcohol.	**Jag dricker inte alkohol.**	yaa(g) **dri**kkerr **in**ter ahlko**hawl**
I'd like a/an ...	**Jag skulle vilja ha ...**	yaa(g) **skew**ler **vil**yah haa
apple juice	**äppeljuice**	**eh**perlyo͞oss
grapefruit juice	**grapefruktjuice**	"**grape**"frewktyo͞oss
iced tea	**iste**	**ees**ta͞y
lemonade	**en läsk**	ehn lehsk
(glass of) milk	**(ett glas) mjölk**	(eht glaass) myurlk
milkshake	**en milkshake**	ehn "milkshake"
mineral water	**mineralvatten**	minerr**aal**vahtern
fizzy (carbonated)	**med kolsyra**	ma͞yd **kawl**se͞wrah
still	**utan kolsyra**	**e͞w**tahn **kawl**se͞wrah
orange juice	**apelsinjuice**	ahperl**seen**yo͞oss
pineapple juice	**ananasjuice**	**ah**nahnahsyo͞oss
tomato juice	**tomatjuice**	too**maat**yo͞oss
tonic water	**tonic**	**to**nnik

Hot drinks *Varma drycker*

The best place to go for your afternoon tea or coffee is a cake shop. Pay for your cake or pastry at the counter and then take it through to the seating area. There's usually a table with tea and coffee on it—self-service—and you can have as many cups as you like! In more elegant or old-fashioned cafés a waitress will serve you.

I'd like a/an ...	**Jag skulle vilja ha ...**	yaa(g) **skew**ler **vil**yah haa
(hot) chocolate	**(varm) choklad**	(vahrm) sho**klaa(d)**
coffee	**kaffe**	**kah**fer
a pot of	**en kanna**	ehn **kah**nah
decaffeinated	**koffeinfritt**	koffeh**een**frit
espresso	**en espresso**	ehn eh**spreh**sso
with cream	**med grädde**	ma͞yd **greh**der
tea	**te**	ta͞y
a cup of	**en kopp**	ehn kop
with lemon	**med citron**	ma͞yd si**tro͞on**
with milk	**med mjölk**	ma͞yd myurlk

Complaints *Klagomål*

There's a ... missing.	**Det fattas ...**	da̅y̅(t) **fah**tahss
plate	**en tallrik**	ehn **tahl**rik
glass	**ett glas**	eht glaass
I don't have a knife/ fork/spoon.	**Jag har inte någon kniv/gaffel/sked.**	yaa(g) haar **in**ter **naw**gon kneev/**gah**ferl/sha̅y̅d
That's not what I ordered.	**Det där har jag inte beställt.**	da̅y̅(t) dæ̅r̅ haar yaa(g) **in**ter ber**stehlt**
I asked for ...	**Jag bad om ...**	yaa(g) baa(d) om
There must be a mistake.	**Det måste vara ett misstag.**	da̅y̅(t) **mos**ter **vaa**rah eht **mis**taag
May I change this?	**Kan jag få byta ut det här?**	kahn yaa(g) faw **be̅w̅**tah e̅w̅t da̅y̅(t) hæ̅r̅
I asked for a small portion (for the child).	**Jag bad om en liten portion (till barnet).**	yaa(g) baa(d) om ehn **lee**tern po^r^**tsho̅o̅n** (til **baa^r^**nert)
The meat is ...	**Köttet är ...**	**khur**tert æ̅r̅
overdone	**för mycket stekt**	fu̅r̅r **mew**ker(t) sta̅y̅kt
underdone	**inte tillräckligt genomstekt**	**in**ter **til**rehkli(g)t **ya̅y̅**nomsta̅y̅kt
too rare	**för blodigt**	fu̅r̅r **blo̅o̅**di(g)t
too tough	**för segt**	fu̅r̅r sa̅y̅gt
This is too ...	**Det här är för ...**	da̅y̅(t) hæ̅r̅ æ̅r̅ fu̅r̅r
bitter	**beskt**	behskt
salty	**salt**	sahlt
sweet	**sött**	surt
I don't like this.	**Jag tycker inte om det här.**	yaa(g) **tew**kerr **in**ter om da̅y̅(t) hæ̅r̅
The food is cold.	**Maten är kall.**	**maa**tern æ̅r̅ kahl
This isn't fresh.	**Det här är inte färskt.**	da̅y̅(t) hæ̅r̅ æ̅r̅ **in**ter fæ^r^skt
What's taking so long?	**Varför tar det så lång tid?**	**vahr**furr taar da̅y̅(t) saw long teed
Have you forgotten our drinks?	**Har ni glömt våra drinkar?**	haar nee glurmt **vaw**rah **drin**kahr
The wine doesn't taste right.	**Vinet smakar inte bra.**	**vee**nert **smaa**kahr **in**ter braa

This isn't clean.	**Det här är inte rent.**	da̅y̅(t) hær ær **in**ter ra̅y̅nt
I'd like to speak to the head waiter.	**Kan jag få tala med hovmästaren?**	kahn yaa(g) faw **taa**lah ma̅y̅d **hawv**mehstah^{r}n

The bill (check) *Notan*

The service charge is automatically included in restaurant bills. Anything extra for the waiter is optional. Credit cards may be used in an increasing number of restaurants.

I'd like to pay.	**Får jag betala?**	fawr yaa(g) ber**taa**lah
We'd like to pay separately.	**Vi skulle vilja betala var och en för sig.**	vee **skew**ler **vil**yah ber**taa**lah vaar ok ehn fu̅r̅ say
I think there's a mistake in this bill.	**Jag tror att det är ett fel på notan.**	yaa(g) tro̅o̅r aht da̅y̅(t) ær eht fa̅y̅l paw **no̅o̅**tahn
What's this amount for?	**Vad står den här summan för?**	vaad stawr den hær **sew**mahn fu̅r̅
Is everything included?	**Är allting inräknat?**	ær **ahl**ting **in**raiknaht
Do you accept traveller's cheques?	**Tar ni emot resechecker?**	taar nee eh**mo̅o̅t** **ra̅y̅**sserkhehkerr
Can I pay with this credit card?	**Kan jag betala med det här kreditkortet?**	kahn yaa(g) ber**taa**lah ma̅y̅d da̅y̅(t) hær kreh**deet**koo^{r}tert
Keep the change.	**Behåll växeln.**	ber**hol** **veh**kserln
That was a delicious meal.	**Det var en utsökt måltid.**	da̅y̅(t) vaar ehn **e̅w̅**tsu̅r̅kt **mawl**teed
We enjoyed it, thank you.	**Det var mycket gott.**	da̅y̅(t) vaar **mew**ker(t) got

SERVERINGSAVGIFT INRÄKNAD
SERVICE INCLUDED

TIPPING, see inside back-cover

Snacks *Mellanmål*

If you want a quick snack, every self-respecting village has its own *gatukök,* street kitchen, where you can get everything from a hot dog to spring rolls, ice cream and soft drinks. If you want to sit down, look for a *café* or *cafeteria,* where you will get pastries, open sandwiches or maybe a salad.

I'll have one of those.	**Jag skulle vilja ha en av de där.**	yaa(g) **skew**ler **vil**yah haa ehn aav dom dæ̅r
Can I have two of these, please.	**Kan jag få två av de här, tack?**	kahn yaa(g) faw tvaw aav dom hæ̅r tahk
to the left/right	**till vänster/höger**	til **vehn**sterr/**hu̅r̅**gerr
above/below	**ovanför/nedanför**	**aw**vahnfu̅r̅r/**na̅y̅**dahnfu̅r̅r
It's to take away.	**Jag tar det med mig.**	yaa(g) taar da̅y̅(t) ma̅y̅d may
I'd like a frankfurter with mashed potatoes.	**Jag skulle vilja ha en varm korv med (potatis)mos.**	yaa(g) **skew**ler **vil**yah haa ehn vahrm korv ma̅y̅d (poo**taa**tis)mo̅o̅ss
I'd like a/an/some ...	**Jag skulle vilja ha ...**	yaa(g) **skew**ler **vil**yah haa
fried sausage	**en grillad korv**	ehn **gril**lahd korv
in a roll	**med bröd**	ma̅y̅d bru̅r̅d
with chips	**med pommes frites**	ma̅y̅d pom frit
ice cream	**en glass**	ehn glahss
chocolate	**choklad-**	shoo**klaa(d)**-
pear	**päron-**	**pæ̅**ron-
strawberry	**jordgubbs-**	**yo̅o̅ʳ**dgewbss-
vanilla	**vanilj-**	vah**nily**-
Can I have an open sandwich with eggs and marinated sprats?	**Kan jag få en smörgås med ägg och ansjovis?**	kahn yaa(g) faw ehn **smurr**gawss ma̅y̅d ehg ok ahn**sho̅o̅**viss
cheese	**ost**	oost
ham	**skinka**	**shin**kah
liver paté	**leverpastej**	**la̅y̅**verrpahstay
shrimps	**räkor**	**rai**koor
meat balls	**köttbullar**	**khurt**bewlahr
spring roll	**vårrulle**	**vawr**rewler

landgång (**lahn(d)**gong) a long open sandwich with at least 3 different toppings

Pastries and cakes *Bakverk och kakor*

Sweden is famous for its pastries and cakes so either buy them in a pastry shop or try some with coffee in a café.

I'd like a ...	**Jag skulle vilja ha en ...**	yaa(g) **skew**ler **vil**yah haa ehn
bun	**bulle**	**bew**ler
cake	**kaka**	**kaa**kah
piece of gâteau	**tårtbit**	**taw^{r}t**beet
kanelbulle	kahn**āyl**bewler	cinnamon bun
mjuk pepparkaka	myēwk **peh**pahrkaakah	gingerbread cake
sockerkaka	**so**kkerrkaakah	sponge cake
wienerbröd	**vee**nerbrūrd	Danish pastry

chokladbiskvi (sho**klaa(d)**biskvee) chocolate-covered macaroon with a filling of chocolate-flavoured butter-cream

drömtårta (**drurm**taw^{r}tah) chocolate Swiss roll with a vanilla-butter filling

gräddtårta (**grehd**taw^{r}tah) cream sponge with jam filling

mazarin (mahssah**reen**) Sweden's most beloved pastry; almond tart topped with icing

napoleonbakelse (nah**pōō**lāyon-baakerlser) iced flaky pastry filled with whipped cream and apple sauce

prinsesstårta (prin**sehs**staw^{r}tah) sponge cake with vanilla custard, whipped cream and strawberry jam, covered with green marzipan

rulltårta (**rewl**taw^{r}tah) Swiss roll filled with jam or chocolate cream

saffransbulle (**sahf**rahnsbewler) saffron bun; traditionally a Christmas bun

semla, fastlagsbulle (**seh**mlah, **fahst**-laagsbewler) bun filled with almond paste and whipped cream, served either as a pastry or in a bowl with hot milk and cinnamon; available from Christmas to Easter

spettekaka (**speh**terkaakah) tall, cone-shaped dry cake, made of egg and sugar paste on a spit; speciality from southern Sweden

Picnic *Picknick*

Just a little information to make shopping for a picnic easier. Almost all butter and margarine in Sweden is salted; unsalted butter does exist but is difficult to find. Or buy easy-spread butter/margarine mixtures (not for frying).

For fillings there's a variety of pre-packed smoked or boiled meat and sausages. You can also buy food at the fresh-meat counter—the sales person will slice it for you. Try *medvurst* (**ma̅y̅d**vewrst), a very popular smoked or boiled sausage (one variety is flavoured with cognac), or juniper-smoked ham, *enrisrökt skinka* (**a̅y̅n**reesru̅r̅kt **shin**kah). You can also buy a whole sausage and slice it yourself. There are different kinds of liver paté worth trying and an interesting selection of cheeses.

And if you like fermented milk, *filmjölk* (**feel**myurlk), try a variety called *filbunke* (**feel**bewnker)—you eat it like yoghurt.

I'd like a/an/ some ...	**Jag skulle vilja ha ...**	yaa(g) **skew**ler **vil**yah haa
biscuits (Br.)	**kex**	kehks
beer	**öl**	u̅r̅l
bread	**bröd**	bru̅r̅d
butter	**smör**	smu̅r̅r
cheese	**ost**	oost
chips (Am.)	**chips**	khips
chocolate bar	**en chokladkaka**	ehn sho**klaa(d)**kaakah
(instant) coffee	**(snabb)kaffe**	**(snahb)kah**fer
cookies	**kex**	kehks
crisps	**chips**	khipss
eggs	**ägg**	ehg
gherkins (pickles)	**ättiksgurka**	**eh**tiksgewrkah
ginger biscuits	**pepparkakor**	**peh**pahrkaakor
ham	**skinka**	**shin**kah
liver paté	**leverpastej**	**la̅y̅**verrpahstay
milk	**mjölk**	myurlk
mustard	**senap**	**sa̅y̅**nahp
sausage	**korv**	korv
sugar	**socker**	**sok**kerr
tea	**te**	ta̅y̅
yoghurt	**en yoghurt**	ehn **yawg**(h)ew[r]t

Travelling around

Plane *Flyg*

Is there a flight to Luleå?	**Finns det något flyg till Luleå?**	finss day(t) **naw**got flewg til **lew**layaw
Is it a direct flight?	**Är det ett direktflyg?**	ær day(t) eht di**rehkt**flewg
When's the next flight to Malmö?	**När går nästa flyg till Malmö?**	nær gawr **neh**stah flewg til **mahl**mur
Is there a connection to ...?	**Finns det någon anslutning till ...?**	finss day(t) **naw**gon **ahn**slewtning til
I'd like a ticket to ...	**Jag skulle vilja ha en biljett till ...**	yaa(g) **skew**ler **vil**yah haa ehn **bil**yeht til
single (one-way)	**enkel**	**ehn**kerl
return (round trip)	**tur och retur**	tewr ok rer**tewr**
aisle seat	**plats vid gången**	plahtss veed **gon**gern
window seat	**plats vid fönstret**	plahtss veed **furn**strert
What time do we take off?	**Hur dags går planet?**	hewr dahgss gawr **plaa**nert
What time should I check in?	**Hur dags måste jag checka in?**	hewr dahgss **mos**ter yaa(g) **khehk**kah in
Is there a bus to the airport?	**Går det någon buss till flygplatsen?**	gawr day(t) **naw**gon bewss til **flewg**plahtsern
What time do we arrive?	**Hur dags är vi framme?**	hewr dahgss ær vee **frah**mer
I'd like to ... my reservation.	**Jag skulle vilja ... min reservation.**	jaa(g) **skew**ler **vil**yah ... min rehsehrvah**shoon**
cancel	**annullera**	ahnew**lay**rah
change	**ändra**	**ehn**drah
confirm	**bekräfta**	ber**krehf**tah
I'd like to cancel my ticket.	**Jag skulle vilja avbeställa min biljett.**	yaa(g) **skew**ler **vil**yah **aav**berstehlah min bil**yeht**

ANKOMST ARRIVAL	**AVGÅNG** DEPARTURE

Train *Tåg*

Trains in Sweden are operated by Swedish State Railways (SJ). They are extremely comfortable—in fact, second class in Sweden is often as luxurious as first class in many other countries. On long-distance trains there is always a restaurant car or a buffet. Some trains have special compartments, marked "Bk", for mothers with infants.

Seat reservations are not normally necessary for short distances but are often compulsory on long-distance trains, and during the Christmas and Easter periods it's recommended to book your seat well ahead.

Eurocity (EC) (ehewroositti)	International express train with first and second class
Intercity (IC) ("Intercity")	Long-distance inter-city train with first and second class; reservation compulsory; has telephone, a shop for small items such as perfume, chocolate, books, etc., and a dining car
City Express ("city-express")	Business train on special runs; reservation compulsory; surcharge payable; telephone
Lokaltåg (loo**kaal**tawg)	Local train
Motorvagnståg (m$\bar{o}\bar{o}$torvahngnstawg)	Small diesel train used on short runs
Pendeltåg (**pehn**derltawg)	Local train serving the city suburbs

Coach (long-distance bus) *Expressbuss*

A cheap, comfortable way to travel is by express coach, mainly run by the Swedish State Railways (SJ). These buses operate between major towns in the southern and central parts of Sweden and between the capital and coastal towns further north. In the northern region, the rail network is extended by a postal bus service.

Note: Most of the phrases on the following pages can be used for both train and bus travel.

To the railway station *Till stationen*

Where's the railway station?	**Var ligger järnvägs-stationen?**	vaar **li**ggerr **yæ̅**^{r}nvaigs-stahsho͞onern
Where's the coach station.	**Var ligger buss-stationen?**	vaar **li**ggerr **bews**-stahsho͞onern
Taxi!	**Taxi!**	**tah**ksi
Take me to the ..., please.	**Till ..., tack.**	til ... tahk

INGÅNG	ENTRANCE
UTGÅNG	EXIT
TILL TÅGEN	TO THE TRAINS
INFORMATION	INFORMATION

Where's the ...? *Var är ...?*

Where is/are (the) ...?	**Var är ...?**	vaar æ̅r
booking office	**biljettexpeditionen**	bil**yeht**ehkspehdisho͞onern
cafeteria	**cafeterian**	kahfer**tāy**reeahn
currency exchange office	**växelkontoret**	**veh**kserlkonto͞orert
left-luggage office (baggage check)	**effektförvaringen**	eh**fehkt**furrvaaringern
lost property (lost and found) office	**hittegods-expeditionen**	**hi**ttergoods-ehkspehdisho͞onern
luggage lockers	**förvaringsboxarna**	furr**vaa**ringsboksah^{r}nah
newsstand	**tidningskiosken**	**tee**(d)ningskhioskern
platform 2	**perrong 2**	peh**rong** 2
reservations office	**biljettexpeditionen**	bil**yeht**ehkspehdi-sho͞onern
restaurant	**restaurangen**	rehsto**rrahng**ern
snack bar	**snackbaren**	**snahk**baarern
ticket office	**biljettluckan**	bil**yeht**lewkahn
track 5	**spår 5**	spawr 5
waiting room	**väntsalen**	**vehnt**saalern
Where are the toilets?	**Var är toaletten?**	vaar æ̅r tooah**leh**tern

TAXI, see page 21

Inquiries *Förfrågningar*

In Sweden **i** means information office.

When is the ... train to Uppsala?	**När går ... tåget till Uppsala?**	nær gawr ... **taw**gert til **ewp**saalah
first/last	**första/sista**	**fur**^{r}stah/**sis**tah
When is the next train to ...?	**När går nästa tåg till ...?**	nær gawr **neh**stah tawg til
What time does the train to Göteborg leave?	**Hur dags går tåget till Göteborg?**	hewr dahgss gawr **taw**gert til yurter**bory**
What's the fare to Örebro?	**Vad kostar en biljett till Örebro?**	vaad **kos**tahr ehn bil**yeht** til urrer**broo**
Is it a through train?	**Är det ett direkt-gående tåg?**	ær day(t) eht di**rehkt**-gawehnder tawg
Is there a connection to ...?	**Finns det någon anslutning till ...?**	finss day(t) **naw**gon **ahns**lewtning til
Do I have to change trains?	**Måste jag byta tåg?**	**mos**ter yaa(g) **bew**tah tawg
Is there enough time to change?	**Hinner man byta tåg?**	**hin**nerr mahn **bew**tah tawg
Is the train running on time?	**Går tåget i tid?**	gawr **taw**gert ee teed
What time does the train arrive in Helsingborg?	**Hur dags är tåget framme i Helsingborg?**	hewr dahgss ær **taw**gert **frah**mer ee hehlsing**bory**
Is there a dining car/ sleeping car on the train?	**Finns det någon restaurangvagn/ sovvagn i tåget?**	finss day(t) **naw**gon rehstor**rahng**vahngn/ **saw**vahngn ee **taw**gert
Does the train stop in Norrköping?	**Stannar tåget i Norrköping?**	**stah**nahr **taw**gert ee **nork**hurping
Which platform does the train to Malmö leave from?	**Från vilken perrong går tåget till Malmö?**	frawn **vil**kern peh**rong** gawr **taw**gert til **mahl**mur
Which track does the train from Göteborg arrive at?	**På vilket spår kommer tåget från Göteborg in?**	paw **vil**kert spawr **kom**merr **taw**gert frawn yurter**bory** in
I'd like a time-table, please.	**Skulle jag kunna få en tidtabell, tack?**	**skew**ler yaa(g) **kew**nah faw ehn **tee(d)**tahbehl tahk

Det är ett direktgående tåg.	It's a through train.
Ni måste byta i ...	You have to change at ...
Byt i ... och ta lokaltåget.	Change at ... and get a local train.
Perrong 2 är ...	Platform 2 is ...
där borta/uppför trappan till vänster/till höger	over there/upstairs on the left/right
Det går ett tåg till Gävle kl ...	There's a train to Gävle at ...
Tåget avgår från spår 8.	Your train will leave from track 8.
Det är ... minuter försenat.	It's running ... minutes late.
Första klass längst fram/ i mitten/längst bak.	First class at the front/in the middle/at the rear.

Tickets—Reservation *Biljetter – Beställning*

I'd like a ticket to Lund.	**Jag skulle vilja ha en biljett till Lund.**	yaa(g) **skew**ler **vil**yah haa ehn bil**yeht** til lewnd
single (one-way)	**enkel**	**ehn**kerl
return (round trip)	**tur och retur**	t$\overline{\text{ew}}$r ok reh**t$\overline{\text{ew}}$r**
first class	**första klass**	**fur^{r}**stah klahss
second class	**andra klass**	**ahn**drah klahss
half price	**halv biljett**	hahlv bil**yeht**
I'd like to reserve a ...	**Jag skulle vilja reservera en ...**	yaa(g) **skew**ler **vil**yah rehsehr**v$\overline{\text{ay}}$**rah ehn
couchette	**liggplats**	**lig**plahtss
window seat	**fönsterplats**	**furn**sterrplahtss
I'd like to reserve a berth in the sleeping car.	**Jag skulle vilja reservera en sovplats.**	yaa(g) **skew**ler **vil**yah rehsehr**v$\overline{\text{ay}}$**rah ehn **sawv**plahts
upper berth	**överbädd**	**$\overline{\text{ur}}$**verrbehd
middle berth	**mellanbädd**	**meh**lahnbehd
lower berth	**underbädd**	**ewn**derrbehd

All aboard *Tag plats*

Is this the right platform for the train to Luleå?	**Är det här rätt perrong för tåget till Luleå?**	æ̅r da̅y̅(t) hæ̅r reht peh**rong** fu̅r̅ **taw**gert til **le̅w̅**la̅y̅aw
Is this the train to Östersund?	**Är det här tåget till Östersund?**	æ̅r da̅y̅(t) hæ̅r **taw**gert til urster^{r}**sewnd**
Excuse me. Could I get by?	**Ursäkta, kan jag få komma förbi?**	**e̅w̅**^{r}sehktah kahn yaa(g) faw **kom**mah furr**bee**
Is this seat taken?	**Är den här platsen upptagen?**	æ̅r dehn hæ̅r **plaht**sern **ewp**taagern

RÖKARE
SMOKER

ICKE RÖKARE
NONSMOKER

I think that's my seat.	**Jag tror att det där är min plats.**	yaa(g) tro̅o̅r aht da̅y̅(t) dæ̅r æ̅r min plahtss
Would you let me know before we get to Växjö?	**Skulle ni kunna säga till innan vi kommer till Växjö?**	**skew**ler nee **kew**nah **seh**yah til **in**nahn vee **kom**merr til **vehks**shu̅r̅
What station is this?	**Vilken station är det här?**	**vil**kern stah**sho̅o̅n** æ̅r da̅y̅(t) hæ̅r
How long does the train stop here?	**Hur länge står tåget här?**	he̅w̅r **lehng**er stawr **taw**gert hæ̅r
When do we get to Kiruna?	**När kommer vi till Kiruna?**	næ̅r **kom**mer vee til **kir**rewnah

Sleeping *I sovvagnen*

Are there any free compartments in the sleeping car?	**Finns det någon ledig kupé i sovvagnen?**	finns da̅y̅(t) **naw**gon **la̅y̅**di(g) kew**pa̅y̅** ee **saw**vahngnern
Where's the sleeping car?	**Var är sovvagnen?**	vaar æ̅r **saw**vahngnern
Where's my berth?	**Var är min sovplats?**	vaar æ̅r min **sawv**plahtss
I'd like a lower berth.	**Jag skulle vilja ha en underbädd.**	yaa(g) **skew**ler **vil**yah haa ehn **ewn**derrbehd

Would you make up our berths?	**Skulle ni kunna göra i ordning våra bäddar?**	**skew**ler nee **kew**nah **yu̅r**rah ee **aw^{r}d**ning **vaw**rah **beh**dahr
Would you wake me at 7 o'clock?	**Kan ni väcka mig kl. 7?**	kahn nee **veh**kah may **klo**kkahn 7

Eating *I restaurangvagnen*

On every long-distance train there's a restaurant car and/or a buffet car for drinks and snacks. In some trains there are cars with table space for each passenger so that you can take your coffee back to your own seat.

Where's the dining car/buffet car?	**Var är restaurangvagnen/cafévagnen?**	vaar æ̅r rehsto**rrang**vahngnern/kah**fa̅y̅**vahngnern

Baggage and porters *Bagage och bärare*

Where can I find a porter?	**Var kan jag få tag på en bärare?**	vaar kahn yaa(g) faw taag paw ehn **bæ̅**rahrer
Can you help me with my luggage?	**Kan ni hjälpa mig med bagaget?**	kahn nee **yehl**pah may ma̅y̅d bah**gaa**shert
Where are the ...?	**Var är ...?**	vaar æ̅r
luggage trolleys (carts)	**bagagekärrorna**	bah**gaash**khæroo^{r}nah
luggage lockers	**förvaringsboxarna**	furr**vaa**ringsboksah^{r}nah
Where's the left-luggage office (baggage check)?	**Var är effektförvaringen?**	vaar æ̅r eh**fehkt**furrvaaringern
I'd like to leave my luggage, please.	**Jag skulle vilja lämna in mitt bagage.**	yaa(g) **skew**ler **vil**yah **lehm**nah in mit bah**gaash**
I'd like to register (check) my luggage.	**Jag skulle vilja pollettera mitt bagage.**	yaa(g) **skew**ler **vil**yah polleh**ta̅y̅**rah mit bah**gaash**

RESGODS
REGISTERING (CHECKING) BAGGAGE

PORTERS, see also page 18

Bus—Tram (streetcar) *Buss – Spårvagn*

Get your ticket from the driver when you board the bus. In major cities it's worthwhile buying a booklet of tickets at a reduced price if you plan to travel extensively. The fare on buses and taxis doubles after midnight.

I'd like a booklet of tickets.	**Jag skulle vilja ha ett biljetthäfte.**	yaa(g) **skew**ler **vil**yah haa eht bil**yeht**hehfter
Which tram (streetcar) goes to the town centre?	**Vilken spårvagn går till centrum?**	**vil**kern **spawr**vahngn gawr til **sehn**trewm
Does this bus stop at ...?	**Stannar den här bussen vid ...?**	**stah**nahr dehn hær **bew**ssern veed
Where can I get a bus to the opera?	**Varifrån går bussen till operan?**	**vaa**rifrawn gawr **bew**ssern til ōōperrahn
Which bus do I take to Skansen?	**Vilken buss skall jag ta till Skansen?**	**vil**kern bewss skah(l) yaa(g) taa til **skahn**sern
Where's the bus stop?	**Var är busshållplatsen?**	vaar ær **bews**holplahtsern
When is the next bus to ...?	**När går nästa buss till ...?**	nær gawr **nehs**tah bewss til
How much is the fare to ...?	**Hur mycket kostar det till ...?**	hewr **mew**ker(t) **kos**tahr day(t) til
Do I have to change buses?	**Måste jag byta buss?**	**mos**ter yaa(g) **bew**tah bewss
How many stops are there to ...?	**Hur många hållplatser är det till ...?**	hewr **mon**gah **hol**plahtserr ær day(t) til
Will you tell me when to get off?	**Kan ni säga till när jag skall stiga av?**	kahn nee **seh**yah til nær yaa(g) skah(l) **stee**gah aav
I want to get off at ...	**Jag vill stiga av vid ...**	yaa(g) vil **stee**gah aav veed

BUSSHÅLLPLATS
BUS STOP

Underground (subway) *Tunnelbana*

Stockholm's underground system, the *Tunnelbana,* extends from the centre of the city to the suburbs. Maps of the entire system are displayed inside every station and aboard every train. Stations are marked with a blue "T". Services begin at 5 a.m. and continue until midnight; reduced service continues late into the night on certain lines. You can transfer from bus to underground on the same ticket, which is valid for one hour.

Where's the nearest underground station?	**Var ligger närmaste tunnelbanestation?**	vaar **lig**gerr **nær**mahster **tew**nerlbaanerstahsh**ōōn**
Does this train go to Central Station?	**Går det här tåget till Centralen?**	gawr dāy(t) hǣr **taw**gert til sehn**traa**lern
Where do I change for ...?	**Var byter jag till ...?**	vaar **bēw**terr yaa(g) til
Is the next station ...?	**Är nästa station ...?**	ǣr **nehs**tah stah**shōōn**
Which line should I take to ...?	**Vilken linje skall jag ta till ...?**	**vil**kern **lin**yer skah(l) yaa(g) taa til

Boat service *Båt*

Regular boat and ferry services, carrying trains and cars as well as passengers, link Sweden to the neighbouring countries. Ferries and steamers also join the Swedish mainland to many of the thousands of islands dotted round the coast. Steamer trips on Sweden's lakes and waterways offer beautiful sightseeing opportunities; one of the best is the Göta Canal tour which takes you from one side of the country to the other.

If you would like to rent a boat you should know the regulations applying to Swedish territorial waters, and where guest harbours are located. Get in touch with the Swedish Touring Club (STF). Or hire a canoe for more leisurely excursions on lakes and canals.

I'd like to take a boat trip.	**Jag skulle vilja göra en båttur.**	yaa(g) **skew**ler **vil**yah **yūr**rah ehn **bawt**tēwr

When does the boat for ... leave?	**När går båten till ...?**	nǣr gawr **baw**tern til
Where's the embarkation point?	**Var lägger båten till?**	vaar **leh**gerr **baw**tern til
How long does the crossing take?	**Hur lång tid tar överfarten?**	hēw̄r lawng teed taar ūrverrfaa^{r}tern
boat	**en båt**	ehn bawt
cabin	**en hytt**	ehn hewt
single/double	**enkel/dubbel**	**ehn**kerl/**dew**berl
canoe	**en kanot**	ehn kah**nōōt**
cruise	**en kryssning**	ehn **krew**sning
deck	**ett däck**	eht dehk
ferry	**en färja**	ehn **fær**yah
gangway	**en landgång**	ehn **lahn(d)**gong
hydrofoil	**en svävare**	ehn **svai**vahrer
jetty	**en brygga**	ehn **brew**gah
life belt	**ett livbälte**	eht **leev**behlter
life boat	**en livbåt**	ehn **leev**bawt
pier	**en pir**	ehn peer
rowing boat	**en roddbåt**	ehn **rood**bawt
sailing boat	**en segelbåt**	ehn **sāȳ**gerlbawt
ship	**ett fartyg**	eht **faa^r**tēw̄g
steamer	**en ångbåt**	ehn **ong**bawt

Bicycle hire *Cykeluthyrning*

It is very easy to hire bicycles in Sweden and the local tourist office can give you all the information you will need.

I'd like to hire a bicycle.	**Jag skulle vilja hyra en cykel.**	yaa(g) **skew**ler **vil**yah **hēw̄**rah ehn **sew**kerl

Other means of transport *Andra transportmedel*

cable car	**en linbana**	ehn **leen**baanah
helicopter	**en helikopter**	ehn **heh**likopterr
moped	**en moped**	ehn moo**pāȳd**
motorbike	**en motorcykel**	ehn **mōō**to^{r}sewkerl
scooter	**en skoter**	ehn **skōō**terr

Or perhaps you prefer:

to hitchhike	**att lifta**	aht **lif**tah
to walk	**att gå**	aht gaw

Car *Bil*

Cars drive on the right in Sweden. All vehicles (including motorcycles) must have dipped headlights switched on at all times, even in broad daylight. A red reflector warning triangle must be carried for use in case of a breakdown, and seat belts *(bilbälte)* are obligatory. Crash helmets are compulsory for both drivers and passengers on motorcycles and scooters.

Where's the nearest filling station?	**Var ligger närmaste bensinstation?**	vaar **lig**gerr **nær**mahster behn**seen**stahshōōn
Fill it up, please.	**Full tank, tack.**	fewl tahnk tahk
Give me ... litres of petrol (gasoline).	**Kan jag få ... liter bensin?**	kahn yaa(g) faw ... **lee**terr behn**seen**
super (premium)	**högoktanig**	**hūrg**oktaanig
regular	**lågoktanig**	**lawg**oktaanig
unleaded	**blyfri**	**blew**free
diesel	**diesel**	**dee**sserl
Please check the ...	**Var snäll och kontrollera ...**	vaar snehl ok kontro**llāy**rah
battery	**batteriet**	bahterr**iert**
brake fluid	**bromsvätskan**	**broms**vehtskahn
oil	**oljan**	**ol**yahn
water	**vattnet**	**vaht**nert
Would you check the tyre pressure?	**Skulle ni kunna kontrollera trycket i däcken?**	**skew**ler nee **kew**nah kontro**llāy**rah **trew**kert ee **deh**kern
1.6 front, 1.8 rear.	**1,6 fram, 1,8 bak.**	1 **kom**mah 6 frahm 1 **kom**mah 8 baak
Could you check the spare tyre, too?	**Kan ni kontrollera reservdäcket också?**	kahn nee kontro**llāy**rah reh**særv**dehkert **ok**so
Can you mend this puncture (fix this flat)?	**Kan ni laga den här punkteringen?**	kahn nee **laa**gah dehn hær pewng**tāy**ringern
Would you change the ..., please?	**Skulle ni kunna byta ... tack?**	**skew**ler nee **kew**nah **bew**tah ... tahk
bulb	**glödlampan**	**glūrd**lahmpahn
fan belt	**fläktremmen**	**flehkt**rehmern
spark(ing) plugs	**tändstiften**	**tehn(d)**stiftern
tyre	**däcket**	**deh**kert
wipers	**vindrutetorkarna**	**vind**rewtertorkah[r]nah

CAR HIRE, see page 20

Would you clean the windscreen (windshield)?	**Skulle ni kunna torka av vindrutan?**	**skew**ler nee **kew**nah **tor**kah aav **vind**rewtahn

TANKA SJÄLV SELF SERVICE

Asking the way — Street directions *Fråga om vägen – Visa vägen*

In which direction is ...?	**I vilken riktning ligger ...?**	ee **vil**kern **rikt**ning **lig**gerr
Can you tell me the way to ...?	**Kan ni tala om hur man kommer till ...?**	kahn nee **taa**lah om hewr mahn **kom**merr til
Can you tell me where ... is?	**Kan ni säga mig var ... ligger?**	kahn nee **seh**yah may vaar ... **lig**gerr
How do I get to ...?	**Hur kommer jag till ...?**	hewr **kom**merr yaa(g) til
Am I on the right road for ...?	**Är det här vägen till ...?**	ær day(t) hær **vai**gern til
How far is the next village?	**Hur långt är det till nästa samhälle?**	hewr longt ær day(t) til **neh**stah **sahm**hehler
How far is it to ... from here?	**Hur långt är det till ... härifrån?**	hewr longt ær day(t) til ... **hær**ifrawn
Is there a motorway (expressway)?	**Är det motorväg?**	ær day(t) **moo**torvaig
Is there a road with little traffic?	**Finns det någon väg med lite trafik?**	finss day(t) **naw**gon vaig mayd **lee**ter trah**feek**
Can I drive to the centre of town?	**Kan jag köra in i centrum?**	kahn yaa(g) **khur**rah in ee **sehn**trewm
How long does it take by car/on foot?	**Hur lång tid tar det med bil/ till fots?**	hewr long teed taar day(t) mayd beel/ til footss
How can I find this place/address?	**Hur kommer jag till den här platsen/ adressen?**	hewr **kom**merr yaa(g) til dehn hær **plaht**sern/ ahd**reh**ssern
Where's this?	**Var ligger det?**	vaar **lig**gerr day(t)
Can you show me on the map where I am?	**Kan ni visa mig på kartan var jag är?**	kahn nee **vee**ssah may paw **kaa**^{r}tahn vaar yaa(g) ær

Ni har kört fel.	You're on the wrong road.
Kör rakt fram.	Go straight ahead.
Det är där nere till vänster/höger.	It's down there on the left/right.
mitt emot/bakom ... bredvid/efter ...	opposite/behind ... next to/after ...
norr/söder/öster/väster	north/south/east/west
Kör till första/andra korsningen.	Go to the first/second crossroads (intersection).
Sväng till vänster vid trafikljusen.	Turn left at the traffic lights.
Sväng till höger vid nästa gathörn.	Turn right at the next corner.
Ta ... vägen.	Take the ... road.
Det är en enkelriktad gata.	It's a one-way street.
Ni måste köra tillbaka till ...	You have to go back to ...
Följ skyltarna mot Malmö.	Follow signs for Malmö.

Parking *Parkering*

In town centres, most street parking is metered. The police are normally lenient with tourists, but don't push your luck. Parking fines are high in Sweden.

Where can I park?	**Var kan jag parkera?**	vaar kahn yaa(g) pahr**kay**rah
Is there a car park nearby?	**Finns det en parkering i närheten?**	finss day(t) ehn pahr**kay**ring ee **nær**haytern
May I park here?	**Får jag parkera här?**	fawr yaa(g) pahr**kay**rah hær
How long can I park here?	**Hur länge får jag stå här?**	hewr **lehng**er fawr yaa(g) staw hær
What's the charge per hour?	**Vad är avgiften per timme?**	vaad ær **aav**yiftern pær **tim**merr
Do you have some change for the parking meter?	**Ni har inte lite växel till parkeringsautomaten?**	nee haar **in**ter **lee**ter **veh**kserl til pahr**kay**rings-ahtommaatern

Breakdown—Road assistance *Motorstopp – Hjälp på vägen*

Where's the nearest garage?	**Var ligger närmaste verkstad?**	vaar **li**ggerr **nær**mahster **værk**staa(d)
My car has broken down.	**Min bil har gått sönder.**	min beel haar got **surn**derr
I've had a breakdown at ...	**Jag har fått motorstopp vid ...**	yaa(g) haar fot **mo͞o**torstop veed
Can you send a mechanic?	**Kan ni skicka en mekaniker?**	kahn nee **shi**kkah ehn meh**kaa**nikkerr
My car won't start.	**Bilen startar inte.**	**bee**lern **stah**rtahr **in**ter
The battery is dead.	**Batteriet är slut.**	bahter**ri**ert ǣr sle͞wt
I've run out of petrol (gasoline).	**Bensinen är slut.**	behn**see**nern ǣr sle͞wt
I have a flat tyre.	**Jag har fått punktering.**	yaa(g) haar fot pewng**tāy**ring
The engine is overheating.	**Motorn har gått varm.**	**mo͞o**torn haar got vahrm
There is something wrong with the ...	**Det är något fel på ...**	dāy(t) ǣr **naw**got fāyl paw
brakes	**bromsarna**	**brom**sahrnah
carburettor	**förgasaren**	furr**gaa**ssahrern
exhaust pipe	**avgasröret**	**aav**gaasrūrrert
radiator	**kylaren**	**ke͞w**lahrern
wheel	**hjulet**	**ye͞w**lert
Can you send a breakdown van (tow truck)?	**Kan ni skicka en bärgningsbil?**	kahn nee **shi**kkah ehn **bæry**ningsbeel
How long will you be?	**När kan ni komma?**	nǣr kahn nee **ko**mmah

Accident—Police *Olycka – Polis*

Please call the police.	**Var snäll och ring polisen.**	vaar snehl ok ring poo**lee**ssern
There's been an accident.	**Det har hänt en olycka.**	dāy(t) haar hehnt ehn **o͞o**lewkah
It's about 2 km. from ...	**Det är cirka 2 kilometer från ...**	dāy(t) ǣr **sir**kah 2 khillo**mmāy**terr frawn
Where's there a telephone?	**Var finns det en telefon?**	vaar finns dāy(t) ehn tehleh**fawn**

Call a doctor/an ambulance quickly.	**Ring fort efter en läkare/ambulans.**	ring foo^{r}t **ehf**terr ehn **lai**kahrer/ahmbew**lahnss**
There are people injured.	**Några är skadade.**	**naw**grah ǣr **skaa**dahder
Here's my driving licence.	**Här är mitt körkort.**	hǣr ǣr mit **khūrr**koo^{r}t
What's your name and address?	**Kan jag få namn och adress?**	kahn yaa(g) faw nahmn ok ah**drehss**
What's your insurance company?	**Vilket är ert försäkringsbolag?**	**vil**kert ǣr āy^{r}t fur^{r}**sai**kringsboolaag

Road signs *Vägmärken*

BEGRÄNSAD FRAMKOMLIGHET	Road narrows
CYKELBANA	Cycle path
EJ MOTORFORDON	No motor vehicles
ENSKILD VÄG	Private road
FARLIG KURVA	Dangerous bend (curve)
HUVUDLED	Main road
INFART	Entrance
JÄRNVÄGSKORSNING	Level (railroad) crossing
KÖR SAKTA	Slow down
KORSANDE ARBETSFORDON	Works vehicles merging
KORSANDE TIMMERVÄG	Lumber-track merging
LIVSFARLIG LEDNING	High-tension cable
LÄMNA FÖRETRÄDE	Give way (yield)
MOTORVÄG	Motorway (expressway)
MÖTESPLATS	Passing place
OMKÖRNING FÖRBJUDEN	No overtaking (no passing)
PARKERING	Parking
PRIVAT VÄG	Private road
RASTPLATS	Roadside picnic site
RIDVÄG	Bridle path
SKOLA	School
STENSKOTT	Loose gravel
STOP	Stop
TJÄLSKOTT	Potholes
TRAFIKOMLÄGGNING	Diversion (detour)
TRAFIKPLATS	Roundabout
TULL	Customs
UTFART	Exit
VÄGARBETE	Roadworks (men working)
VÄNDZON	Turning place
ÅTERVÄNDSVÄG/GATA	No through road

Sightseeing

Where's the tourist office?	**Var ligger turistbyrån?**	vaar **li**ggerr tew**rist**bewrawn
What are the main points of interest?	**Vad finns det för sevärdheter?**	vaad finss day(t) furr **say**væ^{r}dhayterr
We're here for ...	**Vi är här ...**	vee ær hær
only a few hours	**bara några timmar**	**baa**rah **naw**grah **ti**mmahr
a day	**en dag**	ehn daa(g)
a week	**en vecka**	ehn **veh**kah
Can you recommend a/an ...?	**Kan ni föreslå någon ...?**	kahn nee **fur**rerslaw **naw**gon
sightseeing tour	**sightseeingtur**	"sightseeing"tewr
excursion	**rundtur**	**rewn(d)**tewr
Where do we leave from?	**Varifrån startar vi?**	**vaa**rifrawn **stah**^{r}tahr vee
Will the bus pick us up at the hotel?	**Kommer bussen och hämtar oss vid hotellet?**	**ko**mmerr **bew**ssern ok **hehm**tahr oss veed ho**teh**lert
How much does the tour cost?	**Hur mycket kostar turen?**	hewr **mew**ker(t) **ko**stahr **tew**rern
What time does the tour start?	**Hur dags startar turen?**	hewr dahgss **stah**^{r}tahr **tew**rern
Is lunch included?	**Ingår lunch?**	**in**gawr lewnsh
What time do we get back?	**Hur dags är vi tillbaka?**	hewr dahgss ær vee til**baa**kah
Do we have free time in ...?	**Har vi någon ledig tid i ...?**	haar vee **naw**gon **lay**dig teed ee
Is there an English-speaking guide?	**Finns det någon engelsktalande guide?**	finss day(t) **naw**gon **ehn**gerlsktaalahnder "guide"
I'd like to hire a private guide for ...	**Jag skulle vilja ha en privat guide ...**	yaa(g) **skew**ler **vil**yah haa ehn pri**vaat** "guide"
half a day	**en halv dag**	ehn hahlv daa(g)
a day	**en dag**	ehn daa(g)

Where is/Where are the ...?	**Var ligger ...?**	vaar **li**ggerr
artists' quarter	**konstnärskvarteren**	**konst**næ^{r}s-kvah^{r}t$\overline{ay}$rern
art museum	**konstmuseet**	**konst**mewss$\overline{ay}$ert
botanical gardens	**botaniska trädgården**	boo**taa**niskah **trai(d)**gaw^{r}dern
bridge	**bron**	br$\overline{oo}$n
building	**byggnaden**	**bewg**nahdern
business district	**affärskvarteren**	ahfæ^{r}skvah^{r}t$\overline{ay}$rern
castle	**slottet**	**slo**ttert
cathedral	**domkyrkan**	**doom**khewrkahn
cave	**grottan**	**gro**ttahn
cemetery	**kyrkogården**	**khewr**koogaw^{r}dern
chapel	**kapellet**	**kah**pehlert
church	**kyrkan**	**khewr**kahn
citadel	**fästningen**	**fehst**ningern
city centre	**(stads)centrum**	**(stahds)sehn**trewm
city hall	**stadshuset**	**stahds**h$\overline{ew}$ssert
concert hall	**konserthuset**	kon**sær**h$\overline{ew}$ssert
court house	**tingshuset**	**tings**h$\overline{ew}$ssert
downtown area	**(stads)centrum**	**(stahds)sehn**trewm
exhibition	**utställningen**	**$\overline{ew}$t**stehlningern
factory	**fabriken**	fah**bree**kern
fair	**mässan**	**meh**ssahn
fleamarket	**loppmarknaden**	**lop**mahrknahdern
fortress	**borgen**	**bor**yern
fountain	**fontänen**	fon**tai**nern
gardens	**trädgårdarna**	**trai(d)**gaw^{r}dah^{r}nah
harbour	**hamnen**	**hahm**nern
lake	**sjön**	shurn
library	**biblioteket**	biblio**t$\overline{ay}$**kert
memorial	**minnesmärket**	**mi**nnehsmærkert
monastery	**klostret**	**klos**trert
monument	**monumentet**	monew**mehn**tert
museum	**museet**	mew**ss$\overline{ay}$**ert
observatory	**observatoriet**	obsehrvah**t$\overline{oo}$**riert
old town	**gamla stan**	**gahm**lah **staan**
opera house	**operan**	**$\overline{oo}$**perrahn
palace	**slottet**	**slo**ttert
park	**parken**	**pahr**kern
parliament building	**riksdagshuset**	**riks**dah(g)sh$\overline{ew}$ssert
planetarium	**planetariet**	plahner**taa**riert
royal palace	**Kungliga slottet**	**kewng**liggah **slo**ttert
ruins	**ruinerna**	rew**ee**ner^{r}nah
shopping area	**affärscentrum**	ahfæ^{r}ssehntrewm

square	**torget**	to**r**yert
stadium	**stadion**	staadion
statue	**statyn**	stah**te̅w̅n**
stock exchange	**börsen**	**bur^r**sern
television studios	**TV-huset**	**ta̅y̅**veh-**he̅w̅**ssert
theatre	**teatern**	ta̅y̅aater^{r}n
tomb	**graven**	**graa**vern
tower	**tornet**	**to̅o̅^{r}**nert
town hall	**rådhuset**	**rawd**he̅w̅ssert
university	**universitetet**	ewnivæ^r**sitta̅y̅**tert
zoo	**djurparken**	**ye̅w̅r**pahrkern

Admission *Inträde*

Is ... open on Sundays?	**Är ... öppet på söndagar?**	ær ... **ur**pert paw **surn**daagahr
When is it open?	**När är det öppet?**	nær ær da̅y̅(t) **ur**pert
When does it close?	**När stänger det?**	nær **stehng**err da̅y̅(t)
What's the entrance fee?	**Vad kostar det i inträde?**	vaad **kos**tahr da̅y̅(t) ee **in**traider
Is there any reduction for (the) ...?	**Är det någon rabatt för ...?**	ær da̅y̅(t) **naw**gon rah**baht** fu̅r̅
children	**barn**	baa^{r}n
disabled	**handikappade**	hahndi**kah**pahder
groups	**grupper**	**grew**perr
pensioners	**pensionärer**	pahnshoon**æ**rerr
students	**studerande**	stew**da̅y̅**rahnder
Do you have a guide-book (in English)?	**Har ni någon guide-bok (på engelska)?**	haar nee **naw**gon **"guide"**-bo̅o̅k (paw **ehng**erlskah)
Can I buy a catalogue?	**Kan jag få köpa en katalog?**	kahn yaa(g) faw **khu̅r̅**pah ehn kahtah**lawg**
Is it all right to take pictures?	**Är det tillåtet att fotografera?**	ær da̅y̅(t) **till**awtert aht footograh**fa̅y̅**rah

FRITT INTRÄDE	ADMISSION FREE
FOTOGRAFERING FÖRBJUDEN	NO CAMERAS ALLOWED

Who—What—When? *Vem – Vad – När?*

What's that building?	**Vad är det där för byggnad?**	vaad ær day(t) dær furr **bewg**nahd
Who was the ...?	**Vem var ...?**	vehm vaar
architect	**arkitekten**	ahrki**tehk**tern
artist	**konstnären**	**konst**nærern
painter	**konstnären**	**konst**nærern
sculptor	**skulptören**	skewlp**tur**rern
Who built it?	**Vem har byggt den?**	vehm haar bewgt dehn
Who painted that picture?	**Vem har målat den där tavlan?**	vehm haar **maw**laht dehn dær **taav**lahn
When did he live?	**När levde han?**	nær **layv**der hahn
When was it built?	**När byggdes det?**	nær **bewg**derss day(t)
Where's the house where ... lived?	**Var ligger huset där ... bodde?**	vaar **li**ggerr **hew**ssert dær ... **boo**derr
We're interested in ...	**Vi är intresserade av ...**	vee ær intreh**ssay**rahder aav
antiques	**antikviteter**	ahntikvi**tay**terr
archaeology	**arkeologi**	ahrkeholo**ggee**
art	**konst**	konst
botany	**botanik**	bootah**neek**
ceramics	**keramik**	khehrah**meek**
coins	**mynt**	mewnt
folk art	**allmogekonst**	**ahl**moogerkonst
furniture	**möbler**	**mur**blerr
geology	**geologi**	yayolo**ggee**
handicrafts	**konsthantverk**	**konst**hahntværk
history	**historia**	his**too**riah
medicine	**medicin**	mehdi**sseen**
modern art	**modern konst**	moo**dærn** konst
music	**musik**	mew**sseek**
natural history	**naturhistoria**	nah**tewr**histooriah
ornithology	**ornitologi**	ornitolo**ggee**
painting	**måleri**	mawler**ree**
pottery	**lergods**	**layr**goodss
religion	**religion**	rehli**yoon**
sculpture	**skulptur**	skewlp**tewr**
wild life	**djurliv**	**yewr**leev
zoology	**zoologi**	solo**ggee**
Where's the ... department?	**Var ligger avdelningen för ...?**	vaar **li**ggerr **aav**daylningern furr

It's ...	**Det är ...**	da̅y̅(t) ær
amazing	**fantastiskt**	fahn**tahs**tiskt
awful	**förskräckligt**	fur^{r}**skrehk**li(g)t
beautiful	**vackert**	**vah**ker^{r}t
gloomy	**dystert**	**dew**ster^{r}t
impressive	**imponerande**	impon**na̅y̅**rahnder
interesting	**intressant**	intreh**ssahnt**
magnificent	**storslaget**	**sto̅o̅**^{r}slaagert
pretty	**sött**	surt
romantic	**romantiskt**	roo**mahn**tiskt
strange	**konstigt**	**kon**sti(g)t
superb	**utomordentligt**	**e̅w̅**tomo^{r}dehntli(g)t
terrible	**hemskt**	hehmskt
tremendous	**förfärligt**	furr**fær**li(g)t
ugly	**fult**	fe̅w̅lt

Churches – Religious services *Kyrkor – Gudstjänster*

The Swedish state church is Lutheran. But freedom of religion is assured and other denominations have their own churches.

Most churches and cathedrals are open to the public to view except, of course, when a service is being conducted.

Is there a ... near here?	**Finns det någon ... här i närheten?**	finss da̅y̅(t) **naw**gon ... hær ee **nær**ha̅y̅tern
Catholic church	**katolsk kyrka**	kah**to̅o̅lsk khewr**kah
Protestant church	**protestantisk kyrka**	prooter**stahn**tisk **khewr**kah
mosque	**moské**	mos**ka̅y̅**
synagogue	**synagoga**	**se̅w̅**nahgo̅o̅gah
At what time is ...?	**Hur dags börjar ...?**	he̅w̅r dahgss **burr**yahr
mass	**mässan**	**meh**ssahn
the service	**gudstjänsten**	**gewds**khainstern
Where can I find a ... who speaks English?	**Var kan jag få tag på en ... som talar engelska?**	vaar kahn yaa(g) faw taag paw ehn ... som **taa**lahr **ehng**erlskah
priest	**katolsk präst**	kah**to̅o̅lsk** prehst
minister	**protestantisk präst**	prooteh**stahn**tisk prehst
rabbi	**rabbin**	rah**been**
I'd like to visit the church.	**Jag skulle vilja titta på kyrkan.**	yaa(g) **skew**ler **vil**yah **tit**tah paw **khewr**kahn

In the countryside *På landet*

Is there a scenic route to ...?	**Finns det någon vacker väg till ...?**	finss da̅y̅(t) **naw**gon **vah**kerr vaig til
How far is it to ...?	**Hur långt är det till ...?**	he̅w̅r longt æ̅r da̅y̅(t) til
Can we walk there?	**Kan man gå dit?**	kahn mahn gaw deet
How high is that mountain?	**Hur högt är det där berget?**	he̅w̅r hurgt æ̅r da̅y̅(t) dæ̅r **bæ̅**ryert
What kind of ... is that?	**Vad är det där för ...?**	vaad æ̅r da̅y̅(t) dæ̅r fu̅r̅r
animal	**ett djur**	eht ye̅w̅r
bird	**en fågel**	ehn **faw**gerl
flower	**en blomma**	ehn **bloo**mah
tree	**ett träd**	eht traid

Landmarks *Landmärken*

bridge	**en bro**	ehn bro̅o̅
cliff	**en klippa**	ehn **klip**pah
farm	**en bondgård**	ehn **boon(d)**gaw[r]d
field	**ett fält**	eht fehlt
footpath	**en stig**	ehn steeg
forest	**en skog**	ehn sko̅o̅g
garden	**en trädgård**	ehn **trai(d)**gaw[r]d
hill	**en kulle**	ehn **kew**ler
house	**ett hus**	eht he̅w̅ss
lake	**en sjö**	ehn shu̅r̅
meadow	**en äng**	ehn ehng
mountain	**ett berg**	eht bæ̅ry
path	**en stig**	ehn steeg
peak	**en topp**	ehn top
pond	**en damm**	ehn dahm
river	**en flod**	ehn flo̅o̅d
road	**en väg**	ehn vaig
sea	**ett hav**	eht haav
spring	**en källa**	ehn **kheh**lah
stream	**en å**	ehn aw
valley	**en dal**	ehn daal
village	**en by**	ehn be̅w̅
wall	**en mur**	ehn me̅w̅r
waterfall	**ett vattenfall**	eht **vah**ternfahl
well	**en brunn**	ehn brewn
wood	**en skog**	ehn sko̅o̅g

ASKING THE WAY, see page 76

Relaxing

Cinema (movies) – Theatre *Bio – Teater*

To find out what's playing, consult the newspapers and bill-boards, or the weekly (monthly) tourist publication in Stockholm and other towns.

All films are shown in the original language with Swedish subtitles. Advance booking is essential for theatres and the opera.

What's on at the cinema tonight?	**Vad går det för filmer i kväll?**	vaad gawr da̅y̅(t) fu̅r̅r **fil**merr ee kvehl
What's playing at the ... Theatre?	**Vad går det på ... teatern?**	vaad gawr da̅y̅(t) paw ... ta̅y̅**aa**ter[r]n
What sort of play is it?	**Vad är det för slags pjäs?**	vaad æ̅r̅ da̅y̅(t) fu̅r̅r slahgss pyaiss
Who's it by?	**Vem har skrivit den?**	vehm haar **skree**vit dehn
Can you recommend a ...?	**Kan ni rekommendera någon ...?**	kahn nee rehkommern**da̅y̅**rah **naw**gon
good film	**bra film**	braa film
comedy	**komedi**	kommer**dee**
musical	**musikal**	mewssi**kaal**
revue	**revy**	rehv**e̅w̅**
Where's that new film directed by ... being shown?	**Var går den nya filmen av ...?**	vaar gawr dehn **n̅e̅w̅**ah **fil**mern aav
Who's in it?	**Vem spelar i den?**	vehm **spa̅y̅**lahr ee dehn
Who's playing the lead?	**Vem spelar huvudrollen?**	vehm **spa̅y̅**lahr **he̅w̅**vew(d)-rollern
Who's the director?	**Vem har regisserat den?**	vehm haar rehshiss**a̅y̅**raht dehn
At which theatre is that new play by ... being performed?	**På vilken teater går den nya pjäsen av ...?**	paw **vil**kern ta̅y̅**aa**terr gawr dehn **n̅e̅w̅**ah **pyai**ssern aav

What time does it begin?	**Hur dags börjar det?**	he̅w̅r dahgss **burr**yahr da̅y̅(t)
What time does it finish?	**Hur dags slutar det?**	he̅w̅r dahgss **sle̅w̅**tahr da̅y̅(t)
Are there any tickets for tonight?	**Finns det några biljetter till i kväll?**	finss da̅y̅(t) **naw**grah bil**yeh**terr til ee kvehl
How much are the tickets?	**Hur mycket kostar biljetterna?**	he̅w̅r **mew**ker(t) **kos**tahr bil**yeh**terʳnah
I'd like to reserve 2 tickets for the show on Friday evening.	**Jag skulle vilja beställa 2 biljetter till föreställningen på fredag kväll.**	yaa(g) **skew**ler **vil**yah ber**steh**lah 2 bil**yeh**terr til **fu̅r̅**rerstehlningern paw **fra̅y̅**daa(g) kvehl
Can I have a ticket for the matinée on Tuesday?	**Kan jag få en biljett till matinén på tisdag?**	kahn yaa(g) faw ehn bil**yeht** til mahti**na̅y̅n** paw **tees**daa(g)
I'd like a seat in the stalls (orchestra).	**Jag skulle vilja ha en plats på parkett.**	yaa(g) **skew**ler **vil**yah haa ehn plahtss paw pahr**keht**
Not too far back.	**Inte för långt bak.**	**in**ter fu̅r̅ longt baak
Somewhere in the middle.	**Någonstans i mitten.**	**naw**gonstahnss ee **mit**tern
How much are the tickets for the circle (mezzanine)?	**Hur mycket kostar biljetterna på första raden?**	he̅w̅r **mew**ker(t) **kos**tahr bil**yeh**terʳnah paw **fur**ʳstah **raa**dern
May I have a programme, please?	**Kan jag få ett program, tack?**	kahn yaa(g) faw eht proo**grahm** tahk
Where's the cloakroom?	**Var är garderoben?**	vaar æ̅r̅ gahʳder**raw**bern

Tyvärr är det utsålt.	I'm sorry, we're sold out.
Det finns bara några få platser kvar på första raden.	There are only a few seats left in the circle (mezzanine).
Kan jag få se biljetten?	May I see your ticket?
Det här är er plats.	This is your seat.

DAYS OF THE WEEK, see page 150

Opera—Ballet—Concert *Opera - Balett - Konsert*

Can you recommend a/an ...?	**Kan ni rekommendera någon ...?**	kahn nee rehkommern**dāȳ**rah **naw**gon
ballet	**balett**	bah**leht**
concert	**konsert**	kon**sær**
opera	**opera**	**ōō**perrah
operetta	**operett**	ooper**reht**
Where's the opera house/the concert hall?	**Var ligger Operan/ Konserthuset?**	vaar **lig**gerr **ōō**perrahn/ kon**sær**hēw̄ssert
What's on at the opera tonight?	**Vad ger man på Operan i kväll?**	vaad yāȳr mahn paw **ōō**perrahn ee kvehl
Who's singing/ dancing?	**Vem sjunger/ dansar?**	vehm **shewng**err/ **dahn**sahr
Which orchestra is playing?	**Vilken orkester är det som spelar?**	**vil**kern or**kehs**terr ær dāȳ(t) som **spāȳ**lahr
What are they playing?	**Vad spelar man?**	vaad **spāȳ**lahr mahn
Who's the conductor/soloist?	**Vem är dirigent/ solist?**	vehm ær dirri**shehnt** soo**list**

Nightclubs *Nattklubbar*

Can you recommend a good nightclub?	**Kan ni rekommendera någon trevlig nattklubb?**	kahn nee rehkommern**dāȳ**rah **naw**gon **trāȳ**vli(g) **naht**klewb
Is there a floor show?	**Är det någon show?**	ær dāȳ(t) **naw**gon "show"
What time does the show start?	**Hur dags börjar showen?**	hēw̄r dahgss **burr**yahr "**show**"ern
Do I have to wear a tie?	**Är det slipstvång?**	ær dāȳ(t) **slips**tvong

Discos *Diskotek*

Where can we go dancing?	**Var kan man gå och dansa?**	vaar kahn mahn gaw ok **dahn**sah
Is there a discotheque in town?	**Finns det något diskotek i stan?**	finss dāȳ(t) **naw**got disko**tāȳk** ee staan
Would you like to dance?	**Skall vi dansa?**	skah(l) vee **dahn**sah

Sports *Sport*

In summer the most popular sports are golf, tennis, sailing and swimming, not to mention jogging, cycling, riding and hiking. In winter the Swedes are active skiers and skaters. Popular spectator sports are football, ice hockey and tennis.

Is there a football (soccer) match (anywhere) this Saturday?	**Är det någon fotbollsmatch (någonstans) nu på lördag?**	æ̅r da̅y̅(t) **naw**gon **fo͞ot**bolsmahtsh (nawgon**stahnss**) ne̅w̅ paw **lu̅r̅ʳ**daa(g)
Which teams are playing?	**Vilka lag spelar?**	**vil**kah laag **spa̅y̅**lahr
Can you get me a ticket?	**Kan ni skaffa mig en biljett?**	kahn nee **skah**fah may ehn bil**yeht**
I'd like to see a tennis match.	**Jag skulle vilja se en tennismatch.**	yaa(g) **skew**ler **vil**yah sa̅y̅ ehn **teh**nismahtsh
What's the admission charge?	**Vad kostar det i inträde?**	vaad **kos**tahr da̅y̅(t) ee **in**traider

canoeing	**kanot**	kah**no͞ot**
car racing	**biltävling**	**beel**taivling
cycling	**cykel**	**sew**kerl
football (soccer)	**fotboll**	**fo͞ot**bol
horse racing	**hästkapplöpning**	**hehst**kahplu̅r̅pning
(horse-back) riding	**ridning**	**reed**ning
hunting	**jakt**	yahkt
sailing	**segling**	**sa̅y̅**gling
skiing	**skidåkning**	**sheed**awkning
swimming	**simning**	**sim**ning
table tennis	**bordtennis**	**bo͞oʳ**dtehniss
team handball	**handboll**	**hahnd**bol
tennis	**tennis**	**teh**niss

Where's the nearest golf course?	**Var ligger närmaste golfbana?**	vaar **lig**gerr **nær**mahster **golf**baanah
Where are the tennis courts?	**Var ligger tennisbanorna?**	vaar **lig**gerr **teh**nisbaanooʳnah
What's the charge per ...?	**Vad kostar det per ...?**	vaad **kos**tahr da̅y̅(t) pær
day/round/hour	**dag/runda/timme**	daa(g)/**rewn**dah/**tim**mer

Can I hire (rent) rackets?	**Kan man hyra racketar?**	kahn mahn **hewr**ah **rah**kertahr
Where's the race course (track)?	**Var ligger häst-kapplöpningsbanan?**	vaar **lig**gerr **hehst**-kahplurpningsbaanahn
Is there any good fishing around here?	**Finns det något bra fiskevatten i närheten?**	finss day(t) **naw**got braa **fis**kervahtern ee **nær**haytern
Do I need a permit?	**Behöver jag fiskekort?**	ber**hur**verr yaa(g) **fis**kerkoo^{r}t
Where can I get one?	**Var kan jag få tag på ett?**	vaar kahn yaa(g) faw taag paw eht
Can one swim in the lake/river/sea?	**Kan man bada i sjön/floden/havet?**	kahn mahn **baa**dah ee shurn/**floo**dern/**haa**vert
Is there a swimming pool here?	**Finns det någon swimmingpool här?**	finss day(t) **naw**gon "swimmingpool" hær
Is it open-air or indoor?	**Är den utomhus eller inomhus?**	ær dehn **ew**tomhewss **eh**lerr innomhewss
Is it heated?	**Är den uppvärmd?**	ær dehn **ewp**værmd
Is there a sandy beach?	**Finns det någon sandstrand?**	finss day(t) **naw**gon **sahnd**strahnd

On the beach *På stranden*

Is it safe to swim/dive here?	**Är det riskfritt att bada/dyka här?**	ær day(t) **risk**frit aht **baa**dah/**dew**ka hær
Is there a lifeguard?	**Finns det någon badvakt?**	finss day(t) **naw**gon **baad**vahkt
Is it safe for children?	**Är det riskfritt för barn?**	ær day(t) **risk**frit furr baa^{r}n
Could I have swimming lessons?	**Kan man ta simlektioner?**	kahn mahn taa **sim**lehkshoonerr
What's the temperature of the water?	**Hur många grader är det i vattnet?**	hewr **mong**ah **graa**derr ær day(t) ee **vaht**nert
Are there any dangerous currents?	**Finns det några farliga strömmar?**	finss day(t) **naw**grah **faa^r**liggah **strur**mahr
How deep is it?	**Hur djupt är det?**	hewr yewpt ær day(t)
Is it shallow?	**Är det långgrunt?**	ær day(t) **long**grewnt

I want to hire a/an/ some ...	**Jag skulle vilja hyra ...**	yaa(g) **skew**ler **vil**yah **hew**rah
bathing hut (cabana)	**en badhytt**	ehn **baad**hewt
deck chair	**en solstol**	ehn **sool**stool
motorboat	**en motorbåt**	ehn **moo**torbawt
rowing boat	**en roddbåt**	ehn **rood**bawt
sailing boat	**en segelbåt**	ehn **say**gerlbawt
skin-diving equipment	**en dykar-utrustning**	ehn **dew**kahr-ewtrewstning
sunshade (umbrella)	**ett parasoll**	eht pahrah**sol**
water-skis	**vattenskidor**	**vah**ternsheedoor
windsurfer	**en windsurfingbräda**	ehn **wind**sewrfingbraidah

BADNING FÖRBJUDEN	NO SWIMMING
ANKRING FÖRBJUDEN	NO ANCHORAGE

Winter sports *Vintersport*

I'd like to see an ice hockey match.	**Jag skulle vilja se en ishockeymatch.**	yaa(g) **skew**ler **vil**yah say ehn **ees**hokkimahtsh
Is there a skating rink near here?	**Finns det en skrid-skobana i närheten?**	finss day(t) ehn **skri(d)**skoo-baanah ee **nær**haytern
I'd like to ski.	**Jag skulle vilja åka skidor.**	yaa(g) **skew**ler **vil**yah **aw**kah **shee**door
downhill	**utförsåkning**	**ewt**fur^{r}sawkning
crosscountry skiing	**längdåkning**	**lehngd**awkning
Are there any ski runs for ...?	**Finns det några (skid)backar för ...?**	finss day(t) **naw**grah **(sheed)bah**kahr fur
beginners	**nybörjare**	**new**burryahrer
average skiers	**medelgoda åkare**	**may**derlgoodah **aw**kahrer
good skiers	**bra åkare**	braa **aw**kahrer
Which way are the ski lifts?	**Åt vilket håll ligger skidliftarna?**	awt **vil**kert hol **lig**gerr **sheed**liftah^{r}nah
I'd like to hire ...	**Jag skulle vilja hyra ...**	yaa(g) **skew**ler **vil**yah **hew**rah
poles	**stavar**	**staa**vahr
skates	**ett par skridskor**	eht paar **skri(d)**skoor
ski boots	**pjäxor**	**pyehk**soor
skiing equipment	**skidutrustning**	**sheed**ewtrewstning
skis	**skidor**	**shee**door

Making friends

Introductions *Presentation*

May I introduce ...?	**Får jag presentera ...?**	fawr yaa(g) prehssern**tay**rah
John, this is ...	**John, det här är ...**	John day(t) hær ær
My name is ...	**Mitt namn är ...**	mit nahmn ær
Pleased to meet you!	**Trevligt att träffas!**	**tray**vli(g)t aht **treh**fahss
What's your name?	**Vad heter ni/du?***	vaad **hay**terr nee/dew
How are you?	**Hur står det till?**	hewr stawr day(t) til
Fine, thanks. And you?	**Bra, tack. Och du?**	braa tahk. ok dew

Follow up *Lära känna varandra*

How long have you been here?	**Hur länge har du varit här?**	hewr **lehng**er haar dew **vaa**rit hær
I've been here a week.	**Jag har varit här en vecka.**	yaa(g) haar **vaa**rit hær ehn **veh**kah
Is this your first visit to Stockholm?	**Är det ditt första besök i Stockholm?**	ær day(t) dit **fur^{r}**stah bersurk ee **stok**holm
How do you like Sweden?	**Vad tycker du om Sverige?**	vaad **tew**kerr dew om **svær**yer
What do you think of the country/people?	**Vad tycker du om landet/människorna?**	vaad **tew**kerr dew om **lahn**dert/**meh**nishoo^{r}nah
I love the landscape.	**Jag älskar naturen.**	yaa(g) **ehl**skahr nah**tew**rern
Where do you come from?	**Varifrån kommer du?**	**vaa**rifrawn **kom**mer dew
I'm from ...	**Jag är från ...**	yaa(g) ær frawn
What nationality are you?	**Vad har du för nationalitet?**	vaad haar dew furr nahtshoonahli**tay(t)**

* In this section we use *du*, the informal form for "you". If you want to use the polite form *ni*, the rest of the sentence does not change.

COUNTRIES, see page 146

I'm ...	**Jag är ...**	yaa(g) ær
American	**amerikan**	ahm(er)ri**kaan**
British	**britt**	brit
Canadian	**kanadensare**	kahnah**dehn**sahrer
English	**engelsman**	**ehng**erlsmahn
Irish	**irländare**	**ir**lehndahrer
Where are you staying?	**Var bor du här?**	vaar boor dew hær
Are you on your own?	**Är du här ensam?**	ær dew hær **ehn**sahm
I'm with my ...	**Jag är här med ...**	yaa(g) ær hær mayd
wife	**min fru**	min frew
husband	**min man**	min mahn
family	**min familj**	min fah**mily**
children	**mina barn**	**mi**nah baa^{r}n
parents	**mina föräldrar**	**mi**nah furr**ehl**drahr
boyfriend/girlfriend	**min pojkvän/ flickvän**	min **poyk**vehn/ **flik**vehn

father/mother	**far/mor**	faar/moor
son/daughter	**son/dotter**	sawn/**dot**terr
brother/sister	**bror/syster**	broor/**sew**sterr
cousin	**kusin**	kew**sseen**
uncle	**farbror*/morbror****	**fahr**broor/**moor**broor
aunt	**faster*/moster****	**fah**sterr/**moo**sterr

* father's side ** mother's side

Are you married/ single?	**Är du gift/ogift?**	ær dew yeeft/**oo**yeeft
Do you have children?	**Har du barn?**	haar dew baa^{r}n
What do you do?	**Vad har du för yrke?**	vaad haar dew furr **ewr**ker
I'm a student.	**Jag studerar.**	yaa(g) stew**day**rahr
What are you studying?	**Vad studerar du?**	vaad stew**day**rahr dew
I'm here on a business trip.	**Jag är här på affärsresa.**	yaa(g) ær hær paw ahf**æ^{r}s**rayssah
Do you travel a lot?	**Reser du mycket?**	**ray**sserr dew **mew**ker(t)
Do you play cards/ chess?	**Spelar du kort/ schack?**	**spay**lahr dew koo^{r}t/ shahk

The weather *Vädret*

What a lovely day!	**Vilken underbar dag!**	**vil**kern **ewn**derrbaar daa(g)
What awful weather!	**Ett sånt förskräckligt väder!**	eht sont fur^{r}-**skrehk**li(g)t **vai**derr
Isn't it cold/ hot today?	**Är det inte kallt/ varmt idag?**	$\overline{\text{ær}}$ d$\overline{\text{ay}}$(t) **in**ter kahlt/ vahrmt ee daa(g)
Is it usually as warm as this?	**Brukar det vara så här varmt?**	**br$\overline{\text{ew}}$**kahr d$\overline{\text{ay}}$(t) **vaa**rah saw h$\overline{\text{æ}}$r vahrmt
Do you think it's going to ... tomorrow?	**Tror du att det kommer att ... i morgon?**	tr$\overline{\text{oo}}$r d$\overline{\text{ew}}$ aht d$\overline{\text{ay}}$(t) **ko**mmerr aht ... ee **mo**rron
be a nice day	**bli vackert**	blee **vah**ker^{r}t
rain	**regna**	**rehng**nah
snow	**snöa**	**sn$\overline{\text{ur}}$**ah
What is the weather forecast?	**Vilka är väderleks-utsikterna?**	**vil**kah $\overline{\text{ær}}$ **vai**derrl$\overline{\text{ay}}$ks-$\overline{\text{ew}}$tsikter^{r}nah

cloud	**molnet**	**mawl**nert
fog	**dimman**	**di**mmahn
frost	**frosten**	**fros**tern
ice	**isen**	**ee**ssern
lightning	**blixten**	**bleek**stern
midnight sun	**midnattssolen**	**meed**nahts$\overline{\text{oo}}$lern
moon	**månen**	**maw**nern
rain	**regnet**	**rehng**nert
sky	**himlen**	**him**lern
snow	**snön**	snurn
star	**stjärnan**	**sh$\overline{\text{æ}}$^{r}**nahn
sun	**solen**	**s$\overline{\text{oo}}$**lern
thunder	**åskan**	**aws**kahn
thunderstorm	**åskvädret**	**awsk**vaidrert
wind	**vinden**	**vin**dern

Invitations *Inbjudan*

Would you like to have dinner with us on ...?	**Vill du äta middag med oss på ...?**	vil d$\overline{\text{ew}}$ **ai**tah **mi**ddah(g) m$\overline{\text{ay}}$d oss paw
May I invite you to lunch?	**Får jag bjuda på lunch?**	fawr yaa(g) **by$\overline{\text{ew}}$**dah paw lewnsh

DAYS OF THE WEEK, see page 150

Can you come round for a drink this evening?	**Kan du komma på en drink i kväll?**	kahn dew **ko**mmah paw ehn drink ee kvehl
We are having a party. Can you come?	**Vi skall ha fest. Kan du komma?**	vee skah(l) haa fehst. kahn dew **ko**mmah
Great. I'd love to come.	**Tack, jag kommer gärna.**	tahk yaa(g) **ko**mmerr **yær**nah
What time shall I come?	**Hur dags skall jag komma?**	hewr dahgss skah(l) yaa(g) **ko**mmah
May I bring a friend?	**Får jag ta med en vän?**	fawr yaa(g) taa mayd ehn vehn
I'm afraid we've got to leave now.	**Tyvärr måste vi gå nu.**	tew**vær mo**ster vee gaw new
Next time you (pl.) must come to visit us.	**Nästa gång måste ni komma och hälsa på oss.**	**neh**stah gong **mo**ster nee **ko**mmah ok **hehl**sah paw oss
Thanks for the evening.	**Tack för i kväll.**	tahk furr ee kvehl
It was great.	**Det var verkligen trevligt.**	day(t) vaar **vehrk**liggern **trayv**li(g)t

Dating *Träff*

Do you mind if I smoke?	**Har du något emot att jag röker?**	haar dew **naw**got ay**moot** aht yaa(g) **rur**kerr
Would you like a cigarette?	**Vill du ha en cigarrett?**	vil dew haa ehn siggah**reht**
Do you have a light, please?	**Har du eld?**	haar dew ehld
Why are you laughing?	**Varför skrattar du?**	**vahr**furr **skrah**tahr dew
Is my Swedish that bad?	**Är min svenska så dålig?**	ær min **svehn**skah saw **daw**lig
Do you mind if I sit here?	**Har du något emot att jag sätter mig här?**	haar dew **naw**got ay**moot** aht yaa(g) **seh**terr may hær
Can I get you a drink?	**Kan jag hämta en drink åt dig?**	kahn yaa(g) **hehm**tah ehn drink awt day
Are you waiting for someone?	**Väntar du på någon?**	**vehn**tahr dew paw **naw**gon

Are you free this evening?	**Är du ledig i kväll?**	ær dew **lay**di(g) ee kvehl
Would you like to go out with me tonight?	**Skall vi gå ut i kväll?**	skah(l) vee gaw ewt ee kvehl
Would you like to go dancing?	**Har du lust att gå ut och dansa?**	haar dew lewst aht gaw ewt ok **dahn**sah
I know a good discotheque.	**Jag vet ett bra diskotek.**	yaa(g) vayt eht braa disko**tayk**
Shall we go to the cinema (movies)?	**Skall vi gå på bio?**	skah(l) vee gaw paw **bee**oo
Would you like to go for a drive?	**Har du lust att göra en biltur?**	haar dew lewst aht **yur**rah ehn **beel**tewr
Where shall we meet?	**Var skall vi träffas?**	vaar skah(l) vee **treh**fahss
I'll pick you up at your hotel.	**Jag kommer och hämtar dig på hotellet.**	yaa(g) **kom**merr ok **hehm**tahr day paw ho**teh**lert
I'll call for you at 8.	**Jag hämtar dig klockan 8.**	yaa(g) **hehm**tahr day **klok**kahn 8
May I take you home?	**Får jag följa dig hem?**	fawr yaa(g) **furl**yah day hehm
Can I see you again tomorrow?	**Skall vi ses i morgon igen?**	skah(l) vee sayss ee **mor**ron ee**yehn**
I hope we'll meet again.	**Jag hoppas vi ses igen.**	yaa(g) **hop**pahss vee sayss ee**yehn**

... and you might answer:

I'd love to, thank you.	**Mycket gärna, tack.**	**mew**ker(t) **yæʳ**nah tahk
That's very kind of you.	**Det var hemskt snällt av dig.**	day(t) vaar hehmskt snehlt aav day
Thank you, but I'm busy.	**Tack, men jag är tyvärr upptagen.**	tahk mehn yaa(g) ær tew**vær** **ewp**taagern
Leave me alone, please!	**Var snäll och lämna mig ifred.**	vaar snehl ok **lehm**nah may ee**fray(d)**
Thank you, it's been a wonderful evening.	**Tack, det har varit en underbar kväll.**	tahk day(t) haar **vaa**rit ehn **ewn**derrbaar kvehl

Shopping Guide

This shopping guide is designed to help you find what you want with ease, accuracy and speed. It features:

1. A list of all major shops, stores and services (p. 98).
2. Some general expressions required when shopping to allow you to be specific and selective (p. 100).
3. Full details of the shops and services most likely to concern you. Here you'll find advice, alphabetical lists of items and conversion charts listed under the headings below.

LAUNDRY, see page 29/HAIRDRESSER'S, see page 30

Shops, stores and services *Affärer och service*

Most shops are open from 9 or 9.30 a.m. to 6 p.m., Monday to Friday, and on Saturdays closing time varies from 1 to 4 p.m. In larger cities certain supermarkets and the food sections of some of the main department stores remain open till 8 p.m. They open on Sundays, too, as do several corner shops.

Where can I find a (an) ...?	**Var finns det ...?**	vaar finss day(t)
antique shop	**en antikvitetsaffär**	ehn ahntikvi**ttayts**ahfær
art gallery	**ett konstgalleri**	eht **konst**gahlerree
baker's	**ett bageri**	eht baage**rree**
bank	**en bank**	ehn bahnk
barber's	**en herrfrisör**	ehn **hehr**frissurr
beauty salon	**en skönhetssalong**	ehn shurn**hayts**sahlong
bookshop	**en bokhandel**	ehn **book**hahnderl
butcher's	**en slaktare/ ett charkuteri**	ehn **slahk**tahrer/ eht shahrkewter**ree**
cake shop	**ett konditori**	eht kondittо**ree**
camera shop	**en fotoaffär**	ehn **foo**tooahfær
chemist's	**ett apotek**	eht ahpoo**tayk**
dairy	**en ostaffär**	ehn **oost**ahfær
delicatessen	**en delikatessaffär**	ehn dehlikka**tehss**ahfær
dentist	**en tandläkare**	ehn **tahn(d)**laikahrer
department store	**ett varuhus**	eht **vaa**rewhewss
doctor	**en läkare**	ehn **lai**kahrer
drugstore	**ett apotek**	eht ahpoo**tayk**
dry cleaner's	**en kemtvätt**	ehn **khaym**tveht
electricial goods shop	**en elaffär**	ehn **ay**lahfær
fishmonger's	**en fiskaffär**	ehn **fisk**ahfær
flea market	**en loppmarknad**	ehn **lop**mahrknahd
florist's	**en blomsteraffär**	ehn **blom**sterrahfær
furrier's	**en körsnär**	ehn khur**ʳsnær**
glass and china shop	**en glas- och porslinsaffär**	ehn glaass- ok pooʳ**sleens**ahfær
greengrocer's	**en grönsaksaffär**	ehn **grurn**saaksahfær
grocer's	**en livsmedelsaffär**	ehn **livs**mayderlsahfær
hairdresser's (ladies/men)	**en frisör (dam-/herr-)**	ehn fri**surr** (daam-/hehr-)
hardware store	**en järnhandel**	ehn **yæʳ**nhahnderl
health food shop	**en hälsokostaffär**	ehn **hehl**sookostahfær
hospital	**ett sjukhus**	eht **shewk**hewss

ironmonger's	**en järnhandel**	ehn **yæʳn**hahnderl
jeweller's	**en juvelerare/ guldsmedsaffär**	ehn y̅e̅w̅verl**a̅y̅**rahrer/ **gewld**sma̅y̅dsahfær
launderette	**en snabbtvätt**	ehn **snahb**tveht
laundry	**en tvättinrättning**	ehn **tveht**inrehtning
library	**ett bibliotek**	eht biblio**ta̅y̅k**
liquor store	**ett systembolag**	eht sew**sta̅y̅m**boolaag
market	**en marknad/ en torghandel**	ehn **mahrk**nahd **tory**hahnderl
newsstand	**en tidningskiosk**	ehn **tee(d)**ningskhiosk
optician	**en optiker**	ehn **op**tikkerr
pastry shop	**ett konditori**	eht konditto**ree**
perfumery	**ett parfymeri**	eht pahrfewmer**ree**
photographer	**en fotograf**	ehn footoo**graaf**
police station	**en polisstation**	ehn poo**lees**stahsho̅o̅n
post office	**ett postkontor**	eht **post**konto̅o̅r
second-hand shop	**en andrahandsaffär**	ehn **ahn**drahhahndsahfær
shoemaker's (repairs)	**en skomakare**	ehn **sko̅o̅**maakahrer
shoe shop	**en skoaffär**	ehn **sko̅o̅**ahfær
shopping centre	**ett shoppingcenter**	eht **sho**ppingsehnterr
silversmith	**en silversmed**	ehn **sil**verʳsma̅y̅d
souvenir shop	**en souvenirbutik**	ehn sooverneerbewteek
sporting goods shop	**en sportaffär**	ehn **spo**ʳtahfær
stationer's	**en pappershandel**	ehn **pah**perʳshahnderl
supermarket	**ett snabbköp**	eht **snahb**khu̅r̅p
sweet shop	**en godisaffär**	ehn **go̅o̅**dissahfær
tailor's	**en skräddare**	ehn **skreh**dahrer
telegraph office	**en telegraf**	ehn tehleh**graaf**
tobacconist's	**en tobaksaffär**	ehn **to̅o̅**bahksahfær
toy shop	**en leksaksaffär**	ehn **la̅y̅k**saaksahfær
travel agency	**en resebyrå**	ehn **ra̅y̅**sserbe̅w̅raw
vegetable store	**en grönsaksaffär**	ehn **gru̅r̅n**saaksahfær
veterinarian	**en veterinär**	ehn vehterrin**næ̅r**
watchmaker's	**en urmakare**	ehn **e̅w̅r**maakahrer
wine merchant	**ett systembolag**	eht sew**sta̅y̅m**boolaag

INGÅNG	ENTRANCE
UTGÅNG	EXIT
UTNÖD	EMERGENCY EXIT

General expressions *Allmänna uttryck*

Where? *Var?*

Where's there a good ...?	**Var finns det någon bra ...?**	vaar finss da͞y(t) **naw**gon braa
Where can I find a ...?	**Var hittar jag en ...?**	vaar **hit**tahr yaa(g) ehn
Where's the main shopping area?	**Var ligger affärscentrum?**	vaar **lig**gerr ah**fǣ**^{r}ssehntrewm
Is it far from here?	**Är det långt härifrån?**	ǣr da͞y(t) longt hǣri**frawn**
How do I get there?	**Hur kommer jag dit?**	he͞wr **kom**merr yaa(g) deet

REA SALE

Service *Betjäning*

Can you help me?	**Kan ni hjälpa mig?**	kahn nee **yehl**pah may
I'm just looking.	**Jag tittar bara.**	yaa(g) **tit**tahr **baa**rah
Do you sell ...?	**Säljer ni ...?**	**sehl**yerr nee
I'd like to buy ...	**Jag skulle vilja köpa ...**	yaa(g) **skew**ler **vil**yah **khu͞r**pah
Can you show me some ...?	**Kan ni visa mig några ...?**	kahn nee **vee**ssah may **naw**grah
Do you have any ...?	**Har ni några ...?**	haar nee **naw**grah
Where's the ... department?	**Var ligger ... -avdelningen?**	vaar **lig**gerr ... -**aav**da͞ylningern
Where is the lift (elevator)/escalator?	**Var är hissen/ rulltrappan?**	vaar ǣr **his**sern/ **rewl**trahpahn
Where do I pay?	**Var betalar man?**	vaar ber**taa**lahr mahn

That one *Den där*

Can you show me ...?	**Kan ni visa mig ...?**	kahn nee **vee**ssah may
this/that	**det här/det där**	da͞y(t) hǣr/da͞y(t) dǣr/
the one in the window/in the display case	**den i skyltfönstret/ i montern**	dehn ee **shewlt**furnstrert/ ee **mon**ter^{r}n

Defining the article *Beskrivning av varan*

I'd like a ... one.	**Jag skulle vilja ha en ...**	yaa(g) **skew**ler **vil**yah haa ehn
big	**stor**	stoor
cheap	**billig**	**bil**lig
dark	**mörk**	murrk
good	**bra**	braa
heavy	**tung**	tewng
large	**stor**	stoor
light (weight)	**lätt**	leht
light (colour)	**ljus**	yewss
oval	**oval**	oo**vaal**
rectangular	**rektangulär**	rehktanggew**lær**
round	**rund**	rewnd
small	**liten**	**lee**tern
square	**kvadratisk**	kvah**draa**tisk
sturdy	**kraftig**	**krahf**tig
I don't want anything too expensive.	**Jag vill inte ha någonting för dyrt.**	yaa(g) vil **in**ter haa **naw**gonting furr dew[r]t

Preference *Jag föredrar ...*

Can you show me some others?	**Kan ni visa mig några andra?**	kahn nee **vee**ssah may **naw**grah **ahn**drah
Don't you have anything ...?	**Har ni inte någonting ...?**	haar nee **in**ter **naw**gonting
cheaper/better	**billigare/bättre**	**bil**liggahrer/**beh**trer
larger/smaller	**större/mindre**	**stur**rer/**min**drer

How much? *Hur mycket?*

How much is this?	**Hur mycket kostar det här?**	hewr **mew**ker(t) **kos**tahr day(t) hær
How much are they?	**Hur mycket kostar de där?**	hewr **mew**ker(t) **kos**tahr dom dær
I don't understand.	**Jag förstår inte.**	yaa(g) fur[r]**stawr in**ter
Please write it down.	**Kan ni skriva det?**	kahn nee **skree**vah day(t)
I don't want to spend more than ... crowns.	**Jag vill inte lägga ut mer än ... kronor.**	yaa(g) vil **in**ter **leh**gah ewt mayr ehn ... **kroo**noor

COLOURS, see page 113

Decision *Beslut*

It's not quite what I want.	**Det är inte riktigt vad jag vill ha.**	da̅y̅(t) ær **in**ter **rik**ti(g)t vaad yaa(g) vil haa
No, I don't like it.	**Nej, jag tycker inte om det.**	nay yaa(g) **tew**kerr **in**ter om da̅y̅(t)
I'll take it.	**Jag tar det.**	yaa(g) taar da̅y̅(t)

Ordering *Beställning*

Can you order it for me?	**Kan ni beställa det åt mig?**	kahn nee ber**steh**lah da̅y̅(t) awt may
How long will it take?	**Hur lång tid tar det?**	he̅w̅r long teed taar da̅y̅(t)

Delivery *Leverans*

I'll take it with me.	**Jag tar det med mig.**	yaa(g) taar da̅y̅(t) ma̅y̅d may
Deliver it to the ... Hotel.	**Kan ni leverera det till hotell ...?**	kahn nee lehver**ra̅y̅**rah da̅y̅(t) til ho**tehl**
Please send it to this address.	**Skulle ni kunna skicka det till den här adressen?**	**skew**ler nee **kew**nah **shik**kah da̅y̅(t) til dehn hær ah**dreh**ssern
Will I have any difficulty with the customs?	**Kommer jag att få problem i tullen?**	**kom**merr yaa(g) aht faw proo**bla̅y̅m** ee **tew**lern

Paying *Betalning*

How much is it?	**Hur mycket kostar det?**	he̅w̅r **mew**ker(t) **kost**ahr da̅y̅(t)
Can I pay by traveller's cheque?	**Kan jag betala med resecheck?**	kahn yaa(g) ber**taa**lah ma̅y̅d **ra̅y̅**sserkhehk
Do you accept dollars/pounds?	**Tar ni emot dollar/pund?**	taar nee a̅y̅**mo̅o̅t** **dol**lahr/pewnd
Do you accept credit cards?	**Tar ni kreditkort?**	taar nee kreh**deet**koo[r]t
Can I get the VAT (sales tax) back?	**Får jag tillbaka momsen?**	fawr yaa(g) til**baa**kah **mom**sern
I think there's a mistake in the bill.	**Jag tror att det är ett fel på räkningen.**	yaa(g) tro̅o̅r aht da̅y̅(t) ær eht fa̅y̅l paw **raik**ningern

Anything else? *Något annat?*

No, thanks, that's all.	**Nej tack. Det var allt.**	nay tahk da̅y̅(t) vaar ahlt
Yes, I'd like ...	**Ja, jag skulle vilja ha ...**	yaa yaa(g) **skew**ler **vil**yah haa
May I have a bag, please?	**Kan jag få en kasse, tack?**	kahn yaa(g) faw ehn **kah**sser tahk
Could you wrap it up for me, please?	**Kan ni slå in det åt mig, tack?**	kahn nee slaw in da̅y̅(t) awt may tahk

Dissatisfied? *Missnöjd?*

Can you exchange this, please?	**Kan jag få byta det här, tack?**	kahn yaa(g) faw **be̅w̅**tah da̅y̅(t) hær tahk
I want to return this.	**Jag vill lämna tillbaka det här.**	yaa(g) vil **lehm**nah til**baa**kah da̅y̅(t) hær
Could I have a refund? Here's the receipt.	**Kan jag få pengarna tillbaka? Här är kvittot.**	kahn yaa(g) faw **pehng**ah^{r}nah til**baa**kah. hær ær **kvit**tot

Kan jag hjälpa er?	Can I help you?
Vad önskar ni?	What would you like?
Vilken ... önskar ni?	What ... would you like?
färg/form	colour/shape
kvalitet	quality
Jag är ledsen, vi har inga.	I'm sorry, we don't have any.
Det är slut på lagret.	We're out of stock.
Skall vi beställa det åt er?	Shall we order it for you?
Tar ni det med er eller skall vi skicka det?	Will you take it with you or shall we send it?
Något annat?	Anything else?
Det blir ... kronor, tack.	That's ... crowns, please.
Kassan är där borta.	The cash desk is over there.

Bookshop—Stationer's *Bokhandel – Pappershandel*

In Sweden, books and stationery are usually sold in the same shop. Newspapers, magazines and paperbacks are sold at newsstands and tobacconist's.

Where's the nearest ...?	**Var ligger närmaste ...?**	vaar **li**ggerr **nær**mahster
bookshop	**bokhandel**	**bo͞ok**hahnderl
stationer's	**pappershandel**	**pah**per^{r}shahnderl
newsstand	**tidningskiosk**	**tee(d)**ningskhiosk
Where can I buy an English-language newspaper?	**Var kan jag köpa en engelskspråkig tidning?**	vaar kahn yaa(g) **khūr**pah ehn **ehng**erlsksprawki(g) **tee(d)**ning
Where's the guide-book section?	**Var finns guideböckerna?**	vaar finns **"guide"**burker^{r}nah
Where do you keep the English books?	**Var har ni engelska böcker?**	vaar haar nee **ehng**erlskah **bur**kerr
Do you have any of ...'s books in English?	**Har ni någon av ...s böcker på engelska?**	haar nee **naw**gon aav ...s **bur**kerr paw **ehng**erlskah
Do you have second-hand books?	**Har ni antikvariska böcker?**	haar nee ahnti**kvaa**riskah **bur**kerr
I want to buy a/an/some ...	**Jag skulle vilja köpa ...**	yaa(g) **skew**ler **vil**yah **khūr**pah
address book	**en adressbok**	ehn ah**drehs**bo͞ok
adhesive tape	**tejp**	"tape"
ball-point pen	**en kulspetspenna**	ehn **kēwl**spehtspehnah
book	**en bok**	ehn bo͞ok
calendar	**en kalender**	ehn kah**lehn**derr
carbon paper	**karbonpapper**	kahr**bawn**pahperr
crayons	**färgkritor**	**færy**kreetoor
dictionary	**en ordbok**	ehn **o͞o^{r}d**bo͞ok
pocket	**fick-**	fik-
Swedish-English	**Svensk-Engelsk**	svehnsk-**ehng**erlsk
drawing pad	**ett ritblock**	eht **reet**blok
drawing pins	**häftstift**	**hehft**stift
envelopes	**några kuvert**	**naw**grah kew**vær**
eraser	**ett radergummi**	eht rah**dāyr**gewmi
exercise book	**en skrivbok**	ehn **skreev**bo͞ok
felt-tip pen	**en filtpenna**	ehn **filt**pehnah
fountain pen	**en reservoarpenna**	ehn rehsserr**vaar**pehnah

glue	**klister**	**klis**terr
grammar book	**en grammatik**	ehn grahmah**teek**
guidebook	**en reseguide**	ehn **ray**sserr"guide"
ink	**bläck**	blehk
black/red/blue	**svart/rött/blått**	svahrt/rurt/blot
(adhesive) labels	**(självhäftande) etiketter**	(**shehlv**hehftahnder) ehti**keh**terr
magazine	**en veckotidning**	ehn **veh**kootee(d)ning
map	**en karta**	ehn **kaar**tah
street map of ...	**en karta över ...**	ehn **kaar**tah **ur**verr
road map of ...	**en vägkarta över ...**	ehn **vaig**kaartah **ur**verr
mechanical pencil	**en stiftpenna**	ehn **stift**pehnah
newspaper	**en dagstidning**	ehn **dahgs**tee(d)ning
American/English	**amerikansk/ engelsk**	ahm(eh)ri**kaansk**/ **eng**erlsk
notebook	**en anteckningsbok**	ehn **ahn**tehkningsbook
note paper	**brevpapper**	**brayv**pahperr
paintbox	**en färglåda**	ehn **færy**lawdah
paper	**papper**	**pah**perr
paperback	**en pocketbok**	ehn **po**kkertbook
paperclips	**gem**	gaym
paper napkins	**pappersservetter**	**pah**perrssehrvehterr
paste	**klister**	**klis**terr
pen	**en bläckpenna**	ehn blehk**peh**nah
pencil	**en blyertspenna**	ehn **blew**errtspehnah
pencil sharpener	**en pennvässare**	ehn **pehn**vehssahrer
picture-book	**bilderbok**	**bil**derrbook
playing cards	**spelkort**	**spayl**koort
pocket calculator	**en fickräknare**	ehn **fik**ræknahrer
postcard	**ett vykort**	eht **vew**koort
propelling pencil	**en stiftpenna**	ehn **stift**pehnah
refill (for a pen)	**en refill**	ehn reh**fil**
rubber	**ett radergummi**	eht rah**dayr**gewmi
rubber bands	**gummisnoddar**	**gew**misnooddahr
ruler	**en linjal**	ehn lin**yaal**
stapler	**häftapparat**	**hehft**ahpahraat
staples	**häftklammer**	**hehft**klahmerr
string	**ett snöre**	eht **snur**rer
thumbtacks	**häftstift**	**hehft**stift
tissue paper	**silkespapper**	**sil**kerspahperr
travel guide	**en reseguide**	ehn **ray**sser"guide"
typewriter ribbon	**ett skrivmaskins-band**	eht **skreev**mahsheens-bahnd
typing paper	**skrivmaskins-papper**	**skreev**mahsheens-pahperr
wrapping paper	**omslagspapper**	**om**slaagspahperr
writing pad	**ett skrivblock**	eht **skreev**blok

Camping equipment *Campingutrustning*

I'd like a/an/some ...	**Jag skulle vilja ha ...**	yaa(g) **skew**ler **vil**yah haa
air bed	**en luftmadrass**	ehn **lewft**mahdrahss
bottle-opener	**en flasköppnare**	ehn **flahsk**urpnahrer
bucket	**en hink**	ehn hink
butane gas	**butangas**	bew**taan**gaass
campbed	**en tältsäng**	ehn **tehlt**sehng
candles	**några ljus**	**naw**grah ye̅w̅ss
can opener	**en konservöppnare**	ehn kon**sær**vurpnahrer
chair	**en stol**	ehn sto̅o̅l
folding chair	**en fällstol**	ehn **fehl**sto̅o̅l
charcoal	**träkol (briketter)**	**trai**kawl (**bri**kehterr)
clothes pegs	**klädnypor**	**klai(d)**ne̅w̅poor
compass	**en kompass**	ehn kom**pahss**
cool bag	**en kylväska**	ehn **khe̅w̅l**vehskah
cool box	**en kylbox**	ehn **khe̅w̅l**bokss
corkscrew	**en korkskruv**	ehn **kork**skre̅w̅v
crockery	**porslin**	poo^{r}**sleen**
cutlery	**bestick**	ber**stik**
deck chair	**en solstol**	ehn **so̅o̅l**sto̅o̅l
first-aid kit	**en förbandslåda**	ehn furr**bahnds**lawdah
fishing tackle	**fiskeredskap**	**fis**kerra̅y̅dskaap
flashlight	**en ficklampa**	ehn **fik**lahmpah
food box	**en matlåda**	ehn **maat**lawdah
frying pan	**en stekpanna**	ehn **sta̅y̅k**pahnah
groundsheet	**ett tältunderlag**	eht **tehlt**ewnder^{r}laag
hammer	**en hammare**	ehn **hah**mahrer
hammock	**en hängmatta**	ehn **hehng**mahtah
haversack	**en ryggsäck**	ehn **rewg**sehk
ice packs	**några frysklampar**	**naw**grah **fre̅w̅s**klahmpahr
kerosene	**fotogen**	footoo**sha̅y̅n**
knapsack	**en ryggsäck**	ehn **rewg**sehk
lamp	**en lampa**	ehn **lahm**pah
lantern	**en lykta**	ehn **lewk**tah
mallet	**en träklubba**	ehn **træ̅**klewbah
matches	**tändstickor**	**tehn(d)**stikkoor
mattress	**en madrass**	ehn mah**drahss**
methylated spirits	**rödsprit**	**ru̅r̅(d)**spreet
mosquito net	**ett myggnät**	eht **mewg**nait
pail	**en hink**	ehn hink
paper napkins	**pappersservetter**	**pah**per^{r}ssehrvehterr
paraffin	**fotogen**	footoo**sha̅y̅n**
penknife	**en pennkniv**	ehn **pehn**kneev
picnic basket	**en picknickkorg**	ehn **pik**nikkory

CAMPING, see page 32

plastic bags	**plastpåsar**	**plahst**pawssahr
pump	**pump**	pewmp
rope	**ett rep**	eht ra̅y̅p
rucksack	**en ryggsäck**	ehn **rewg**sehk
saucepan	**en kastrull**	ehn kah**strewl**
scissors	**en sax**	ehn sahkss
screwdriver	**en skruvmejsel**	ehn **skre̅w̅v**mayserl
sleeping bag	**en sovsäck**	ehn **sawv**sehk
stew pot	**en gryta**	ehn **gre̅w̅**tah
table	**ett bord**	eht bo̅o̅^{r}d
folding table	**ett fällbord**	eht **fehl**bo̅o̅^{r}d
tent	**ett tält**	eht tehlt
tent pegs	**tältpinnar**	**tehlt**pinnahr
tent pole	**en tältstång**	ehn **tehlt**stawng
tinfoil	**aluminiumfolie**	ahlewm**een**yewmfo̅o̅lyer
tin opener	**en konservöppnare**	ehn kon**særv**urpnahrer
tongs	**en tång**	ehn tong
torch	**en ficklampa**	ehn **fik**lahmpah
vacuum flask	**en termosflaska**	ehn **tær**mosflahskah
washing powder	**tvättmedel**	**tveht**ma̅y̅derl
washing-up liquid	**diskmedel**	**disk**ma̅y̅derl
water flask	**en fältflaska**	ehn **fehlt**flahskah
wood alcohol	**rödsprit**	**ru̅r̅(d)**spreet

Crockery *Porslin*

cups	**koppar**	**kop**pahr
mugs	**muggar**	**mew**gahr
plates	**tallrikar**	**tahl**rikkahr
saucers	**tefat**	**ta̅y̅**faat
tumblers	**dricksglas**	**driks**glaass

Cutlery *Bestick*

forks	**gafflar**	**gahf**lahr
knives	**knivar**	**knee**vahr
spoons	**skedar**	**sha̅y̅**dahr
teaspoons	**teskedar**	**ta̅y̅**sha̅y̅dahr
(made of) plastic	**(av) plast**	(aav) plahst
(made of) stainless steel	**(av) rostfritt stål**	(aav) **rost**frit stawl

Chemist's (drugstore) *Apotek*

Swedish chemists' normally don't stock the great range of goods that you'll find in Britain or the U.S.A. For example, they don't sell photographic equipment or books. And for perfume, cosmetics, etc. you must go to a *parfymeri* (**pahr**fewmerree). Note that you need a prescription for most medicines.

In the window you'll see a notice telling you where the nearest all-night chemist's is.

This section is divided into two parts:

1. Pharmaceutical—medicine, first-aid, etc.
2. Toiletry—toilet articles, cosmetics

General *Allmänt*

Where's the nearest (all-night) chemist's?	**Var ligger närmaste (jour)apotek?**	vaar **li**ggerr **nær**mahster **(sho̅o̅r)**ahpoota̅y̅k
What time does the chemist's open/close?	**Hur dags öppnar/stänger apoteket?**	he̅w̅r dahgss **urp**nahr/ **stehng**err ahpoo**ta̅y̅**kert

1—Pharmaceutical *Medicin – Förbandsartiklar*

I'd like something for ...	**Jag skulle vilja ha något mot ...**	yaa(g) **skew**ler **vil**yah haa **naw**got mo̅o̅t
a cold	**förkylning**	fur^{r}**khe̅w̅l**ning
a cough	**hosta**	**hoo**stah
a hangover	**baksmälla**	**baak**smehlah
hay fever	**hösnuva**	**hu̅r̅**sne̅w̅vah
insect bites	**insektsbett**	**in**sehktsbeht
sunburn	**solsveda**	**so̅o̅l**sva̅y̅dah
travel sickness	**åksjuka**	**awk**she̅w̅kah
an upset stomach	**orolig mage**	o̅o̅ro̅o̅lig **maa**ger
Can you prepare this prescription for me?	**Kan ni göra i ordning det här receptet åt mig?**	kahn nee **yu̅r̅**rah ee o^{r}**d**ning da̅y̅(t) hær reh**sehp**tert awt may
Can I get it without a prescription?	**Kan jag få det utan recept?**	kahn yaa(g) faw da̅y̅(t) **e̅w̅**tahn reh**sehpt**
Shall I wait?	**Skall jag vänta?**	skah(l) yaa(g) **vehn**tah

DOCTOR, see page 137

Can I have a/an/ some ...?	**Skulle jag kunna få ...?**	**skew**ler yaa(g) **kew**nah faw
analgesic	**något smärt-stillande**	**naw**got **smæʳt**stillahnder
antiseptic cream	**en antiseptisk salva**	ehn ahnti**ssehp**tisk **sahl**vah
aspirin	**aspirin**	ahspi**reen**
bandage	**ett förband**	eht furʳ**bahnd**
elastic bandage	**en elastisk binda**	ehn eh**lahs**tisk **bin**dah
Band-Aids	**plåster**	**plos**terr
charcoal tablets	**koltabletter**	**kawl**tahblehterr
condoms	**kondomer**	kon**daw**merr
contraceptives	**preventivmedel**	prehvehn**teev**ma̅y̅derl
corn plasters	**liktornsplåster**	**leek**to̅o̅ʳnsplosterr
cotton wool (absorbent cotton)	**ett paket bomull**	eht pah**ka̅y̅t boo**mewl
cough drops	**några halstabletter**	**naw**grah **hahls**tahblehterr
disinfectant	**desinficeringsmedel**	dehssinfi**ssa̅y̅**rings-ma̅y̅derl
ear drops	**örondroppar**	**u̅r̅**rondroppahr
Elastoplast	**plåster**	**plos**terr
eye drops	**ögondroppar**	**u̅r̅**gondroppahr
(roll of) gauze	**en gasbinda**	ehn **gaas**bindah
insect repellent/ insect spray	**ett insektsmedel/ insektsspray**	eht **in**sehktsma̅y̅derl/ **in**sehkts"spray"
iodine	**jod**	yod
laxative	**ett laxermedel**	eht lah**ksa̅y̅r**ma̅y̅derl
mouthwash	**ett munvatten**	eht **mewn**vahtern
nose drops	**näsdroppar**	**nais**droppahr
painkiller	**något smärt-stillande**	**naw**got **smæʳt**stillahnder
sanitary towels (napkins)	**ett paket dambindor**	eht pah**ka̅y̅t daam**bindoor
suppositories	**några stolpiller**	**naw**grah **sto̅o̅l**pillerr
... tablets	**... tabletter**	... tah**bleh**terr
tampons	**tamponger**	tahm**pong**err
thermometer	**en termometer**	ehn tehrmoo**ma̅y̅**terr
throat lozenges	**några halstabletter**	**naw**grah **hahls**tahblehterr
vitamin pills	**vitamintabletter**	vittah**meen**tahblehterr

GIFT	POISON
ENDAST FÖR UTVÄRTES BRUK	FOR EXTERNAL USE ONLY

2—Toiletry *Toalettartiklar*

I'd like a/an/some ...	**Jag skulle vilja ha ...**	yaa(g) **skew**ler **vil**yah haa
after-shave lotion	**ett rakvatten**	eht **raak**vahtern
bath salts	**ett badsalt**	eht **baad**sahlt
blusher (rouge)	**rouge**	ro̅o̅sh
bubble bath	**ett skumbad**	eht **skewm**baad
cream	**en kräm/crème**	ehn kraim
cleansing cream	**en rengöringskräm**	ehn **ra̅y̅**nyu̅r̅ringskraim
foot cream	**en fotkräm**	ehn **fo̅o̅t**kraim
foundation cream	**ett puderunderlag**	eht **pe̅w̅**derrewnderrlaag
hand cream	**en handkräm**	ehn **hahn(d)**kraim
moisturizing cream	**en fuktighets-bevarande kräm**	ehn **fewk**tigha̅y̅ts-bervaarahnder kraim
night cream	**en nattkräm**	ehn **naht**kraim
sun-tan cream	**en solkräm**	ehn **so̅o̅l**kraim
cuticle remover	**nagelbandsvatten**	**naa**gerlbahndsvahtern
deodorant	**deodorant**	da̅y̅odo**rahnt**
emery boards	**sandpappersfilar**	**sahnd**pahper^{r}sfeelahr
eyebrow pencil	**en ögonbrynspenna**	ehn u̅r̅gonbre̅w̅nspehnah
eye liner	**en eyeliner**	ehn "eye liner"
eye shadow	**en ögonskugga**	ehn u̅r̅gonskewgah
face flannel	**en tvättlapp**	ehn **tveht**lahp
face powder	**puder**	**pe̅w̅**derr
lipbrush	**en läppstiftpensel**	ehn **leh**pstiftpehnserl
lipsalve	**ett cerat**	eht seh**raat**
lipstick	**ett läppstift**	eht **leh**pstift
make-up bag	**en sminkväska**	ehn **smink**vehskah
make-up remover pads	**make-up remover pads**	"make-up remover pads"
mascara	**en mascara**	ehn mah**skaa**rah
nail brush	**en nagelborste**	ehn **naa**gerlbo^{r}ster
nail clippers	**en nageltång**	ehn **naa**gerltong
nail file	**en nagelfil**	ehn **naa**gerlfeel
nail polish	**ett nagellack**	eht **naa**gerllahk
nail polish remover	**nagellacks-borttagningsmedel**	eht **naa**gerllahks-bo^{r}ttaagningsma̅y̅derl
nail scissors	**en nagelsax**	ehn **naa**gerlsahkss
perfume	**en parfym**	ehn pahr**fe̅w̅m**
powder	**puder**	**pe̅w̅**derr
powder puff	**en pudervippa**	ehn **pe̅w̅**derrvippah
razor	**en rakhyvel**	ehn **raak**he̅w̅verl
razor blades	**rakblad**	**raak**blaad
rouge	**rouge**	ro̅o̅sh
safety pins	**säkerhetsnålar**	**sai**kerrha̅y̅tsnawlahr

shaving brush	**en rakborste**	ehn **raak**bo^{r}ster
shaving cream	**en rakkräm**	ehn **raak**kraim
soap	**en tvål**	ehn tvawl
sponge	**en tvättsvamp**	ehn **tveht**svahmp
sponge bag	**en necessär**	ehn nehsser**sær**
sun-tan oil	**sololja**	ehn **soo**lolyah
talcum powder	**talkpuder**	**tahlk**pewderr
tissues	**pappersnäsdukar**	**pah**per^{r}snaisdewkahr
toilet paper	**toalettpapper**	tooah**leht**pahperr
toilet water	**eau de toilette**	aw der tooah**leht**
toothbrush	**en tandborste**	**ehn tahn(d)**bo^{r}ster
toothpaste	**en tandkräm**	ehn **tahn(d)**kraim
towel	**en handduk**	ehn **hahn(d)**dewk
tweezers	**en pincett**	ehn pin**seht**

For your hair *För håret*

bobby pins	**hårklämmor**	**hawr**klehmoor
colour shampoo	**tonande schampo**	**too**nahnder **shahm**poo
comb	**en kam**	ehn kahm
curlers	**papiljotter**	pahpil**yott**err
dry shampoo	**torrschampo**	**tor**shahmpoo
hairbrush	**en hårborste**	ehn **hawr**bo^{r}ster
hair dye	**hårfärgnings-medel**	**hawr**færynings-mayderl
hair gel	**frisyrgelé**	**fris**sewrshehlay
hair mousse	**mousse**	mooss
hairgrips	**hårklämmor**	**hawr**klehmoor
hair lotion	**hårvatten**	**hawr**vahtern
hairpins	**hårnålar**	**haw^{r}**nawlahr
hair slide	**ett hårspänne**	eht **haw^{r}**spehner
hair spray	**hårspray**	**haw^{r}**"spray"
setting lotion	**en läggningsvätska**	ehn **lehg**ningsvehtskah
shampoo	**ett shampo**	eht **shahm**poo
for dry/greasy (oily) hair	**för torrt/ fett hår**	furr to^{r}t/ feht hawr
tint	**ett toningsmedel**	eht **too**ningsmayderl
wig	**en peruk**	ehn peh**rewk**

For the baby *För babyn*

baby food	**barnmat**	**baa^{r}n**maat
dummy (pacifier)	**en napp**	ehn nahp
feeding bottle	**en nappflaska**	ehn **nahp**flahskah
nappies (diapers)	**blöjor**	**blur**yoor

Clothing *Kläder*

If you want to buy something specific, prepare yourself in advance. Look at the list of clothing on page 116. Get some idea of the colour, material and size you want. They're all listed on the next few pages.

General *Allmänt*

I'd like …	**Jag skulle vilja ha …**	yaa(g) **skew**ler **vil**yah haa
I want … for a 10-year-old boy/girl.	**Jag skulle vilja ha … till en 10-årig pojke/flicka.**	yaa(g) **skew**ler **vil**yah haa … til ehn 10-**aw**ri(g) **poy**ker/**flik**kah
I want something like this.	**Jag skulle vilja ha något som det här.**	yaa(g) **skew**ler **vil**yah haa **naw**got som dāy(t) hǣr
I like the one in the window.	**Jag tycker om den i fönstret.**	yaa(g) **tew**kerr om dehn ee **furn**strert
How much is that per metre?	**Hur mycket kostar det där per meter?**	hēwr **mew**ker(t) **kos**tahr dāy(t) dǣr pǣr **māy**terr

1 centimetre (cm.)	= 0.39 in.	1 inch =	2.54 cm.
1 metre (m.)	= 39.37 in.	1 foot =	30.5 cm.
10 metres	= 32.81 ft.	1 yard =	0.91 m.

Colour *Färg*

I want something in …	**Jag skulle vilja ha något i …**	yaa(g) **skew**ler **vil**yah haa **naw**got ee
I'd like a darker/lighter shade.	**Jag skulle vilja ha en nyans mörkare/ljusare.**	yaa(g) **skew**ler **vil**yah haa ehn nēw**ahngss** **murr**kahrer/**yēw**ssahrer
I want something to match this.	**Jag vill ha något som passar till det här.**	yaa(g) vil haa **naw**got som **pah**ssahr til dāy(t) hǣr
I don't like the colour/pattern.	**Jag tycker inte om färgen/mönstret.**	yaa(g) **tew**kerr **in**ter om **fær**yern/**murn**strert

beige	**beige**	baish
black	**svart**	svah^{r}t
blue	**blå**	blaw
brown	**brun**	brewn
fawn	**gulbrun**	**gewl**brewn
golden	**guldfärgad**	**gewld**færyahd
green	**grön**	grurn
grey	**grå**	graw
mauve	**lila**	**lee**lah
orange	**orange**	orahnsh
pink	**rosa**	**raws**sah
purple	**violett**	veeooleht
red	**röd**	rurd
scarlet	**scharlakansröd**	shah^{r}**laa**kahnsrurd
silver	**silverfärgad**	**sil**verrfæryahd
turquoise	**turkos**	tewr**kooss**
white	**vit**	veet
yellow	**gul**	gewl
light ...	**ljus ...**	yewss
dark ...	**mörk ...**	murrk

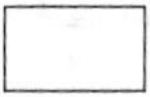
enfärgad (**ayn**færyahd)

randig (**rahn**dig)

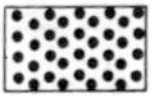
prickig (**prik**kig)

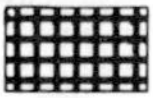
rutig (**rew**tig)

mönstrad (**murn**strahd)

Fabric *Tyg*

Do you have anything in ...?	**Har ni någonting i ...?**	haar nee **naw**gonting ee
Is that ...?	**Är det där ...?**	ær day(t) dær
handmade	**handgjort**	**hahn(d)**yoo^{r}t
imported	**importerat**	impo^{r}**tay**raht
made in Sweden	**svensktillverkat**	**svehnsk**tilvehrkaht
I'd like something thinner.	**Jag skulle vilja ha någonting tunnare.**	yaa(g) **skew**ler **vil**yah haa **naw**gonting **tew**nahrer
Do you have anything of better quality?	**Har ni någon bättre kvalitet?**	haar nee **naw**gon **beh**trer kvahli**tay(t)**

What's it made of? **Vad är det gjort av?** vaad ær day(t) yoo^r^t aav

cambric	**batist**	bah**tist**
camelhair	**kamelhår**	kah**mayl**hawr
chiffon	**chiffon**	shif**fong**
corduroy	**manchester**	mahn**kheh**sterr
cotton	**bomull**	boomewl
crepe	**crêpe**	krehp
denim	**denim**	deh**neem**
felt	**filt**	filt
flannel	**flanell**	flah**nehl**
gabardine	**gabardin**	gahbahr**deen**
lace	**spets**	spehtss
leather	**läder/skinn**	**lai**der/shin
linen	**linne**	**lin**ner
poplin	**poplin**	pop**leen**
satin	**satin**	sah**tehng**
silk	**siden/silke**	**see**dern/**sil**ker
suede	**mocka**	**mok**kah
towelling	**frotté**	frot**tay**
velvet	**sammet**	**sah**mert
velveteen	**bomullssammet**	**boo**mewlssahmert
wool	**ylle**	**ew**ler
worsted	**kamgarn**	**kahm**gaa^r^n

Is it ...? **Är det ...?** ær day(t)

pure cotton/wool **ren bomull/ull** rayn **boo**mewl/ewl
synthetic **syntetiskt** sewn**tay**tiskt
colourfast **färgäkta** **færy**ehktah
crease (wrinkle) resistant **skrynkelfritt** **skrewn**kerlfrit

Is it hand washable/machine washable? **Skall det tvättas för hand/i maskin?** skah(l) day(t) **tveh**tahss furr hahnd/ee mah**sheen**

Will it shrink? **Krymper det?** **krewm**perr day(t)

Size *Storlek*

I take size 38. **Jag har storlek 38.** yaa(g) haar **stoo^r^**layk 38

Could you measure me? **Kan ni ta mina mått?** kahn nee taa **mee**nah mot

I don't know the Swedish sizes. **Jag känner inte till de svenska storlekarna.** yaa(g) **kheh**nerr **in**ter til dom **svehn**skah **stoo^r^**laykah^r^nah

Sizes vary from country to country and from one manufacturer to another, so be sure to try on the clothes before you buy.

Women *Damer*

Dresses/Suits						
American	8	10	12	14	16	18
British	10	12	14	16	18	20
Continental	36	38	40	42	44	46

Stockings						
American / British	8	8½	9	9½	10	10½
Continental	1		2		3	

Shoes				
American	5½	6½	7½	8½
British	4	5	6	7
Continental	37	38	39	40

Men *Herrar*

Suits/Overcoats						
American / British	36	38	40	42	44	46
Continental	46	48	50	52	54	56

Shirts				
American / British	15	16	17	18
Continental	38	40	42	44

Shoes							
American / British	5	6	7	8	9	10	11
Continental	38	39	40	41	42	43	44

A good fit? *Passar det?*

Can I try it on?	**Kan jag få prova den?**	kahn yaa(g) faw **prōō**vah dehn
Where's the fitting room?	**Var är provhytten?**	vaar ǣr **prōō**vhewtern
Is there a mirror?	**Finns det någon spegel?**	finss dāȳ(t) **naw**gon **spāȳ**gerl
It fits very well.	**Den sitter mycket bra.**	dehn **si**tterr **mew**ker(t) braa
It doesn't fit.	**Den passar inte.**	dehn **pah**ssahr **in**ter

NUMBERS, see page 147

It's too ...	**Den är för ...**	dehn æ̅r fu̅r̅r
short/long	**kort/lång**	ko^{r}t/long
tight/loose	**trång/vid**	trong/veed
How long will it take to alter it?	**Hur lång tid tar det att ändra den?**	he̅w̅r long teed taar da̅y̅(t) aht **ehn**drah dehn

Clothes and accessories *Kläder och accessoarer*

I would like a/an/ some ...	**Jag skulle vilja ha ...**	yaa(g) **skew**ler **vil**yah haa
anorak	**en anorak**	ehn **ah**norahk
bathing cap	**en badmössa**	ehn **baad**murssahr
bathrobe	**en badrock**	ehn **baad**rok
blouse	**en blus**	ehn ble̅w̅ss
bow tie	**en fluga**	ehn **fle̅w̅**gah
bra	**en behå**	ehn **ba̅y̅**haw
braces	**ett par hängslen**	eht paar **heng**slehn
cap	**en mössa**	ehn **murs**sah
cardigan	**en kofta**	ehn **kof**tah
coat (man's)	**en rock**	ehn rok
coat (woman's)	**en kappa**	ehn **kah**pah
dress	**en klänning**	ehn **kleh**ning
with long sleeves	**med lång ärm**	ma̅y̅d long æ̅rm
with short sleeves	**med kort ärm**	ma̅y̅d ko^{r}t æ̅rm
sleeveless	**utan ärm**	**e̅w̅**tahn æ̅rm
dressing gown	**en morgonrock**	ehn **mo**rronrok
evening dress (woman's)	**en aftonklänning**	ehn **ahf**tonklehning
fur coat	**en päls**	ehn pehlss
girdle	**en höfthållare**	ehn **hurft**hollahrer
gloves	**ett par handskar**	eht paar **hahn(d)**skahr
handbag	**en handväska**	ehn **hahn(d)**vehskah
handkerchief	**en näsduk**	ehn **nais**de̅w̅k
hat	**en hatt**	ehn haht
jacket	**en kavaj**	ehn kah**vahy**
jeans	**ett par jeans**	**eht paar yeenss**
jersey	**en jumper/tröja**	**ehn jew**mperr/**trur**yah
kneesocks	**ett par knästrumpor**	eht paar **knai**strewmpoor
nightdress	**ett nattlinne**	eht **naht**linner
overalls	**en overall**	ehn ovver**rawl**
pair of ...	**ett par ...**	eht paar
panties	**ett par trosor**	eht paar **tro̅o̅**ssoor
pants (Am.)	**ett par (lång)byxor**	eht paar **(long)bew**ksoor
panty girdle	**en byxgördel**	ehn **bewks**yu̅r̅^{r}derl

panty hose	**ett par strump-byxor**	eht paar **strewmp**-bewksoor
parka	**en anorak**	ehn **ah**norahk
pullover	**en jumper/tröja**	ehn **yewm**perr/**tru**ryah
polo (turtle)-neck	**med polokrage**	ma̅y̅d **p̅o̅o̅**lookraager
round-neck	**rundringad**	**rewnd**ringahd
V-neck	**V-ringad**	**va̅y̅**-ringahd
pyjamas	**en pyjamas**	ehn pew**yaa**mahss
raincoat (man's)	**en regnrock**	ehn **rehngn**rok
raincoat (woman's)	**en regnkappa**	ehn **rehngn**kahpah
scarf	**en scarf**	ehn skaarf
shirt	**en skjorta**	ehn **shoo^r^tah**
shorts	**ett par shorts**	eht paar sho^r^tss
skirt	**en kjol**	ehn kh̅o̅o̅l
slip	**en underklänning**	ehn **ewn**derrklehning
socks	**ett par sockor**	eht paar **sok**koor
stockings	**ett par strumpor**	eht paar **strewm**poor
suit (man's)	**en kostym**	ehn **kost̅e̅w̅m**
suit (woman's)	**en dräkt**	ehn drehkt
suspenders (Am.)	**ett par hängslen**	eht paar **heng**slern
sweater	**en tröja**	ehn **tru**ryah
sweatshirt	**en sweatshirt**	ehn "sweatshirt"
swimming trunks	**ett par badbyxor**	eht paar **baad**bewksoor
swimsuit	**en baddräkt**	ehn **baa(d)**drehkt
T-shirt	**en T-shirt**	ehn "T-shirt"
tie	**en slips**	ehn slipss
tights	**ett par strump-byxor**	eht paar **strewmp**-bewksoor
tracksuit	**en träningsoverall**	ehn **trai**ningsovverrawl
trousers	**ett par (lång)byxor**	eht paar **(long)bewk**soor
umbrella	**ett paraply**	eht pahrah**pl̅e̅w̅**
underpants	**ett par kalsonger**	eht paar kahl**song**err
undershirt	**en undertröja**	ehn **ewn**derrtruryah
vest (Am.)	**en väst**	ehn vehst
vest (Br.)	**en undertröja**	ehn **ewn**derrtruryah
waistcoat	**en väst**	ehn vehst

belt	**ett bälte/skärp**	eht **behl**ter/shairp
buckle	**ett spänne**	eht **speh**ner
button	**en knapp**	ehn knahp
collar	**en krage**	ehn **kraa**ger
pocket	**en ficka**	ehn **fik**kah
press stud (snap fastener)	**en tryckknapp**	ehn **trewk**knahp
zip (zipper)	**ett blixtlås**	**bliks(t)**lawss

Shoes *Skor*

I'd like a pair of ...	**Jag skulle vilja ha ett par ...**	yaa(g) **skew**ler **vil**yah haa eht paar
boots	**stövlar**	**sturv**lahr
moccasins	**loafers**	"loafers"
plimsolls (sneakers)	**tennisskor**	**teh**nissko̅o̅r
sandals	**sandaler**	sahn**daa**lerr
shoes	**skor**	sko̅o̅r
flat	**platta**	**plah**tah
with a heel	**med klack**	ma̅y̅d klahk
with leather soles	**med lädersula**	ma̅y̅d **lai**der^{r}se̅w̅law
with rubber soles	**med gummisula**	ma̅y̅d **gew**misse̅w̅lah
slippers	**tofflor**	**tof**loor
These are too ...	**De här är för ...**	dom hæ̅r æ̅r fu̅r̅r
narrow/wide	**smala/breda**	**smaa**lah/**bra̅y̅**dah
big/small	**stora/små**	**sto̅o̅**rah/smaw
Do you have a smaller/larger size?	**Har ni en storlek mindre/större**	haar nee ehn **sto̅o̅**^{r}la̅y̅k **min**drer/**stur**rer
Do you have the same in black?	**Har ni samma i svart?**	haar nee **sah**mah ee svah^{r}t
cloth	**tyg**	te̅w̅g
leather	**läder/skinn**	**lai**derr/shin
rubber	**gummi**	**gew**mi
suede	**mocka**	**mok**kah
Is it real leather?	**Är det äkta läder?**	æ̅r da̅y̅(t) **ehk**tah **lai**derr
I need some ...	**Jag behöver ...**	yaa(g) ber**hu̅r̅**verr
shoe polish	**skokräm**	**sko̅o̅**kraim
shoelaces	**skosnören**	**sko̅o̅**snu̅r̅rern

Shoes worn out? Here's the way to get them mended:

Can you repair these shoes?	**Kan ni laga de här skorna?**	kahn nee **laa**gah dom hæ̅r **sko̅o̅**^{r}nah
Can you stitch this?	**Kan ni sy ihop det här?**	kahn nee se̅w̅ ee**hoop** da̅y̅(t) hæ̅r
I want new soles and heels.	**Jag vill ha nya sulor och klackar.**	yaa(g) vil haa **ne̅w̅**ah **se̅w̅**loor ok **klah**kahr
When will they be ready?	**När blir de klara?**	næ̅r bleer dom **klaa**rah

COLOURS, see page 113

Electrical appliances *Elektriska artiklar*

220-volt, 50-cycle A.C. is used almost everywhere in Sweden.

Do you have a battery for this?	**Har ni ett batteri till den här?**	haar nee eht bahter**ree** til dehn hǣr
This is broken. Can you repair it?	**Den här har gått sönder. Kan ni laga den?**	dehn hǣr haar got **surn**derr. kahn nee **laa**gah dehn
Can you show me how it works?	**Kan ni visa mig hur den fungerar?**	kahn nee **vee**ssah may he̅w̅r dehn fewng**ga̅y̅**rahr
How do I switch it on?	**Hur sätter jag på den?**	he̅w̅r **seh**terr yaa(g) paw dehn
I'd like to buy/hire a video cassette.	**Jag skulle vilja köpa/hyra en videokassett.**	yaa(g) **skew**ler **vil**yah **khu̅r̅**pah/**he̅w̅**rah ehn **veed**yokahsseht
I'd like a/an/ some ...	**Jag skulle vilja ha ...**	yaa(g) **skew**ler **vil**yah haa
adaptor	**en adapter**	ehn ah**dahp**terr
amplifier	**en förstärkare**	ehn fur^{r}**stǣr**kahrer
bulb	**en glödlampa**	ehn **glu̅r̅d**lahmpah
clock-radio	**en klockradio**	ehn **klok**raadyo
electric toothbrush	**en elektrisk tandborste**	ehn eh**lehk**trisk **tahn(d)**bo^{r}ster
extension lead (cord)	**en förlängnings-sladd**	ehn fur^{r}**lehng**ningsslahd
hair dryer	**en hårtork**	ehn **haw^{r}**tork
headphones	**ett par hörlurar**	eht paar **hur^{r}**le̅w̅rahr
(travelling) iron	**ett (rese)strykjärn**	eht (**ra̅y̅**sser)**stre̅w̅k**yǣ^{r}n
lamp	**en lampa**	ehn **lahm**pah
plug	**en stickkontakt**	ehn **stik**kontahkt
portable ...	**en bärbar ...**	ehn **bǣr**baar
radio	**en radio**	ehn **raa**dyo
car radio	**en bilradio**	ehn **beel**raadyo
(cassette) recorder	**en (kassett)-bandspelare**	ehn (kah**sseht**)-**bahnd**spa̅y̅lahrer
record player	**en skivspelare**	ehn **sheev**spa̅y̅lahrer
shaver	**en rakapparat**	ehn **raa**kahpahraat
speakers	**högtalare**	**hu̅r̅g**taalahrer
(colour) television	**en (färg)TV**	ehn (**fǣry**)**ta̅y̅**va̅y̅
transformer	**en transformator**	ehn trahnsfor**maa**tor
video recorder	**en videoband-spelare**	ehn **veed**yobahnd-spa̅y̅lahrer

Grocer's *Livsmedelsaffär*

I'd like some bread, please.	**Jag skulle vilja ha lite bröd, tack.**	yaa(g) **skew**ler **vil**yah haa **lee**ter bru̅r̅d tahk
crispbread	**hårt bröd**	haw^{r}t bru̅r̅d
sliced bread	**skivat bröd**	**shee**vaht bru̅r̅d
white bread	**vitt bröd**	vit bru̅r̅d
What sort of cheese do you have?	**Vad har ni för sorts ostar?**	vaad haar nee fu̅r̅r so^{r}tss **oos**tahr
A piece of that one, please.	**En bit av den där, tack.**	ehn beet aav dehn dæ̅r tahk
I'll have one of those, please.	**Kan jag få en av de där, tack?**	kahn yaa(g) faw ehn aav dom dæ̅r tahk
May I help myself?	**Kan jag ta själv?**	kahn yaa(g) taa shehlv
I'd like ...	**Jag skulle vilja ha ...**	yaa(g) **skew**ler **vil**yah haa
a kilo of apples	**ett kilo äpplen**	eht **khee**loo **ehp**lern
half a kilo of tomatoes	**ett halvt kilo tomater**	eht hahlft **khee**loo too**maa**terr
250 grams of butter	**¼ kg smör**	eht kvah^{r}tss **khee**loo smu̅r̅r
3 hg. (300 g.) of pâté	**3 hekto paté**	3 **hehk**too pah**ta̅y̅**
a litre of milk	**en liter mjölk**	ehn **lee**terr myurlk
4 slices of ham	**4 skivor skinka**	4 **shee**voor **shin**kah
a packet of tea	**ett paket te**	eht pah**ka̅y̅t** ta̅y̅
a jar of jam	**en burk sylt**	ehn bewrk sewlt
a tin (can) of peaches	**en burk persikor**	ehn bewrk **pæ^{r}**sikkor
a tube of mustard	**en tub senap**	ehn te̅w̅b **sa̅y̅**nahp
a box of chocolates	**en ask choklad**	ehn ahsk shoo**klaa(d)**

Weights and measures

1 kilogram or kilo (kg.) = 1000 grams (g.)

100 g. = 3.5 oz.	½ kg. = 1.1 lb.
200 g. = 7.0 oz.	1 kg. = 2.2 lb.

1 oz. = 28.35 g.
1 lb. = 453.60 g.

1 litre (l.) = 0.88 imp. qt. or 1.06 U.S. qt.

1 imp. qt. = 1.14 l.	1 U.S. qt. = 0.95 l.
1 imp. gal. = 4.55 l.	1 U.S. gal. = 3.8 l.

FOOD, see also page 64

Jeweller's—Watchmaker's *Juvelerare – Urmakare*

Jeweller's are also known as *guldsmedsaffär*.

I want a present for ...	**Jag skulle vilja ha en present till ...**	yaa(g) **skew**ler **vil**yah haa ehn preh**sehnt** til
Could I see that, please?	**Kan jag få se på det där?**	kahn yaa(g) faw sa̅y̅ paw da̅y̅(t) dæ̅r
Do you have anything in gold?	**Har ni någonting i guld?**	haar nee **naw**gonting ee gewld
How many carats is this?	**Hur många karat är det?**	he̅w̅r **mon**gah kah**raat** æ̅r da̅y̅(t)
Is this real silver?	**Är det här äkta silver?**	æ̅r da̅y̅(t) hæ̅r **ehk**tah **sil**verr
Can you engrave these initials on it?	**Kan ni gravera in de här initialerna?**	kahn nee grah**va̅y̅**rah in dom hæ̅r initsi**aaler**[r]nah
Can you repair this watch?	**Kan ni laga den här klockan?**	kahn nee **laa**gah dehn hæ̅r **klo**kkahn
I'd like a/an/some ...	**Jag skulle vilja ha ...**	yaa(g) **skew**ler **vil**yah haa
alarm clock	**en väckarklocka**	ehn **veh**kahrklokkah
bangle	**en armring**	ehn **ahrm**ring
battery	**ett batteri**	eht bahter**ree**
bracelet	**ett armband**	eht **ahrm**bahnd
chain bracelet	**en armlänk**	ehn **ahrmleh**nk
charm bracelet	**ett berlockarmband**	eht ber[r]**lokk**ahrmbahnd
brooch	**en brosch**	ehn brawsh
chain	**en kedja**	ehn **kha̅y̅**dyah
charm	**en berlock**	ehn ber[r]**lok**
cigarette case	**ett cigarrettetui**	eht siggah**reht**ehtewee
cigarette lighter	**en cigarrettändare**	ehn siggah**reht**tehndahrer
clock	**en klocka**	ehn **klo**kkah
cross	**ett kors**	eht ko[r]ss
cuff links	**ett par manschettknappar**	eht paar mahn**sheht**knahpahr
cutlery	**ett bestick**	eht ber**stik**
earrings	**ett par örhängen**	eht paar **u̅r̅r**hehngern
gem	**en ädelsten**	ehn **ai**derlsta̅y̅n
jewel box	**ett smyckeskrin**	eht **smew**kerskreen
mechanical pencil	**en stiftpenna**	ehn **stift**pehnah
music box	**en speldosa**	ehn **spa̅y̅l**d**o̅o̅**ssah
necklace	**ett halsband**	eht **hahls**bahnd
pendant	**ett hängsmycke**	eht **hehng**smewker
pocket watch	**ett fickur**	eht **fik**e̅w̅r

powder compact	**en puderdosa**	ehn **pe͞w**derʳdo͞ossah
propelling pencil	**en stiftpenna**	ehn **stift**pehnah
ring	**en ring**	ehn ring
engagement ring	**en förlovningsring**	ehn furʳ**lawv**ningsring
signet ring	**en signetring**	ehn sig**na͞y**tring
wedding ring	**en vigselring**	ehn **vig**serlring
silverware	**något i silver**	**naw**got ee **sil**verr
tie clip	**en slipshållare**	ehn **slips**hollahrer
tie pin	**en kravattnål**	ehn krah**vaht**nawl
watch	**en klocka**	ehn **klo**kkah
automatic	**automatisk**	aa(ew)too**maa**tisk
digital	**digital**	diggi**taal**
quartz	**quartz**	kvahʳtss
with a second hand	**med sekundvisare**	ma͞yd seh**kewnd**veessahrer
waterproof	**vattentät**	**vah**terntait
watchstrap	**ett klockarmband**	eht **klokk**ahrmbahnd
wristwatch	**ett armbandsur**	eht **ahrm**bahndse͞wr

amber	**bärnsten**	**bæʳn**sta͞yn
amethyst	**ametist**	ahmer**tist**
chromium	**krom**	krawm
copper	**koppar**	**ko**ppahr
coral	**korall**	koo**rahl**
crystal	**kristall**	kri**stahl**
cut glass	**slipat glas**	**slee**paht glaass
diamond	**diamant**	diah**mahnt**
emerald	**smaragd**	smah**rahgd**
enamel	**emalj**	eh**mahly**
gold	**guld**	gewld
gold plate	**gulddoublé**	**gewl(d)**dobla͞y
ivory	**elfenben**	**ehl**fernba͞yn
jade	**jade**	yehyd
onyx	**onyx**	**o͞o**newkss
mother-of-pearl	**pärlemor**	**pæʳ**lermo͞or
pearl	**pärla**	**pæʳ**lah
pewter	**tenn**	tehn
platinum	**platina**	plah**tee**nah
ruby	**rubin**	rew**been**
sapphire	**safir**	sah**feer**
silver	**silver**	**sil**verr
silver plate	**nysilver**	**ne͞w**silverr
stainless steel	**rostfritt stål**	**rost**frit stawl
topaz	**topas**	too**paass**
turquoise	**turkos**	tewr**ko͞oss**

Optician *Optiker*

I've broken my glasses.	**Mina glasögon har gått sönder.**	**mee**nah **glaassur**gon haar got **surn**derr
Can you repair them for me?	**Kan ni laga dem åt mig?**	kahn nee **laa**gah dom awt may
When will they be ready?	**När är de klara?**	nær ær dom **klaa**rah
Can you change the lenses?	**Kan ni byta ut glasen?**	kahn nee **bew**tah ewt **glaa**ssern
I'd like tinted lenses.	**Jag skulle vilja ha färgade glas.**	yaa(g) **skew**ler **vil**yah haa **fær**yahder glaass
The frame is broken.	**Bågen har gått sönder.**	**baw**gern haar got **surn**derr
I'd like a spectacles case.	**Jag skulle vilja ha ett glasögon-fodral.**	yaa(g) **skew**ler **vil**yah haa eht **glaassur**gon-foodraal
I'd like to have my eyesight checked.	**Jag skulle vilja få min syn kontrollerad.**	yaa(g) **skew**ler **vil**yah faw min sewn kontro**llay**rahd
I'm short-sighted/ long-sighted.	**Jag är närsynt/ långsynt.**	yaa(g) ær **nær**sewnt/ **long**sewnt
I'd like some contact lenses.	**Jag skulle vilja ha kontaktlinser.**	yaa(g) **skew**ler **vil**yah haa kon**tahkt**linserr
I've lost one of my contact lenses.	**Jag har tappat en kontaktlins.**	yaa(g) haar **tah**paht ehn kon**tahkt**linss
Could you give me another one?	**Skulle jag kunna få en ny?**	**skew**ler yaa(g) **kew**nah faw ehn new
I have hard/soft lenses.	**Jag har hårda/ mjuka linser.**	yaa(g) haar **haw**rdah/ **myew**kah **lin**serr
Do you have any contact-lens fluid?	**Har ni någon kontaktlinsvätska?**	haar nee **naw**gon kon**tahkt**linsvehtskah
I'd like to buy a pair of sunglasses.	**Jag skulle vilja köpa ett par solglasögon.**	yaa(g) **skew**ler **vil**yah **khur**pah eht paar **sool**glaassurgon
May I look in the mirror?	**Får jag se i spegeln?**	fawr yaa(g) say ee **spay**gerln
I'd like to buy a pair of binoculars.	**Jag skulle vilja köpa en kikare.**	yaa(g) **skew**ler **vil**yah **khur**pah ehn **khee**kahrer

Photography *Fotografering*

I'd like a(n) ... camera.	**Jag skulle vilja köpa en ... kamera.**	yaa(g) **skew**ler **vil**yah khurpah ehn ... **kaam**(er)rah
automatic	**automatisk**	aa(ew)too**maa**tisk
inexpensive	**billig**	**bil**li(g)
simple	**enkel**	**ehn**kerl
Can you show me some ..., please?	**Kan jag få se på ...?**	kahn yaa(g) faw say paw
cine (movie) cameras	**en filmkamera**	ehn **film**kaam(eh)rah
video cameras	**en videokamera**	ehn **veed**yokaam(eh)rah
I'd like to have some passport photos taken.	**Jag skulle vilja ha ett passfoto taget.**	yaa(g) **skew**ler **vil**yah haa eht **pahs**footoo **taa**gert

Film *Film*

I'd like a film for this camera.	**Jag skulle vilja ha film till den här kameran.**	yaa(g) **skew**ler **vil**yah haa film til dehn hær **kaam**(er)rahn
black and white	**svart-vit**	svah[r]t-veet
colour	**färg**	færy
colour negative	**färgnegativ**	**færy**nehgahteev
colour slide	**färgdiapositiv**	**færy**diahpoositteev
cartridge	**en kassett**	ehn kah**sseht**
disc film	**en disc**	ehn disk
roll film	**en filmrulle**	ehn **film**rewler
video cassette	**en videokassett**	ehn **veed**yokahsseht
24/36 exposures	**tjugofyra/trettio-sex bilder**	khewgoo**few**rah/trehti**ssehks bil**derr
this size	**det här formatet**	day(t) hær for**maa**tert
this ASA/DIN number	**det här ASA/DIN numret**	day(t) hær **aa**ssah/deen **newm**rert
artificial light type	**för inomhusljus**	furr innomhewsyewss
daylight type	**för dagsljus**	furr **dahgs**yewss
fast (high-speed)	**snabb**	snahb
fine grain	**finkornig**	**feen**koo[r]nig

Processing *Framkallning*

Does the price include processing?	**Ingår framkallning i priset?**	**in**gawr **frahm**kahlning ee **pree**ssert

How much do you charge for processing?	**Hur mycket kostar framkallning?**	hewr **mew**ker(t) **kos**tahr **frahm**kahlning
I'd like ... prints of each negative.	**Jag skall be att få ... kopior av varje negativ.**	yaa(g) skahl bay aht faw ... koo**pee**oor aav **vah**ryer **neh**gahteev
with a mat finish	**med matt yta**	mayd maht **ew**tah
with a glossy finish	**med glansig yta**	mayd **glahn**si(g) **ew**tah
Will you enlarge this, please?	**Kan ni förstora det här?**	kahn nee fur^r**stoo**rah day(t) hær
When will the photos be ready?	**När blir korten klara?**	nær bleer **koo**^{r}tern **klaa**rah

Accessories and repairs *Tillbehör och reparationer*

I'd like a/an/some ...	**Jag skulle vilja ha ...**	yaa(g) **skew**ler **vil**yah haa
battery	**ett batteri**	eht bahter**ree**
cable release	**en trådutlösare**	ehn **trawd**ewtlurssahrer
camera case	**ett kamerafodral**	eht **kaam**(er)rahfoodraal
(electronic) flash	**en (elektronisk) blixt**	ehn (ehlehk**traw**nisk) blikst
filter	**ett filter**	eht **fil**terr
for black and white	**för svart-vit**	furr svah^{r}t-vit
for colour	**för färg**	furr færy
lens	**ett objektiv**	eht obyehk**teev**
telephoto lens	**ett teleobjektiv**	eht **tay**lerobyehkteev
wide-angle lens	**ett vidvinkel-objektiv**	eht **veed**vinkerl-obyehkteev
lens cap	**ett linsskydd**	eht **lins**shewd
Can you repair this camera?	**Kan ni laga den här kameran?**	kahn nee **laa**gah dehn hær **kaam**(er)rahn
The film is jammed.	**Filmen har fastnat.**	**fil**mern haar **fahs**naht
There's something wrong with the ...	**Det är något fel på ...**	day(t) ær **naw**got fayl paw
exposure counter	**exponeringsmätaren**	ehkspoo**nay**rings-maitahrern
film winder	**frammatningen**	**frahm**maatningern
flash attachment	**blixtaggregatet**	**blikst**ahgrergaatert
lens	**objektivet**	obyehk**tee**vert
light meter	**ljusmätaren**	**yews**maitahrern
rangefinder	**avståndsväljaren**	**aav**stondsvehlyahrern
shutter	**slutaren**	**slew**tahrern

NUMBERS, see page 147

Tobacconist's *Tobaksaffär*

Tobacco is a state monopoly in Sweden. Virtually all international brands are available in tobacco shops, kiosks, supermarkets and so on. Sweden is especially known for its quality pipe tobaccos and snuff.

A packet of cigarettes, please.	**Ett paket cigarretter, tack.**	eht pah**kāyt** siggah**reh**terr tahk
Do you have any American/English cigarettes?	**Har ni några amerikanska/engelska cigarretter?**	haar nee **naw**grah ahm(er)ri**kaan**skah/**ehng**erlskah siggah**reh**terr
Could I have a carton, please?	**Kan jag få en limpa, tack?**	kahn yaa(g) faw ehn **lim**pah tahk
I'd like a/some ...	**Jag skall be att få ...**	yaa(g) skah(l) bāy aht faw
candy	**lite godis**	**lee**ter **gōō**diss
chewing gum	**ett tuggummi**	eht **tew**gewmi
chewing tobacco	**lite tuggtobak**	**lee**ter **tewg**tōōbahk
chocolate bar	**en chokladkaka**	shoo**klaa(d)**kaakah
cigarette case	**ett cigarrettetui**	eht siggah**reht**ehtēwee
cigarette holder	**ett cigarrett-munstycke**	eht siggah**reht**-mewnstewker
cigarettes	**cigarretter**	siggah**reh**terr
filter-tipped	**med filter**	māyd **fil**terr
without filter	**utan filter**	**ēw**tahn **fil**terr
light/dark tobacco	**ljus/mörk tobak**	yēwss/murrk **tōō**bahk
mild/strong	**svaga/starka**	**svaa**gah/**stahr**kah
menthol	**mentol-**	mehn**tawl**
king-size	**king-size**	"king-size"
cigars	**några cigarrer**	**naw**grah siggah**rerr**
lighter	**en tändare**	ehn **tehn**dahrer
lighter fluid/gas	**bensin/gas till en tändare**	behn**seen**/gaass til ehn **tehn**dahrer
matches	**tändstickor**	**tehn(d)**stikkoor
pipe	**en pipa**	ehn **pee**pah
pipe cleaners	**piprensare**	**peep**rehnsahrer
pipe tobacco	**piptobak**	**peep**tōōbahk
pipe tool	**pipverktyg**	**peep**værktēwg
postcard	**ett vykort**	eht **vēw**koo[r]t
snuff	**en dosa snus**	ehn **dōō**ssah snēwss
stamps	**några frimärken**	**naw**grah **free**mærkern
sweets	**lite godis**	**lee**ter **gōō**diss
wick	**en veke**	ehn **vāy**ker

Miscellaneous *Diverse*

Souvenirs *Souvenirer*

Finding something typically Swedish to take home is not a problem. If anything, the choice is daunting. You'll find colourful textiles, modern pottery and silverware, leather goods, wood- and horncarvings. And, of course, beautiful glassware, even more tempting after seeing the glassblowers at work in "The Kingdom of Crystal", the glassmaking district near Växjö in southeastern Sweden.

And don't forget the wide range of edible souvenirs: sausages and salmon, smoked reindeer meat, caviar, canned herring, crispbread, not to mention aquavit.

I'd like a souvenir from ...	**Jag skulle vilja ha en souvenir från ...**	yaa(g) **skew**ler **vil**yah haa ehn sooverneer frawn
Something typically Swedish, please.	**Något typiskt svenskt.**	**naw**got **tēw**piskt svehnskt
ceramics	**keramik**	khehrah**meek**
clogs	**träskor**	**trǣ**skōōr
Dala horse	**en dalahäst**	ehn **daa**lahhehst
glassware	**glas**	glaass
bowl	**en skål**	ehn skawl
vase	**en vas**	ehn vaass
Lapp handicrafts	**sameslöjd**	**saa**mersluryd
birch-bark work	**något i näver**	**naw**got ee **næ**verr
horn work	**något i horn**	**naw**got ee hōōʳn
knife	**en kniv**	ehn kneev
silverware	**något i silver**	**naw**got ee **sil**verr
jewellery	**ett smycke**	eht **smew**ker
textiles	**textilvaror**	tehks**teel**vaaroor
woodwork	**något i trä**	**naw**got ee trǣ
butter knife	**en smörkniv**	ehn **smūrr**kneev
candlestick	**en ljusstake**	ehn **yēw**sstaaker

Records—Cassettes *Skivor – Kassetter*

I'd like a ...	**Jag skulle vilja ha ...**	yaa(g) **skew**ler **vil**yah haa
cassette	**en kassett**	ehn kah**sseht**
video cassette	**en videokassett**	ehn **veed**yokahsseht
compact disc	**en CD-skiva**	ehn **sāy**-dāy **shee**vah

L.P. (33 rpm)	**LP (33 varvs)**	**ehl**pa͞y (trehti**tra͞y** vahrvss)
E.P. (45 rpm)	**EP (45 varvs)**	**a͞y**pa͞y (fur**ʳ**ti**fehm** vahrvss)
single	**singel**	**sing**erl

Do you have any records by ...?	**Har ni några skivor med ...?**	haar nee **naw**grah **shee**voor ma͞yd
Can I listen to this record?	**Kan jag få lyssna på den här skivan?**	kahn yaa(g) faw **lewss**nah paw dehn hæ̅r **shee**vahn
chamber music	**kammarmusik**	**kah**mahrmewsseek
classical music	**klassisk musik**	**klah**ssisk mew**sseek**
folk music	**folkmusik**	**folk**mewsseek
folk songs	**folksånger**	**folk**sawngerr
instrumental music	**instrumentalmusik**	instrewmehn**taal**mewsseek
jazz	**jazz**	yahss
light music	**lätt musik**	leht mew**sseek**
orchestral music	**orkestermusik**	or**kehs**terrmewsseek
pop music	**pop**	pop

Toys *Leksaker*

I'd like a toy/ game ...	**Jag skulle vilja ha en leksak/ ett spel ...**	yaa(g) **skew**ler **vil**yah haa ehn **la͞y**ksaak/ eht spa͞yl
for a boy	**till en pojke**	til ehn **poy**ker
for a 5-year-old girl	**till en 5-årig flicka**	til ehn 5-**aw**rig **fli**kkah
(beach) ball	**en (bad)boll**	ehn (**baad**)bol
bucket and spade (pail and shovel)	**hink och spade**	hink ok **spaa**der
building blocks (bricks)	**byggklotsar**	**bewg**klossahr
card game	**ett kortspel**	eht **kooʳts**pa͞yl
chess set	**ett schackspel**	eht **shahk**spa͞yl
doll	**en docka**	ehn **do**kkah
electronic game	**ett elektroniskt spel**	eht ehlehk**traw**niskt spa͞yl
roller skates	**ett par rullskridskor**	eht paar **rewl**-skri(d)sko͞or
snorkel	**en snorkel**	ehn **snor**kerl

Your money: banks—currency

At most banks there's sure to be someone who speaks English. You'll find small currency-exchange offices in most tourist centres, especially during the summer season. Remember to take your passport along with you, as you may need it for identification.

Traveller's cheques and credit cards are widely accepted in tourist-oriented shops, hotels, restaurants, etc. However, if you're exploring way off the beaten track, you'll probably come across village stores where they are not taken. The same goes for garages and filling stations—generally, only the main agency garages in the large cities will accept payment in traveller's cheques or by credit card.

Opening hours: Banks are closed all day Saturday, Sunday and on public holidays. Opening hours are from 9.30 a.m. to 3 p.m. Monday to Friday; some banks also open between 4.30 and 6 p.m. one day a week. At the main railway station in Stockholm and at Arlanda airport, the currency exchange offices are open all day, including weekends.

Monetary unit: The crown (*krona*—**kro͞o**nah, plural *kronor*—**kro͞o**noor), is the monetary unit of Sweden, Norway and Denmark, but its value differs in each country. The krona (abbreviation *kr*) is divided into 100 *öre* (**u͞r**rer).

Coins: 10 and 50 öre, 1 and 5 kronor.
Banknotes: 10, 50, 100, 500, 1,000 and 10,000 kronor.

Where's the nearest bank?	**Var ligger närmaste bank?**	vaar **li**ggerr **nær**mahster bahnk
Where's the nearest currency exchange office?	**Var ligger närmaste växelkontor?**	vaar **li**ggerr **nær**mahster **veh**kserlkonto͞or
When is it open?	**När är det öppet?**	nær ær da͞y(t) **ur**pert

At the bank *På banken*

I'd like to change some dollars/pounds.	**Jag skulle vilja växla några dollar/ pund.**	yaa(g) **skew**ler **vil**yah **vehks**lah **naw**grah **do**llahr/ pewnd
I'd like to cash a traveller's cheque.	**Jag skulle vilja lösa in en resecheck.**	yaa(g) **skew**ler **vil**yah **lu̅r̅**ssah in ehn **ra̅y̅**sserkhehk
What's the exchange rate?	**Vilken är växelkursen?**	**vil**kern æ̅r̅ **veh**kserlkew^{r}sern
How much commission do you charge?	**Hur stor är expeditionsavgiften?**	he̅w̅r sto̅o̅r æ̅r̅ ehks-pehdi**sho̅o̅n**saavyiftern
Can you cash a personal cheque?	**Kan ni lösa in en personlig check?**	kahn nee **lu̅r̅**ssah in ehn pæ^{r}**sho̅o̅n**lig khehk
Can you telex my bank in London?	**Kan ni skicka ett telex till min bank i London?**	kahn nee **shik**kah eht **ta̅y̅**lehks til min bahnk ee **lon**don
I have a/an/some ...	**Jag har ...**	yaa(g) haar
credit card	**kreditkort**	kreh**deet**koo^{r}t
Eurocheques	**Eurochecker**	**eh**ewrookhehkerr
letter of credit	**en remburs**	ehn rehm**bew^{r}s**
I'm expecting some money from New York. Has it arrived?	**Jag väntar pengar från New York. Har de kommit?**	yaa(g) **vehn**tahr **pehng**ahr frawn new york. haar dom **kom**mit
Please give me ... in notes (bills) and some small change.	**Kan jag få ... i sedlar och lite växel, tack?**	kahn yaa(g) faw ... ee **sa̅y̅d**lahr ok **lee**ter **veh**kserl tahk
Give me ... in large notes and the rest in small notes.	**Kan jag få ... i stora sedlar och resten i små sedlar?**	kahn yaa(g) faw ... ee **sto̅o̅**rah **sa̅y̅d**lahr ok **reh**stern ee smaw **sa̅y̅d**lahr

Deposits—Withdrawals *Insättning – Uttag*

I'd like to ...	**Jag skulle vilja ...**	yaa(g) **skew**ler **vil**yah
open an account	**öppna ett konto**	**urp**nah eht **kon**too
withdraw ... crowns	**ta ut ... kronor**	taa e̅w̅t ... **kro̅o̅**noor
Where should I sign?	**Var skall jag skriva under?**	vaar skah(l) yaa(g) **skree**vah **ewn**derr

NUMBERS, see page 147

I'd like to pay this into my account.	**Jag skulle vilja sätta in det här på mitt konto.**	yaa(g) **skew**ler **vil**yah **seh**tah in da̅y̅(t) hǣr paw mit **kon**too

Business terms *Affärstermer*

My name is ...	**Mitt namn är ...**	mit nahmn ǣr
Here's my card.	**Här är mitt kort.**	hǣr ǣr mit koo^{r}t
I have an appointment with ...	**Jag har avtalat ett möte med ...**	yaa(g) haar **aav**taalaht eht **mu̅r̅**ter ma̅y̅d
Can you give me an estimate of the cost?	**Kan ni ge mig en uppskattning av kostnaden?**	kahn nee ya̅y̅ may ehn **ewp**skahtning aav **kost**nahdern
What's the rate of inflation?	**Hur hög är inflationen?**	he̅w̅r hu̅r̅g ǣr inflah**sho̅o̅**nern
Can you provide me with an interpreter/ a secretary?	**Kan ni skaffa mig en tolk/ en sekreterare?**	kahn nee **skah**fah may ehn tolk/ ehn sehkrer**ta̅y̅**rahrer
Where can I make photocopies?	**Var kan jag göra fotokopior?**	vaar kahn yaa(g) **yu̅r̅**rah **fo̅o̅**tookoopeeor

amount	**en summa**	ehn **sew**mah
balance	**en balansräkning**	ehn bah**lahns**raikning
capital	**ett kapital**	eht kahpi**taal**
cheque book	**ett checkhäfte**	eht **khehk**hehfter
contract	**ett kontrakt**	eht kon**trahkt**
discount	**en rabatt**	ehn rah**baht**
expenses	**omkostnader**	**om**kostnahderr
interest	**en ränta**	ehn **rehn**tah
investment	**en investering**	ehn invehs**ta̅y̅**ring
invoice	**en faktura**	ehn fahk**te̅w̅**rah
loss	**en förlust**	ehn fur^{r}**lewst**
mortgage	**ett hypotek**	eht hewpoo**ta̅y̅k**
payment	**en betalning**	ehn ber**taal**ning
percentage	**en procentsats**	ehn proo**sehnt**sahtss
profit	**en vinst**	ehn vinst
purchase	**ett köp**	eht khu̅r̅p
sale	**en försäljning**	ehn fur^{r}**sehl**yning
share	**en aktie**	ehn **ahk**tsier
transfer	**en överföring**	ehn **u̅r̅**verrfu̅r̅ring
value	**ett värde**	eht **vǣ**^{r}der

At the post office

The post office only handles mail; for telephone and telegram or telex services you have to go to a *Tele* office. Post offices are indicated by a yellow sign with a blue horn, and mailboxes are also bright yellow except those for local mail which are blue. Business hours are generally from 9 a.m. to 6 p.m., Monday to Friday, but they might change in the summer months. The main post office in Stockholm is open from 7 a.m. to 9 p.m., Monday to Friday, and 10 a.m. to 1 p.m. on Saturdays.

In bigger post offices there's a queue system: you take a number when you enter. It will come up on a screen together with the number of the free window when it's your turn (there's a beep every time the number changes).

Where's the nearest post office?	**Var ligger närmaste postkontor?**	vaar **lig**gerr **nær**mahster **post**kontōōr
What time does the post office open/close?	**Hur dags öppnar/stänger posten?**	hēwr dahgss **urp**nahr/**stehng**err **pos**tern
A stamp for this letter/postcard, please.	**Ett frimärke till det här brevet/kortet, tack.**	eht **free**mærker til dāy(t) hær **brāy**vert/**koo**^{r}tert tahk
A ...-öres stamp, please.	**Ett ... -öres frimärke, tack.**	eht ... -**ūr**rerss **free**mærker tahk
What's the postage for a letter to England?	**Vad är portot för ett brev till England?**	vaad ǣr **po**^{r}tot fūrr eht brāyv til **eng**lahnd
What's the postage for a postcard to the U.S.A.?	**Vad är portot för ett vykort till USA?**	vaad ǣr **po**^{r}tot fūrr eht **vēw**koo^{r}t til **ēw**ehssaa
Where's the letter box (mailbox)?	**Var är brevlådan?**	vaar ǣr **brāyv**lawdahn
I want to send this parcel.	**Jag vill skicka det här paketet.**	yaa(g) vil **shik**kah dāy(t) hær pah**kāy**tert

I'd like to send this by ...	**Jag vill skicka det här ...**	yaa(g) vil **shikk**ah dāy(t) hær
airmail	**med flyg**	māyd flēwg
express (special delivery)	**express**	ehks**prehss**
registered mail	**rekommenderat**	rehkommern**dāy**raht
At which counter can I cash an international money order?	**I vilken lucka kan jag lösa in en internationell postanvisning?**	ee **vil**kern **lew**kah kahn yaa(g) **lurs**sah in ehn interrnahtshoo**nehl** **post**ahnveesning
Where's the poste restante (general delivery)?	**Var är poste restanteluckan?**	vaar ær post reh**stahn**terlewkahn
Is there any post (mail) for me?	**Finns det någon post till mig?**	finss dāy(t) **naw**gon post til may
My name is ...	**Mitt namn är ...**	mit nahmn ær

FRIMÄRKEN	STAMPS
PAKET	PARCELS
POSTANVISNINGAR	MONEY ORDERS

Telegrams *Telegram*

Where's the nearest telegraph office?	**Var ligger närmaste telegraf?**	vaar **lig**gerr **nær**mahster tehleh**graaf**
I'd like to send a ...	**Jag skulle vilja skicka ett ...**	yaa(g) **skew**ler **vil**yah **shik**kah eht
fax/telegram/telex	**telefax/telegram/telex**	tehleh**fahkss**/tehleh**grahm**/**tāy**lehks
May I have a form, please?	**Kan jag få en blankett, tack?**	kahn yaa(g) faw ehn blahn**keht** tahk
How much is it per word?	**Vad kostar det per ord?**	vaad **kos**tahr dāy(t) pær ōōʳd
How long will a cable to Boston take?	**Hur lång tid tar ett telegram till Boston?**	hēwr long teed taar eht tehleh**grahm** til **bos**ton
How much will this telex cost?	**Hur mycket kostar det här telexet?**	hēwr **mew**kert **kos**tahr dāy(t) hær **tāy**lehksert

Telephoning *Telefon*

The telephone system in Sweden is entirely automatic. International or long-distance calls can be made from phone booths, but if you need help in making a call, go to the special telegraph offices marked *Tele* or *Telebutik*. Dialling instructions in foreign languages, including English, are posted inside the booth or can be found at the front of every telephone directory.

To call Britain from Sweden dial 00944, wait for a second dialling tone and then dial the number minus the initial 0 in the dialling (area) code. For the U.S.A. the prefix is 0091.

Where's the telephone?	**Var är telefonen?**	vaar ǣr tehleh**faw**nern
Where's the nearest telephone booth?	**Var finns närmaste telefonkiosk?**	vaar finss **nær**mahster tehleh**fawn**khiosk
May I use your phone?	**Får jag låna telefonen?**	fawr yaa(g) **law**nah tehleh**faw**nern
Do you have a telephone directory for Uppsala?	**Har ni en telefonkatalog över Uppsala?**	haar nee ehn tehleh**fawn**kahtahlawg ūrverr **ewp**saalah
I'd like to call someone in England.	**Jag vill ringa någon i England.**	yaa(g) vil **ring**ah **naw**gon ee **ehng**lahnd
What's the dialling (area) code for ...?	**Vad är riktnumret till ...?**	vaad ǣr **rikt**newmrert til
How do I get the international operator?	**Vilket nummer är det till utlands-telefonisten?**	**vil**kert **new**merr ǣr dāy(t) til **ēw**tlahn(d)s-tehlehfonnistern

Operator *Telefonist*

I'd like Lund 23 45 67.	**Jag vill ha ett samtal till Lund, nummer 23 45 67.**	yaa(g) vil haa eht **sahm**taal til lewnd **new**merr 23 45 67
Can you help me get this number?	**Kan ni hjälpa mig att komma till det här numret?**	kahn nee **yehl**pah may aht **ko**mmah til dāy(t) hǣr **new**mrert
I'd like to place a personal (person-to-person) call.	**Jag vill beställa ett personligt samtal.**	yaa(g) vil ber**steh**lah eht pǣ**ʳshōōn**li(g)t **sahm**taal

NUMBERS, see page 147

I'd like to reverse the charges (call collect).	**Jag skulle vilja beställa ett Ba-samtal.**	yaa(g) **skew**ler **vil**yah ber**stehl**ah eht **bay**aa-sahm**taal**

Telephone alphabet *Bokstaveringsalfabet*

A	**Adam**	aadahm	P	**Petter**	pehterr
B	**Bertil**	bæ^{r}til	Q	**Qvintus**	kvintewss
C	**Cesar**	sayssahr	R	**Rudolf**	rewdolf
D	**David**	daavid	S	**Sigurd**	seegew^{r}d
E	**Erik**	ayrik	T	**Tore**	toorer
F	**Filip**	feelip	U	**Urban**	ewrbahn
G	**Gustav**	gewstahv	V	**Viktor**	viktor
H	**Helge**	hehlger	W	**Wilhelm**	vilhehlm
I	**Ivar**	eevahr	X	**Xerxes**	ksehrksehss
J	**Johan**	yoo(h)ahn	Y	**Yngve**	ewngver
K	**Kalle**	kahler	Z	**Zäta**	saitah
L	**Ludvig**	lewdvig	Å	**Åke**	awker
M	**Martin**	mah^{r}tin	Ä	**Ärlig**	æ^{r}lig
N	**Niklas**	niklahss	Ö	**Östen**	urstern
O	**Olof**	oolof			

Speaking *Samtal*

Hello. This is ...	**Hallå, det här är ...**	hah**law** **day**(t) hær ær
I'd like to speak to ...	**Kan jag få tala med ...?**	kahn yaa(g) faw **taa**lah mayd
Extension ...	**Anknytning ...**	**ahn**knewtning
Speak louder/more slowly, please.	**Kan ni tala lite högre/långsammare, tack?**	kahn nee **taa**lah **lee**ter hurgrer/**long**sahmahrer tahk

Bad luck *Otur*

Would you try again later, please?	**Kan ni försöka igen lite senare?**	kahn nee fur^{r}**sur**kah ee**yehn** **lee**ter **say**nahrer
Operator, you gave me the wrong number.	**Jag tror ni gav mig fel nummer.**	yaa(g) troor nee gaav may fayl **new**merr

Operator, we were cut off.	**Hallå, vi blev avbrutna.**	hah**law** vee bla̅y̅v **aav**bre̅w̅tnah

Not there *Inte inne*

When will he/she be back?	**När kommer han/hon tillbaka?**	næ̅r **kom**merr hahn/hoon **til**baakah
Will you tell him/her I called?	**Kan ni tala om för honom/henne att jag har ringt?**	kahn nee **taa**lah om fu̅r̅r **hon**nom/**heh**ner aht yaa(g) haar ringt
My name is ...	**Mitt namn är ...**	mit nahmn æ̅r
Would you ask him/her to phone me?	**Skulle ni kunna be honom/henne ringa mig?**	**skew**ler nee **kew**nah ba̅y̅ **hon**nom/**heh**ner **ring**ah may
Would you take a message, please?	**Skulle ni kunna lämna ett meddelande?**	**skew**ler nee **kew**nah **lehm**nah eht **ma̅y̅**da̅y̅lahnder

Charges *Avgifter*

How much did the call cost?	**Hur mycket kostade samtalet?**	he̅w̅r **mew**kert **kos**tahder **sahm**taalert
I'd like to pay for the call.	**Jag skulle vilja betala samtalet.**	yaa(g) **skew**ler **vil**yah ber**taa**lah **sahm**taalert

Det är telefon till er.	There's a telephone call for you.
Vilket nummer ringer ni?	What number are you calling?
Det är upptaget.	The line's engaged.
Det är ingen som svarar.	There's no answer.
Ni har slagit fel nummer.	You've got the wrong number.
Telefonen är trasig.	The phone is out of order.
Ett ögonblick.	Just a moment.
Var god dröj.	Hold on, please.
Han/hon är ute för ögonblicket.	He's/She's out at the moment.

Doctor

British subjects are covered by Sweden's national health insurance plan. Other nationalities should check to see if their health insurance policy covers medical treatment in Sweden before leaving home.

General *Allmänt*

Can you get me a doctor?	**Kan ni skaffa mig en läkare?**	kahn nee **skah**fah may ehn **lai**kahrer
Is there a doctor here?	**Finns det någon läkare här?**	finss dāy(t) **naw**gon **lai**kahrer hær
I need a doctor, quickly.	**Jag behöver en läkare fort.**	yaa(g) ber**hūr**verr ehn **lai**kahrer fooʳt
Where can I find a doctor who speaks English?	**Var kan jag få tag på en läkare som talar engelska?**	vaar kahn yaa(g) faw taag paw ehn **lai**kahrer som **taa**lahr **eng**erlskah
Where's the surgery (doctor's office)?	**Var ligger läkarmottagningen?**	vaar **li**ggerr **lai**kahr-**mōō**taagningern
What are the surgery (office) hours?	**Vilka är mottagningstiderna?**	**vil**kah ær **mōō**taagnings-teederʳnah
Could the doctor come to see me here?	**Kan doktorn komma hit och undersöka mig?**	kahn **dok**toʳn **ko**mmah heet ok **ewn**derʳsūrkah may
What time can the doctor come?	**Hur dags kan doktorn komma?**	hēwr dahgss kahn **dok**toʳn **ko**mmah
Can you recommend a/an ...?	**Kan ni rekommendera en ...?**	kahn nee rehkom-mern**dāy**rah ehn
general practitioner	**allmänpraktiker**	**ahl**mehnprahktikkerr
children's doctor	**barnläkare**	**baaʳn**laikahrer
eye specialist	**ögonspecialist**	**ūr**gonspehssiahlist
gynaecologist	**gynekolog**	yewnerkoo**lawg**
Can I have an appointment ...?	**Kan jag få en tid ...?**	kahn yaa(g) faw ehn teed
tomorrow	**i morgon**	ee **mo**rron
as soon as possible	**så snart som möjligt**	saw snaaʳt som **mur**yli(g)t

CHEMIST'S, see page 108

Parts of the body *Kroppsdelar*

appendix	**blindtarmen**	**blin(d)**tahrmern
arm	**armen**	**ahr**mern
artery	**pulsådern**	**pewls**awder^{r}n
back	**ryggen**	**rew**gern
bladder	**urinblåsan**	**$\overline{\text{ew}}$reen**blawssahn
bone	**benen (i kroppen)**	**b$\overline{\text{ay}}$**nern (ee **kro**ppern)
bowel	**tarmen**	**tahr**mern
breast	**bröstet**	**brurs**tert
chest	**bröstkorgen**	**brurst**koryern
ear	**örat**	**$\overline{\text{ur}}$**raht
face	**ansiktet**	**ahn**siktert
finger	**fingret**	**fing**rert
foot	**foten**	**f$\overline{\text{oo}}$**tern
genitals	**könsorganen**	**kh$\overline{\text{ur}}$ns**orgaanern
gland	**körteln**	**khur**^{r}terln
hand	**handen**	**hahn**dern
head	**huvudet**	**h$\overline{\text{ew}}$**v(ewd)ert
heart	**hjärtat**	**yæ**^{r}taht
jaw	**käken**	**khai**kern
joint	**leden**	**l$\overline{\text{ay}}$**dern
kidney	**njuren**	**ny$\overline{\text{ew}}$**rern
knee	**knä(e)t**	knai(er)t
leg	**benet**	**b$\overline{\text{ay}}$**nert
lip	**läppen**	**leh**pern
liver	**levern**	**l$\overline{\text{ay}}$**ver^{r}n
lung	**lungan**	**lewng**ahn
mouth	**munnen**	**mew**nern
muscle	**muskeln**	**mews**kerln
neck	**nacken**	**nah**kern
nerve	**nerven**	**nær**vern
nervous system	**nervsystemet**	**nærv**sewst$\overline{\text{ay}}$mert
nose	**näsan**	**nais**sahn
rib	**revbenet**	**r$\overline{\text{ay}}$v**b$\overline{\text{ay}}$nert
shoulder	**skuldran/axeln**	**skewl**drahn/**ahk**serln
skin	**huden**	**h$\overline{\text{ew}}$**dern
spine	**ryggraden**	**rew**graadern
stomach	**magen**	**maa**gern
tendon	**senan**	**s$\overline{\text{ay}}$**nahn
thigh	**låret**	**law**rert
throat	**halsen**	**hahl**sern
thumb	**tummen**	**tew**mern
toe	**tån**	tawn
tongue	**tungan**	**tewng**ahn
tonsils	**mandlarna**	**mahnd**lah^{r}nah
vein	**venen/ådern**	**v$\overline{\text{ay}}$**nern/**aw**der^{r}n

Accident—Injury *Olycksfall – Skada*

There's been an accident.	**Det har hänt en olycka.**	da̅y̅(t) haar hehnt ehn o̅o̅lewkah
My child has had a fall.	**Mitt barn har ramlat.**	mit baa^{r}n haar **rahm**laht
He/She has hurt his/her head.	**Han/Hon har slagit sig i huvudet.**	hahn/hoon haar **slaa**git say ee **he̅w̅**v(ewd)ert
He's/She's unconscious.	**Han/Hon är medvetslös.**	hahn/hoon æ̅r **ma̅y̅d**va̅y̅tslu̅r̅ss
He's/She's bleeding (heavily).	**Han/Hon blöder (kraftigt).**	hahn/hoon **blu̅r̅**derr (**krahf**tigt)
He's/She's (seriously) injured.	**Han/Hon är (allvarligt) skadad.**	hahn/hoon æ̅r (**ahl**vaa^{r}ligt) **skaa**dahd
His/Her ankle is swollen.	**Hans/Hennes vrist är svullen.**	hahnss/**heh**nerss vrist æ̅r **svew**lern
I've broken my arm.	**Jag har brutit armen.**	yaa(g) haar **bre̅w̅**tit **ahr**mern
I've been stung.	**Jag har blivit biten.**	yaa(g) haar **blee**vit **bee**tern
I've got something in my eye.	**Jag har fått något i ögat.**	yaa(g) haar fot **naw**got ee **u̅r̅**gaht
I've got a/an ...	**Jag har (fått) ...**	yaa(g) haar (fot)
blister	**en blåsa**	ehn **blaw**ssah
boil	**en böld**	ehn burld
bruise	**ett blåmärke**	eht **blaw**mærker
bump	**en bula**	ehn **be̅w̅**lah
burn	**ett brännsår**	eht **brehn**sawr
cut	**ett skärsår**	eht **shæ̅^{r}**sawr
graze	**ett skrubbsår**	eht **skrewb**sawr
insect bite	**ett insektsbett**	eht **in**sehktsbeht
lump	**en knöl**	ehn knu̅r̅l
rash	**ett utslag**	eht **e̅w̅t**slaag
sting	**ett stick**	eht stik
swelling	**en svullnad**	ehn **svewl**nahd
wound	**ett sår**	eht sawr
Could you have a look at it?	**Skulle ni kunna titta på det?**	**skew**ler nee **kew**nah **tit**tah paw da̅y̅(t)
I can't move my ...	**Jag kan inte röra ...**	yaa(g) kahn **in**ter **ru̅r̅**rah
It hurts.	**Det gör ont.**	da̅y̅(t) yu̅r̅r oont

Var gör det ont?	Where does it hurt?
Vad för slags smärta är det?	What kind of pain is it?
dov/intensiv/ pulserande/konstant/ kommer och går	dull/sharp/ throbbing/constant/ on and off
Det är ...	It's ...
brutet/vrickat/ur led	broken/sprained/dislocated
Ni har ett avslitet ligament.	You have a torn ligament.
Vi måste ta en röntgenbild.	I'd like you to have an X-ray.
Vi måste gipsa det.	We'll have to put it in plaster.
Det är infekterat.	It's infected.
Har ni vaccinerats mot stelkramp?	Have you been vaccinated against tetanus?
Jag skall ge er något smärtstillande.	I'll give you a painkiller.

Illness *Sjukdom*

I'm not feeling well.	**Jag mår inte bra.**	yaa(g) mawr **in**ter braa
I'm ill.	**Jag är sjuk.**	yaa(g) $\overline{ae}$r sh$\overline{ew}$k
I feel ...	**Jag känner mig ...**	yaa(g) **khehn**err may
dizzy	**yr**	$\overline{ew}$r
nauseous	**illamående**	illahmawehnder
weak	**svag**	svaag
I feel shivery.	**Jag har frossbrytningar.**	yaa(g) haar **fros**br$\overline{ew}$tningahr
I have a temperature (fever).	**Jag har feber.**	yaa(g) haar **f$\overline{ay}$**berr
I've been vomiting.	**Jag har kräkts.**	yaa(g) haar kraiktss
I'm constipated.	**Jag har förstoppning.**	yaa(g) haar furʳ**stop**ning
I've got diarrhoea.	**Jag har diarré.**	yaa(g) haar diahr$\overline{ay}$
My ... hurt(s).	**Jag har ont i ...**	yaa(g) haar oont ee

I've got (a/an) ...	**Jag har ...**	yaa(g) haar
asthma	**astma**	**ahs**tmah
backache	**ont i ryggen**	oont ee **rew**gern
cough	**hosta**	**hoos**tah
cramps	**kramp**	krahmp
earache	**ont i örat**	oont ee **u̅r̅r̅**aht
hay fever	**hösnuva**	**hu̅r̅**sne̅w̅vah
headache	**huvudvärk**	**he̅w̅**vew(d)værk
indigestion	**dålig matsmältning**	**daw**li(g) **maat**smehltning
nosebleed	**näsblod**	**nais**blo̅o̅d
palpitations	**hjärtklappning**	**yæ^{r}t**klahpning
rheumatism	**reumatism**	rehmah**tism**
sore throat	**ont i halsen**	oont ee **hahl**sern
stiff neck	**stel nacke**	sta̅y̅l **nah**ker
stomach ache	**ont i magen**	oont ee **maa**gern
sunstroke	**solsting**	**so̅o̅l**sting
I've got a cold.	**Jag är förkyld.**	yaa(g) æ̅r̅ fur^r**khe̅w̅ld**
I have difficulties breathing.	**Jag har svårt att andas.**	yaa(g) haar svaw^{r}t aht **ahn**dahss
I have chest pains.	**Jag har ont i bröstet.**	yaa(g) haar oont ee **brur**stert
I had a heart attack ... years ago.	**Jag hade en hjärt-attack för ... år sedan.**	yaa(g) **hah**der ehn **yæ^{r}t**-ahtahk fu̅r̅r̅ ... awr sehn
My blood pressure is too high/too low.	**Mitt blodtryck är för högt/för lågt.**	mit **blo̅o̅(d)**trewk æ̅r̅ fu̅r̅r̅ hurgt/lawgt
I'm allergic to ...	**Jag är allergisk mot ...**	yaa(g) æ̅r̅ ah**lær**gisk mo̅o̅t
I'm diabetic.	**Jag är diabetiker.**	yaa(g) æ̅r̅ diah**ba̅y̅**tikkerr

Women's section *För kvinnor*

I have period pains.	**Jag har mens(truations)smärtor.**	yaa(g) haar **mehns**-(trewah**sho̅o̅ns**)smæ^{r}toor
I have a vaginal infection.	**Jag har en infek-tion i underlivet.**	yaa(g) haar ehn infehk-**sho̅o̅n** ee **ewn**derrleevert
I'm on the pill.	**Jag tar p-piller.**	yaa(g) taar **pa̅y̅**-pillerr
I haven't had a period for 2 months.	**Jag har inte haft mens(truation) på 2 månader.**	yaa(g) haar **in**ter hahft mehns(trewah**sho̅o̅n**) paw 2 **maw**nahderr
I'm pregnant.	**Jag är gravid.**	yaa(g) æ̅r̅ grah**veed**

Hur länge har ni känt er så här?	How long have you been feeling like this?
Är det första gången ni har det här?	Is this the first time you've had this?
Jag skall ta temperaturen/ blodtrycket.	I'll take your temperature/ blood pressure.
Kavla upp ärmen, tack.	Roll up your sleeve, please.
Var snäll och klä av er (på överkroppen).	Please undress (down to the waist).
Var snäll och lägg er här.	Please lie down over here.
Öppna munnen.	Open your mouth.
Andas djupt.	Breathe deeply.
Hosta.	Cough, please.
Var gör det ont?	Where does it hurt?
Ni har ...	You've got (a/an) ...
en allergi	allergy
blindtarmsinflammation	appendicitis
gulsot	jaundice
en inflammation i ...	inflammation of ...
influensa	flu
en könssjukdom	venereal disease
lunginflammation	pneumonia
en magförgiftning	food poisoning
en magkatarr	gastritis
mässling	measles
urinvägsinfektion	cystitis
Det smittar (inte).	It's (not) contagious.
Jag skall ge er en spruta.	I'll give you an injection.
Jag vill ha ett blodprov/ avföringsprov/urinprov.	I want a specimen of your blood/stools/urine.
Ni bör ligga till sängs i ... dagar.	You must stay in bed for ... days.
Jag vill att ni vänder er till en specialist.	I want you to see a specialist.
Jag vill att ni gör en allmän hälsokontroll på sjukhuset.	I want you to go to the hospital for a general check-up.

Prescription—Treatment *Ordination – Behandling*

This is my usual medicine.	**Det här är min vanliga medicin.**	d$\overline{ay}$(t) h$\overline{æ}$r $\overline{æ}$r min **vaan**liggah mehdi**sseen**
Can you give me a prescription for this?	**Kan ni ge mig ett recept på det här?**	kahn nee y$\overline{ay}$ m$\overline{ay}$ eht reh**sehpt** paw d$\overline{ay}$(t) h$\overline{æ}$r
Can you prescribe a/an/some ...?	**Kan ni skriva ut ...**	kahn nee **skree**vah $\overline{ew}$t
antidepressant	**något uppiggande**	**naw**got **ew**piggahnder
sleeping pills	**några sömntabletter**	**naw**grah **surmn**tahblehterr
tranquillizer	**något nervlugnande**	**naw**got **nærv**lewngnahnder
I'm allergic to certain antibiotics/ penicillin.	**Jag är allergisk mot viss antibiotika/ penicillin.**	yaa(g) $\overline{æ}$r ah**lehr**gisk m$\overline{oo}$t viss ahntibi**aw**tikkah/ pehnissi**leen**
I don't want anything too strong.	**Jag vill inte ha någonting för starkt.**	yaa(g) vil **in**ter haa **naw**gonting f$\overline{ur}$r stahrkt
How many times a day should I take it?	**Hur många gånger om dagen skall jag ta det?**	h$\overline{ew}$r **mon**gah **gong**err om **daa**(ger)n skah(l) yaa(g) taa d$\overline{ay}$(t)
Must I swallow them whole?	**Måste jag svälja dem hela?**	**mos**ter yaa(g) **svehl**yah dom **h$\overline{ay}$**lah

Vad får ni för behandling?	What treatment are you having?
Vilken medicin tar ni?	What medicine are you taking?
Intravenöst eller oralt?	By injection or orally?
Ta ... teskedar av den här medicinen ...	Take ... teaspoons of this medicine ...
Ta en tablett med ett glas vatten ...	Take one pill with a glass of water ...
var ... timme	every ... hours
... gånger om dagen	... times a day
före/efter varje måltid	before/after each meal
på morgonen/på kvällen	in the morning/at night
vid smärta	if there is any pain
i ... dagar	for ... days

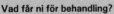

CHEMIST'S, see page 108

Fee *Arvode*

How much do I owe you?	**Hur mycket är jag skyldig?**	hewr **mew**ker(t) ær yaa(g) **shewl**dig
May I have a receipt for my health insurance?	**Kan jag få ett kvitto för min sjukförsäkring?**	kahn yaa(g) faw eht **kvi**tto furr min **shewk**fur^{r}saikring
Can I have a medical certificate?	**Kan jag få ett läkarintyg?**	kahn yaa(g) faw eht **lai**kahrintewg
Would you fill in this health insurance form, please?	**Skulle ni kunna fylla i den här sjukförsäkrings-blanketten?**	**skew**ler nee **kew**nah **few**lah ee dehn hær **shewk**fur^{r}saikrings-blahnkehtern

Hospital *Sjukhus*

Please notify my family.	**Var snäll och underrätta min familj.**	vaar snehl ok **ewn**der-rehtah min fah**mily**
What are the visiting hours?	**När är det besökstid?**	nær ær day(t) bay**surks**-teed?
When can I get up?	**När får jag stiga upp?**	nær fawr yaa(g) **stee**gah ewp
When will the doctor come?	**När kommer doktorn?**	nær **kom**mer **dok**to^{r}n
I'm in pain.	**Jag har ont.**	yaa(g) haar oont
I can't eat/sleep.	**Jag kan inte äta/sova.**	yaa(g) kahn **in**ter **ai**tah/**saw**vah
Where is the bell?	**Var är ringklockan?**	vaar ær **ring**klokkahn

nurse	**en sköterska**	ehn **shur**ter^{r}skah
patient	**en patient**	ehn pahssi**ehnt**
anaesthetic	**en narkos**	ehn nahr**kawss**
blood transfusion	**en blodtransfusion**	ehn **blood**trahnsfewshoon
injection	**en injektion**	ehn inyehk**shoon**
operation	**en operation**	ehn ooperrah**shoon**
bed	**en säng**	ehn sehng
bedpan	**ett bäcken**	eht **beh**kehn
thermometer	**en termometer**	ehn tehrmo**may**terr

Dentist *Tandläkare*

Can you recommend a good dentist?	**Kan ni rekommendera en bra tandläkare?**	kahn nee rehkommern-**dāȳ**rah ehn braa **tahn(d)**laikahrer
Can I make an (urgent) appointment to see Dr...?	**Kan jag få en tid (så fort som möjligt) hos doktor ...?**	kahn yaa(g) faw ehn teed (saw foo^{r}t som **mury**li(g)t) hooss **dok**tor
Couldn't you make it earlier?	**Går det inte tidigare?**	gawr dāȳ(t) **in**ter **tee**diggahrer
I have a broken tooth.	**Jag har bitit av en tand.**	yaa(g) haar **bee**tit aav ehn tahnd
I have a loose tooth.	**Jag har en lös tand.**	yaa(g) haar ehn lūr̄ss tahnd
I have a toothache.	**Jag har tandvärk.**	yaa(g) haar **tahn(d)**værk
Is it an abscess?	**Är det en varbildning?**	ær dāȳ(t) ehn **vaar**-bildning
This tooth hurts.	**Den här tanden gör ont.**	dehn hær **tahn**dern yūr̄r oont
at the top/bottom	**där uppe/nere**	dær **ew**per/**nāȳ**rer
at the front/back	**där framme/bak**	dær **frah**mer/baak
Can you fix it temporarily?	**Kan ni laga den provisoriskt?**	kahn nee **laa**gah dehn proovis**sōō**riskt
I don't want it taken out.	**Jag vill inte ha den utdragen.**	yaa(g) vil **in**ter haa dehn **ēw̄t**draagern
Could you give me an anaesthetic?	**Kan jag få bedövning?**	kahn yaa(g) faw ber**dūr̄v**ning
I've lost a filling.	**Jag har tappat en plomb.**	yaa(g) haar **tah**paht ehn plomb
The gums ...	**tandköttet ...**	**tahn(d)**khurtert
are very sore	**är mycket ömt**	ær **mew**ker(t) urmt
are bleeding	**blöder**	**blūr̄**derr
I've broken my dentures.	**Min tandprotes har gått sönder.**	min **tahn(d)**prootāȳss haar got **surn**derr
Can you repair my dentures?	**Kan ni laga min tandprotes?**	kahn nee **laa**gah min **tahn(d)**prootāȳss
When will they be ready?	**När blir den klar?**	nær bleer dehn klaar

Reference section

Where do you come from? *Varifrån kommer ni?*

I'm from ...	**Jag är från ...**	yaa(g) ǣr frawn
Africa	**Afrika**	aafrikkah
Asia	**Asien**	aassiern
Australia	**Australien**	aaew**straa**liern
Europe	**Europa**	ehew**rōō**pah
North America	**Nordamerika**	**nōōʳ**dahmāȳrikkah
South America	**Sydamerika**	**sēw**dahmāȳrikkah
Austria	**Österrike**	ursterreeker
Belgium	**Belgien**	**behl**giern
Canada	**Kanada**	**kah**nahdah
China	**Kina**	**khee**nah
Czechoslovakia	**Tjeckoslovakien**	khehkoosloo**vaa**kiern
Denmark	**Danmark**	**dahn**mahrk
England	**England**	**eng**lahnd
Finland	**Finland**	**fin**lahnd
France	**Frankrike**	**frahnk**rikker
Germany	**Tyskland**	**tewsk**lahnd
Great Britain	**Storbritannien**	**stōōr**brittahniern
Greece	**Grekland**	**grāȳk**lahnd
Iceland	**Island**	**ees**lahnd
India	**Indien**	**in**diern
Ireland	**Irland**	**ir**lahnd
Israel	**Israel**	**ees**raherl
Italy	**Italien**	i**taa**liern
Japan	**Japan**	**yaa**pahn
Luxembourg	**Luxemburg**	**lew**ksermbewry
Netherlands	**Nederländerna/ Holland**	**nāȳ**derrlehnderʳnah/ hollahnd
New Zealand	**Nya Zealand**	**nēw**ah **sāȳ**lahnd
Norway	**Norge**	**nor**yer
Poland	**Polen**	**po**lern
Portugal	**Portugal**	**po**ʳtewgahl
Scotland	**Skottland**	**skot**lahnd
South Africa	**Sydafrika**	**sēw**daafrikkah
Soviet Union	**Sovjetunionen**	sov**yeh**tewniōōnern
Spain	**Spanien**	**spah**niern
Sweden	**Sverige**	**svær**yer
Switzerland	**Schweiz**	shvehytss
Turkey	**Turkiet**	tewr**kee**ert
United States	**USA**	**ēw**ehssaa
Wales	**Wales**	"wales"
Yugoslavia	**Jugoslavien**	yewgoo**slaa**viern

Numbers *Räkneord*

0	**noll**	nol
1	**ett**	eht
2	**två**	tvaw
3	**tre**	tray
4	**fyra**	**few**rah
5	**fem**	fehm
6	**sex**	sehks
7	**sju**	shew
8	**åtta**	**o**ttah
9	**nio**	**nee**oo
10	**tio**	**tee**oo
11	**elva**	**ehl**vah
12	**tolv**	tolv
13	**tretton**	**treh**ton
14	**fjorton**	**fyoo^r**ton
15	**femton**	**fehm**ton
16	**sexton**	**sehks**ton
17	**sjutton**	**shew**ton
18	**arton**	**aa^r**ton
19	**nitton**	**nit**ton
20	**tjugo**	**khew**goo
21	**tjugoett**	khewgo**eht**
22	**tjugotvå**	khewgo**tvaw**
23	**tjugotre**	khewgo**tray**
24	**tjugofyra**	khewgo**few**rah
25	**tjugofem**	khewgo**fehm**
26	**tjugosex**	khewgo**ssehks**
27	**tjugosju**	khewgo**shew**
28	**tjugoåtta**	khewgo**o**ttah
29	**tjugonio**	khewgo**nee**oo
30	**trettio**	**treh**ti
31	**trettioett**	trehti**eht**
32	**trettiotvå**	trehti**tvaw**
33	**trettiotre**	trehti**tray**
40	**fyrtio**	**fur^r**ti
50	**femtio**	**fehm**ti
60	**sextio**	**sehks**ti
70	**sjuttio**	**shew**ti
80	**åttio**	**o**tti
90	**nittio**	**nit**ti
100	**(ett)hundra**	**(eht)hewn**drah
101	**hundraett**	hewndra**heht**
102	**hundratvå**	hewndraht**vaw**
110	**hundratio**	hewndrah**tee**oo
120	**hundratjugo**	hewndrah**khew**goo

200	**tvåhundra**	**tvaw**hewndrah
300	**trehundra**	**tr$\overline{ay}$**hewndrah
400	**fyrahundra**	**f$\overline{ew}$**rahhewndrah
500	**femhundra**	**fehm**hewndrah
600	**sexhundra**	**sehks**hewndrah
700	**sjuhundra**	**sh$\overline{ew}$**hewndrah
800	**åttahundra**	ottahhewndrah
900	**niohundra**	**nee**oohewndrah
1000	**(ett)tusen**	**(eht)t$\overline{ew}$**ssern
1100	**ettusenetthundra**	**ehtt$\overline{ew}$ssernehthewndrah**
1200	**ettusentvåhundra**	**ehtt$\overline{ew}$sserntvawhewndrah**
2000	**tvåtusen**	**tvawt$\overline{ew}$**ssern
10,000	**tiotusen**	**teeoot$\overline{ew}$**ssern
50,000	**femtiotusen**	**fehm**tit$\overline{ew}$ssern
100,000	**(ett)hundratusen**	**(eht)hewn**draht$\overline{ew}$ssern
1,000,000	**en miljon**	ehn mil**y$\overline{oo}$n**
1,000,000,000	**en miljard**	ehn mil**yaa^{r}d**
first	**första**	**fur^r**stah
second	**andra**	**ahn**drah
third	**tredje**	**tr$\overline{ay}$**dyer
fourth	**fjärde**	**fyæ^r**der
fifth	**femte**	**fehm**ter
sixth	**sjätte**	**sheh**ter
seventh	**sjunde**	**shewn**der
eighth	**åttonde**	**ot**tonder
ninth	**nionde**	**nee**onder
tenth	**tionde**	**tee**onder
once/twice	**en gång/två gånger**	ehn gong/tvaw **gong**err
three times	**tre gånger**	tr$\overline{ay}$ **gong**err
a half	**en halva**	ehn **hahl**vah
half a ...	**en halv ...**	ehn hahlv
half of ...	**hälften av ...**	**hehlf**tern aav
half (adj.)	**halv**	hahlv
a quarter	**en fjärdedel**	ehn **fyæ^r**derd$\overline{ay}$l
a third	**en tredjedel**	ehn **tr$\overline{ay}$d**yerd$\overline{ay}$l
a pair of	**ett par**	eht paar
a dozen	**ett dussin**	eht **dew**ssin
3.4%	**3,4 procent**	tr$\overline{ay}$ **kom**mah **f$\overline{ew}$**rah proo**sehnt**
1981	**nittonhundra-åttioett**	nittonhewndrah-otti**eht**
1992	**nittonhundra-nittiotvå**	nittonhewndrah-nitti**tvaw**
2003	**tvåtusentre**	tvawt$\overline{ew}$ssern**tr$\overline{ay}$**

Year and age *År och ålder*

year	**året**	awrert
leap year	**skottåret**	skotawrert
decade	**årtiondet**	aw^{r}teeondert
century	**århundradet**	awrhewndrahdert
this year	**det här året**	da̅y̅(t) hǣr awrert
last year	**förra året**	furrah awrert
next year	**nästa år**	nehstah awr
each year	**varje år**	vahryer awr
2 years ago	**för 2 år sedan**	fu̅r̅r tvaw awr sehn
in one year	**om ett år**	om eht awr
in the eighties	**på åttiotalet**	paw ottitaalert
the 17th century	**1600-talet**	sehkstonhewndrahtaalert
in the 20th century	**på 1900-talet**	paw nittonhewndrahtaalert
old/young	**gammal/ung**	gahmahl/ewng
old/new	**gammal/ny**	gahmahl/ne̅w̅
How old are you?	**Hur gammal är du?**	he̅w̅r gahmahl ǣr de̅w̅
I'm 30 years old.	**Jag är 30 år.**	yaa(g) ǣr trehti awr
At my age ...	**Vid min ålder ...**	veed min awlderr
He/She was born in 1960.	**Han/Hon är född 1960.**	hahn/hon ǣr furd nittonhewndrahsehksti
Children under 16 are not admitted.	**Barn under 16 år äger ej tillträde.**	baa^{r}n ewnderr sehkston awr aigerr ay tiltraider

Seasons *Årstider*

spring	**vår**	vawr
summer	**sommar**	sommahr
autumn	**höst**	hurst
winter	**vinter**	vinterr
in spring	**på våren**	paw vawrern
during the summer	**under sommaren**	ewnderr sommahrern
in autumn	**på hösten**	paw hurstern
during the winter	**under vintern**	ewnderr vinterrn
high season	**högsäsong**	hu̅r̅gsaissong
low season	**lågsäsong**	lawgsaissong

Months *Månader*

January	**januari***	yahnewaari
February	**februari**	fehbrewaari
March	**mars**	mah^{r}ss
April	**april**	ahpril
May	**maj**	mahy
June	**juni**	yewni
July	**juli**	yewli
August	**augusti**	ahgewsti
September	**september**	sehptehmberr
October	**oktober**	oktooberr
November	**november**	noovehmberr
December	**december**	dehssehmberr
after June	**efter juni**	ehfterr yewni
before July	**före juli**	furrer yewli
during the month of August	**under augusti månad**	ewnderr ahgewsti mawnahd
in September	**i september**	ee sehptehmberr
until October	**till oktober**	til oktooberr
not until November	**inte före november**	inter furrer noovehmberr
since December	**sedan december**	sehn dehssehmberr
last month	**förra månaden**	furrah mawnahdern
next month	**nästa månad**	nehstah mawnahd
the month before	**månaden innan**	mawnahdern innahn
the month after	**följande månad**	furlyahnder mawnahd
the beginning of January	**början av januari**	burryahn aav yahnewaari
the middle of February	**mitten av februari**	mittern aav fehbrewaari
the end of March	**slutet av mars**	slewtert aav mah^{r}ss

Days and Date *Dagar och datum*

What day is it today?	**Vad är det för dag idag?**	vaad ær day(t) furr daa(g) eedaa(g)
Sunday	**söndag***	surndaa(g)
Monday	**måndag**	mondaa(g)
Tuesday	**tisdag**	teesdaa(g)
Wednesday	**onsdag**	oonsdaa(g)
Thursday	**torsdag**	too^{r}sdaa(g)
Friday	**fredag**	fraydaa(g)
Saturday	**lördag**	lur^{r}daa(g)

* The names of months and days aren't capitalized in Swedish.

What's the date today?	**Vad är det för datum idag?**	vaad ær day(t) furr **daa**tewm ee**daa(g)**
It's . . .	**Det är . . .**	day(t) ær
July 1	**den 1 juli**	dehn **furʳ**stah **yew**li
March 31	**den 31 mars**	dehn trehti**furʳ**stah mahʳss
When's your birthday?	**När är det din födelsedag?**	nær ær day(t) din **fur**(deh)lserdaa(g)
August 3rd.	**3 augusti.**	**tray**dyer ah**gew**sti
in the morning	**på morgonen**	paw **mor**ronern
during the day	**under dagen**	**ew**nderr **daa**gern
in the afternoon	**på eftermiddagen**	paw **ehf**terrmiddahn
in the evening	**på kvällen**	paw **kveh**lern
at night	**på natten**	paw **nah**tern
the day before yesterday	**i förrgår**	ee **fur**rgawr
yesterday	**i går**	ee gawr
today	**idag**	ee**daa(g)**
tomorrow	**i morgon**	ee **mor**ron
the day after tomorrow	**i övermorgon**	ee **ur**verrmorron
the day before	**dagen innan**	**daa**(ger)n innahn
the next day	**nästa dag**	**neh**stah daa(g)
two days ago	**för två dagar sedan**	furr tvaw **daa**(gah)r sehn
in three days' time	**om tre dagar**	om tray **daa**(gah)r
last week	**förra veckan**	**fu**rrah **veh**kahn
next week	**nästa vecka**	**neh**stah **veh**kah
for a fortnight (two weeks)	**i fjorton dagar**	ee **fyooʳ**ton **daa**(gah)r
day off	**en ledig dag**	ehn **lay**dig daa(g)
holiday	**en helgdag**	ehn **hehly**daa(g)
holidays/vacation	**en semester**	ehn seh**meh**sterr
school holidays	**ett skollov**	eht **skoo**lawv
week	**en vecka**	ehn **veh**kah
weekend	**en weekend**	ehn **vee**kehnd
working day	**en arbetsdag**	ehn **ahr**baytsdaa(g)

Greetings and wishes *Hälsningar och gratulationer*

Merry Christmas!	**God jul!**	good yewl
Happy New Year!	**Gott nytt år!**	got newt awr

Happy Easter!	**Glad påsk!**	glaad pawsk
Happy birthday!	**Gratulerar på födelsedagen!**	grahtewla̅y̅rahr paw fu̅r̅(deh)lserdaa(ger)n
Best wishes!	**Bästa välgångs-önskningar!**	**beh**stah **vail**gongs-urnskningahr
Congratulations!	**Gratulerar!**	grahtewla̅y̅rahr
Good luck/ All the best!	**Lycka till!**	**lew**kah til
Have a good trip!	**Trevlig resa!**	tra̅y̅vli(g) ra̅y̅ssah
Have a good holiday!	**Trevlig semester!**	tra̅y̅vli(g) sehmehsterr
Regards from ...	**Hälsningar från ...**	**hehl**sningahr frawn
My regards to ...	**Hälsa till ...**	**hehl**sah til

Public holidays *Allmänna helgdagar*

Note that on the days before most public holidays, offices, banks, post offices and shops usually observe shorter working hours.

January 1	**Nyårsdagen**	New Year's Day
January 6	**Trettondagen**	Epiphany
May 1	**Första maj**	May Day
Saturday that falls between June 20 and 26	**Midsommardagen**	Midsummer Day
Saturday that falls between Oct. 31 and Nov. 6	**Allhelgonadagen**	All Saints' Day
December 25	**Juldagen**	Christmas Day
December 26	**Annandag jul**	Boxing Day
Movable Dates:	**Långfredagen**	Good Friday
	Påskdagen	Easter Sunday
	Annandag påsk	Easter Monday
	Kristi himmelsfärds-dag	Ascension
	Pingstdagen	Whit Sunday
	Annandag pingst	Whit Monday

What time is it? *Hur mycket är klockan?*

Excuse me. Can you tell me the time?	**Ursäkta. Kan ni säga vad klockan är?**	**ew**^{r}sehktah. kahn nee **seh**yah vaad **klo**kkahn ær
It's ...	**Den är ...**	dehn ær
five past one	**fem över ett***	fehm urverr eht
ten past two	**tio över två**	**tee**oo urverr tvaw
a quarter past three	**kvart över tre**	kvah^{r}t urverr tray
twenty past four	**tjugo över fyra**	**khew**goo urverr **few**rah
twenty-five past five	**fem i halv sex**	fehm ee hahlv sehks
half past six	**halv sju**	hahlv shew
twenty-five to seven	**fem över halv sju**	fehm urverr hahlv shew
twenty to eight	**tjugo i åtta**	**khew**goo ee **o**ttah
a quarter to nine	**kvart i nio**	kvah^{r}t ee **nee**oo
ten to ten	**tio i tio**	**tee**oo ee **tee**oo
five to eleven	**fem i elva**	fehm ee **ehl**vah
twelve o' clock	**tolv**	tolv
noon	**klockan tolv (på dagen)**	**klo**kkahn tolv (paw **daa**gern)
midnight	**midnatt**	**meed**naht
in the morning	**på morgonen**	paw **mo**rronern
in the afternoon	**på eftermiddagen**	paw **ehf**terrmiddahn
in the evening	**på kvällen**	paw **kveh**lern
What time does the train leave?	**Hur dags går tåget?**	hewr dahgss gawr **taw**gert
It leaves at ...	**Det går klockan ...**	day(t) gawr **klo**kkahn
13.04 (1.04 p.m.)	**tretton noll fyra**	**treh**ton nol **few**rah
0.40 (0.40 a.m.)	**noll fyrtio**	nol **fur**^{r}ti
in five minutes	**om fem minuter**	om fehm mi**new**terr
in a quarter of an hour	**om en kvart**	om ehn kvah^{r}t
half an hour ago	**för en halvtimme sedan**	furr ehn **hahlv**timmer sehn
about two hours	**cirka två timmar**	**sir**kah tvaw **ti**mmahr
more than 10 minutes	**över tio minuter**	urverr **tee**oo mi**new**terr
a few seconds	**ett par sekunder**	eht paar seh**kewn**derr
The clock is fast/ slow.	**Klockan går före/ efter.**	**klo**kkahn gawr **fur**rer/ **ehf**terr

* In everyday conversation, time is expressed as shown here. However, official time uses a 24-hour clock which means that after noon hours are counted from 13 to 24.

Common abbreviations *Vanliga förkortningar*

AB	**aktiebolag**	Ltd.
av.	**aveny**	avenue
avd.	**avdelning**	department
avs.	**avsändare**	sender
ca	**cirka**	around
Co.	**kompani**	company
D	**Damer**	Ladies
dir.	**direktör**	manager/(Am.) president
e.Kr.	**efter Kristus**	A.D.
e.m.	**eftermiddagen**	p.m.
f.Kr.	**före Kristus**	B.C.
FN	**Förenta Nationerna**	United Nations
f.m.	**förmiddagen**	a.m.
f.n.	**för närvarande**	at present
g	**gram**	gram
g.	**gata**	street
H	**Herrar**	Gentlemen
hg	**hekto(gram)**	hectogram
Hr	**Herr**	Mr.
KAK	**Kungliga Automobil-klubben**	Royal Automobile Club
kg	**kilo(gram)**	kilogram
kl.	**klockan**	o' clock
km	**kilometer**	kilometer
kr	**kronor**	crowns
moms	**mervärdeskatt**	value added tax
nr	**nummer**	number
n.b.	**nedre botten**	ground floor
obs.	**observera**	N.B.
o.s.a.	**om svar anhålles**	R.S.V.P.
osv.	**och så vidare**	etc.
SJ	**Statens Järnvägar**	Swedish State Railways
SR	**Sveriges Radio**	Swedish Radio
STF	**Svenska Turist-föreningen**	Swedish Touring Club
STTF	**Svenska Turisttrafik-förbundet**	Swedish Tourist Transport Association
t.ex.	**till exempel**	e.g. (for example)
tfn	**telefon**	telephone
t.o.m.	**till och med**	up to, including
tr.	**trappor**	stairs
UD	**Utrikes-departementet**	Ministry for Foreign Affairs
v.	**vägen**	road
VD	**verkställande direktör**	managing director

Signs and notices *Skyltar och anslag*

Att hyra	For hire/For rent/To let
Damer	Ladies
Drag	Pull
Ej ingång	No entrance
Ej tillträde	No trespassing
Fara	Danger
Fritt inträde	Admission free
Får ej vidröras	Do not touch
... förbjuden	... forbidden
Herrar	Gentlemen
Hiss	Lift (elevator)
Högspänningsledning	High voltage
Icke rökare	Nonsmoker
Ingång	Entrance
Kallt	Cold
Kassa	Cash desk
Ledigt	Free (vacant)
Livsfara	Danger of death
Nymålat	Wet paint
Nödutgång	Emergency exit
Privat	Private
Privat väg	Private road
Rea(lisation)	Sale
Reserverat	Reserved
Rökare	Smoker
Rökning förbjuden	No smoking
Rökning tillåten	Smoking allowed
Skjut	Push
Stängt	Closed
Stör ej	Do not disturb
Till salu	For sale
Tillträde förbjudet	No trespassing
Upplysningar	Information
Upptaget	Occupied
Ur funktion	Out of order
Utgång	Exit
Utsålt	Sold out
Var god ring	Please ring
Var god stäng dörren	Close the door
Var god vänta	Please wait
Varmt	Hot
Varning	Caution
Varning för hunden	Beware of the dog
Öppet	Open
Öppettider	Opening hours

Emergency *Nödsituation*

Call the police	**Ring polisen**	ring poo**lee**ssern
Consulate	**Konsulat**	konsew**laat**
DANGER	**FARA**	**faa**rah
Embassy	**Ambassad**	ahmbah**ssaad**
FIRE	**DET BRINNER**	da̅y̅(t) **brin**nerr
Gas	**Gas**	gaass
Get a doctor	**Hämta en läkare**	**hehm**tah ehn **lai**kahrer
Go away	**Ge er i väg**	ya̅y̅ a̅y̅r ee vaig
HELP	**HJÄLP**	yehlp
Get help quickly	**Skaffa hjälp fort**	**skah**fah yehlp fooʳt
I'm ill	**Jag är sjuk**	yaa(g) æ̅r she̅w̅k
I'm lost	**Jag har gått vilse**	yaa(g) haar got **vil**ser
Leave me alone	**Lämna mig ifred**	**lehm**nah may ee**fra̅y̅(d)**
LOOK OUT	**SE UPP**	sa̅y̅ ewp
Poison	**Gift**	yift
POLICE	**POLIS**	poo**leess**
Stop that man/ woman	**Stoppa den där mannen/kvinnan**	**stop**pah dehn dær **mah**nern/**kvin**nahn
STOP THIEF	**STOPPA TJUVEN**	**stop**pah **khe̅w̅**vern

Emergency telephone numbers *I nödsituation ring . . .*

Fire Ambulance Police	90 000

Lost property – Theft *Borttappat – Stöld*

Where's the . . .?	**Var ligger . . .?**	vaar **lig**gerr
lost property (lost and found) office	**hittegods-expeditionen**	**hit**tergoods-ehkspehdi**sho̅o̅**nern
police station	**polisstationen**	poo**lees**stahsho̅o̅nern
I want to report a theft.	**Jag vill anmäla en stöld.**	yaa(g) vil **ahn**mailah ehn sturld
My . . . has been stolen.	**. . . har stulits.**	. . . haar **ste̅w̅**litss
I've lost my . . .	**Jag har tappat . . .**	yaa(g) haar **tah**paht
handbag	**min handväska**	min **hahn(d)**vehskah
passport	**mitt pass**	mit pahss
wallet	**min plånbok**	min **plawn**bo̅o̅k

CAR ACCIDENTS, see page 78

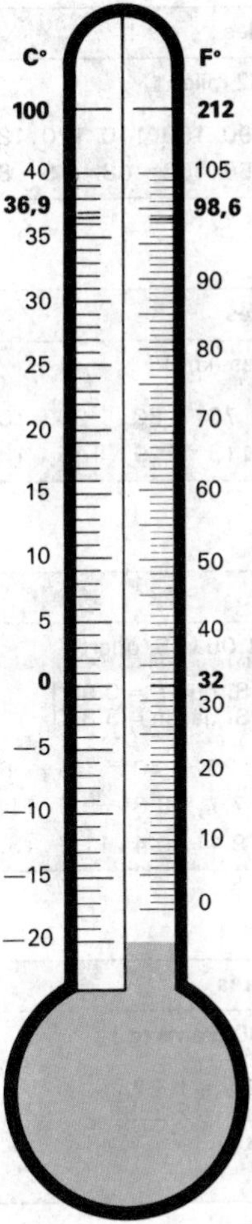

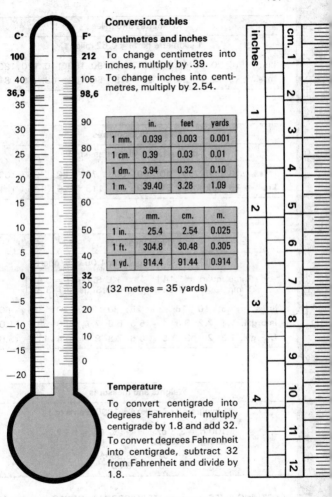

Conversion tables

Centimetres and inches

To change centimetres into inches, multiply by .39.

To change inches into centimetres, multiply by 2.54.

	in.	feet	yards
1 mm.	0.039	0.003	0.001
1 cm.	0.39	0.03	0.01
1 dm.	3.94	0.32	0.10
1 m.	39.40	3.28	1.09

	mm.	cm.	m.
1 in.	25.4	2.54	0.025
1 ft.	304.8	30.48	0.305
1 yd.	914.4	91.44	0.914

(32 metres = 35 yards)

Temperature

To convert centigrade into degrees Fahrenheit, multiply centigrade by 1.8 and add 32.

To convert degrees Fahrenheit into centigrade, subtract 32 from Fahrenheit and divide by 1.8.

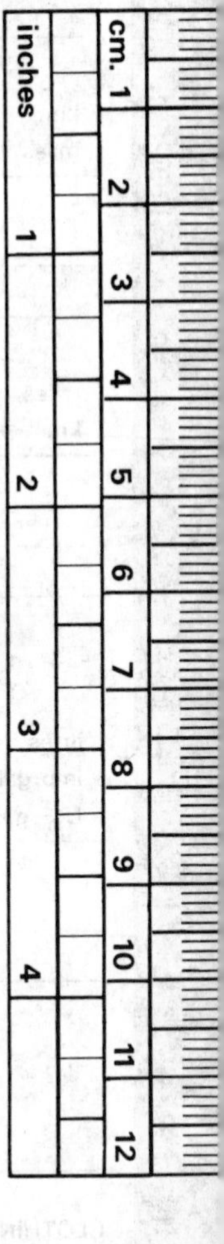

Kilometres into miles

1 kilometre (km.) = 0.62 miles

km.	10	20	30	40	50	60	70	80	90	100	110	120	130
miles	6	12	19	25	31	37	44	50	56	62	68	75	81

Miles into kilometres

1 mile = 1.609 kilometres (km.)

miles	10	20	30	40	50	60	70	80	90	100
km.	16	32	48	64	80	97	113	129	145	161

Fluid measures

1 litre (l.) = 0.88 imp. quart or 1.06 U.S. quart

1 imp. quart = 1.14 l.　　1 U.S. quart = 0.95 l.
1 imp. gallon = 4.55 l.　　1 U.S. gallon = 3.8 l.

litres	5	10	15	20	25	30	35	40	45	50
imp. gal.	1.1	2.2	3.3	4.4	5.5	6.6	7.7	8.8	9.9	11.0
U.S. gal.	1.3	2.6	3.9	5.2	6.5	7.8	9.1	10.4	11.7	13.0

Weights and measures

1 kilogram or kilo (kg.) = 1000 grams (g.)

100 g. = 3.5 oz.　　½ kg. = 1.1 lb.
200 g. = 7.0 oz.　　1 kg. = 2.2 lb.

1 oz. = 28.35 g.
1 lb. = 453.60 g.

CLOTHING SIZES, see page 115/YARDS AND INCHES, see page 112

Basic grammar

Articles

All Swedish nouns are either common or neuter in gender.

1. Indefinite article (a/an)

common:	***en* man**	a man
neuter:	***ett* barn**	a child

2. Definite article (the)

Where we, in English, say "the house", the Swedes say the equivalent of "house-the", i.e. they tag the definite article onto the end of the noun. Common nouns take an **-(e)n** ending, neuter nouns an **-(e)t** ending.

common:	**mann*en***	*the* man
neuter:	**barn*et***	*the* child

Nouns

1. As already noted, nouns are either common or neuter. There are no easy rules for determining gender. Learn each new word with its accompanying article.

2. The plural is formed according to one of five declensions.

		singular		indefinite plurals	
Declension	1	**flicka**	girl	**flick*or***	girls
	2	**bil**	car	**bil*ar***	cars
	3	**dam**	lady	**dam*er***	ladies
		sko	shoe	**sko*r***	shoes
	4	**äpple**	apple	**äpple*n***	apples
	5	**hus**	house	**hus**	houses
				definite plurals	
				flickor*na*	the girls
				äpplen*a*	the apples
				hus*en*	the houses

There are also various irregular plurals.

3. Possession is shown by adding **-s** (singular and plural). *Note:* There is no apostrophe.

Görans bror	George's brother
hotellets ägare	the owner of the hotel
veckans första dag	the first day of the week
den resandes väska	the traveller's suitcase
barnens rum	the children's room

Adjectives

1. Adjectives agree with the noun in gender and number. For the indefinite form, the neuter is formed by adding **-t**; the plural by adding **-a.**

(en) stor hund	(a) big dog	**stora hundar**	big dogs
(ett) stort hus	(a) big house	**stora hus**	big houses

2. For the definite declension of the adjective, add the ending **-a** (common, neuter and plural). This form is used when the adjective is preceded by **den, det, de** (the definite article used with adjectives) or by a demonstrative or a possessive adjective.

den stora hunden	the big dog
de stora hundarna	the big dogs
det stora huset	the big house
de stora husen	the big houses

3. Demonstrative adjectives:

	common	neuter	plural
this/these	**den här/ denna**	**det här/ detta**	**de här/ dessa**
that/those	**den där/ den**	**det där/ det**	**de där/ de**

4. Possessive adjectives agree in number and gender with the noun they modify, i.e. with the thing possessed and not the possessor.

	common	neuter	plural
my	**min**	**mitt**	**mina**
your	**din**	**ditt**	**dina**
his / her / its	**sin**	**sitt**	**sina**
our	**vår**	**vårt**	**våra**
your	**er**	**ert**	**era**
their	**sin**	**sitt**	**sina**

The forms **er, ert, era** correspond to the personal pronoun **ni** and refer to one or several possessors.

The forms **sin, sitt, sina** always refer back to the subject:

Han har sin bok. He has his (own) book.
De har sina böcker. They have their (own) books.

The genitive forms of the personal pronouns (see p. 162) are also used to show possession, however, the meaning changes:

Han har hans bok. He has his (another person's) book.

5. Comparative and superlative:

The comparative and superlative are normally formed either by adding the endings **-(a)re** and **-(a)st,** respectively, to the adjective or by putting **mer** and **mest** (more, most) before the adjective.

Hans arbete är lätt. His work is easy.
Hans arbete är lätt*are*. His work is easier.
Hans arbete är lätt*ast*. His work is easiest.

Er bil är stor. Your car is big.
Er bil är stör*re*. Your car is bigger.
Er bil är stör*st*. Your car is the biggest.

Det är imponerande. It's impressive.
Det är *mer* imponerande. It's more impressive.
Det är *mest* imponerande. It's most impressive.

Adverbs

Adverbs are generally formed by adding **-t** to the corresponding adjective.

Hon går snabbt. She walks quickly.

Personal pronouns

	subject	object	genitive
I	**jag**	**mig**	—
you	**du/ni**	**dig/er**	—
he	**han**	**honom**	**hans**
she	**hon**	**henne**	**hennes**
it	**den/det**	**den/det**	**dess**
we	**vi**	**oss**	—
you	**ni**	**er**	—
they	**de**	**dem**	**deras**

Like many other languages, Swedish has two forms for "you". The formal word **ni,** traditionally the correct form of address between all but close friends and children, is now giving way to the informal **du.**

Verbs

Here we are concerned only with the infinitive, imperative, and present tense. The present tense is simple, because it has the same form for all persons. The infinitive of most Swedish verbs ends in **-a** (a few verbs of one syllable end in other vowels). Here are three useful auxiliary verbs:

	to be	to have	to be able to
Infinitive	**(att) vara**	**(att) ha**	**(att) kunna**
Present tense (same form for all persons)	**är**	**har**	**kan**
Imperative	**var**	**ha**	—

The present tense of Swedish verbs ends in **-r**:

	to ask	to buy	to believe	to do/make
Infinitive	**(att) fråga**	**(att) köpa**	**(att) tro**	**(att) göra**
Present tense (same form for all persons)	**frågar**	**köper**	**tror**	**gör**
Imperative	**fråga**	**köp**	**tro**	**gör**

There is no equivalent to the English present continuous tense. Thus:

Jag reser. I travel/I am travelling.

Negatives

Negation is expressed by using the adverb **inte** (not). It is usually placed immediately after the verb in a main clause. In compound tenses **inte** comes between the auxiliary and the main verb.

Jag talar svenska. I speak Swedish.
Jag talar inte svenska. I do not speak Swedish.
Hon har inte skrivit. She has not written.

Questions

Questions are formed by reversing the order of the subject and the verb:

Bussen stannar här. The bus stops here.
Stannar bussen här? Does the bus stop here?

Jag kommer i kväll. I am coming tonight.
Kommer ni i kväll? Are you coming tonight?

Dictionary
and alphabetical index

English–Swedish

c common *nt* neuter *pl* plural

a en, ett 159
abbreviation förkortning *c* 154
able, to be kunna 162
about *(approximately)* cirka 78, 153
above ovanför 15, 62
abscess varbildning *c* 145
absorbent cotton bomull *c* 109
accept, to ta emot 61, 102
accessories accessoarer *c/pl* 116; tillbehör *nt* 125
accident olycka *c* 78, 139; olycksfall *nt* 139
accommodation logi *nt* 22
account konto *nt* 130, 131
ache värk *c* 141
adaptor adapter *c* 119
address adress *c* 21, 76, 79, 102
address book adressbok *c* 104
adhesive självhäftande 105
adhesive tape tape *c* 104
admission inträde *nt* 82, 89, 155
admitted, to be äga tillträde 149
Africa Afrika *(nt)* 146
after efter 15, 77, 150; följande 150
afternoon eftermiddag *c* 151, 153
after-shave lotion rakvatten *nt* 110
age ålder *c* 149
ago för ... sedan 149, 153
air bed luftmadrass *c* 106
air conditioning luftkonditionering *c* 23, 28
airmail med flyg 133
airplane flyg *nt* 65
airport flygplats *c* 16, 21, 65
alarm clock väckarklocka *c* 121
alcohol alkohol *c* 37, 59
alcoholic alkoholhaltig 56
all allt 103
allergic allergisk 141, 143
allowed tillåten 155
almond mandel *c* 54
alphabet alfabet *nt* 9
also också 15
alter, to ändra 116
amazing fantastisk 84
amber bärnsten *c* 122
ambulance ambulans *c* 79, 156
American amerikansk 105, 126
American amerikan *c* 93
American plan helpension *c* 24
amount summa *c* 61, 131
amplifier förstärkare *c* 119
anaesthetic narkos *c* 144; bedövning *c* 145
analgesic något smärtstillande 109
anchovy sardell *c* 46
and och 15
animal djur *nt* 85
ankle vrist *c* 139
anorak anorak *c* 116
answer, to svara 136
antibiotic antibiotika *nt/pl* 143
antidepressant uppiggande 143
antique antikvitet *c* 83
antique shop antikvitetsaffär *c* 98
antiseptic antiseptisk 109
any inga 15
anyone någon 12
anything något 17, 25, 103; någonting 101, 113
anywhere någonstans 89
aperitif aperitif *c* 58
appendicitis blindtarms-inflammation *c* 142

appendix blindtarm *c* 138
appetizer förrätt *c* 43
apple äpple *nt* 54, 120
apple juice äppeljuice *c* 59
appointment tid *c* 30, 137, 145; möte *nt* 131
apricot aprikos *c* 54
April april *(c)* 150
aquavit brännvin *nt* 56
archaeology arkeologi *c* 83
architect arkitekt *c* 83
area code riktnummer *nt* 134
arm arm *c* 138, 139
around i närheten 35; cirka 154
arrival ankomst *c* 16, 65
arrive, to vara framme 65, 68; komma fram 68
art konst *c* 83
artery pulsåder *c* 138
art gallery konstgalleri *nt* 98
art museum konstmuseum *nt* 81
artichoke kronärtskocka *c* 51
article vara *c* 101
artificial sweetener sötningsmedel *nt* 37
artist konstnär *c* 81, 83
ashtray askkopp *c* 27, 36
Asia Asien *(nt)* 146
ask, to fråga 76, 163
ask for, to be om 25, 60, 136
asparagus sparris *c* 51
aspirin aspirin *c* 109
asthma astma *c* 141
at vid 15
at least minst 24
at once genast 31
aubergine äggplanta *c* 51
August augusti *(c)* 150
aunt faster *c*, moster *c* 93
Australia Australien *(nt)* 146
Austria Österrike *(nt)* 146
automatic automatisk 122, 124; *(car)* med automatlåda 20
autumn höst *c* 149
average medelgod 91
awful förskräcklig 84, 94

B

baby baby *c* 24, 111
baby food barnmat *c* 111
babysitter barnvakt *c* 27
back rygg *c* 138
backache ont i ryggen 141
bacon bacon *nt* 38
bacon and eggs bacon och ägg 38
bad dålig 14, 95
bag bag *c* 17, 18; kasse *c* 103
baggage bagage *nt* 18, 26, 31, 71; *(registered)* resgods *nt/pl* 71
baggage cart bagagekärra *c* 18, 71
baggage check effektförvaring *c* 67, 71
baked bakad 52; ugnstekt 46
baker's bageri *nt* 98
balance *(account)* balansräkning *c* 131
balcony balkong *c* 23
ball *(inflated)* boll *c* 128
ballet balett *c* 88
ball-point pen kulspetspenna *c* 104
banana banan *c* 54
bandage förband *nt*; *(elastic)* binda *c* 109
Band-Aid plåster *nt* 109
bangle armring *c* 121
bank *(finance)* bank *c* 98, 129, 130
banknote sedel *c* 130
bar bar *c* 33; *(chocolate)* kaka *c* 64
barber's herrfrisör *c* 30, 98
bath *(hotel)* bad *nt* 23, 25, 27
bathing cap badmössa *c* 116
bathing hut badhytt *c* 91
bathrobe badkappa *c* 116
bathroom badrum *nt* 27
bath salts badsalt *nt* 110
bath towel badlakan *nt* 27
battery batteri *nt* 75, 78, 119, 121, 125
be, to vara 162
beach strand *c* 90
beach ball badboll *c* 128
bean böna *c* 49, 51
bear björn *c* 50
beard skägg *nt* 31
beautiful vacker 14, 84
beauty salon skönhetssalong *c* 30, 98
bed säng *c* 24, 144
bed and breakfast rum med frukost 24
bedpan bäcken *nt* 144
beef oxkött *nt* 48, 49
beef steak biff *c* 48, 49
beer öl *c* 56, 64
beet(root) rödbeta *c* 51
before *(place)* framför 15; *(time)* före 15, 143, 149; innan 15, 150, 151
begin, to börja 87, 88; starta 80
beginner nybörjare *c* 91

beginning början *c* 150
behind bakom 15, 77
beige beige 113
believe, to tro 163
bell *(electric)* ringklocka *c* 144
bellboy pickolo *c* 26
below nedanför 15, 62
belt *(man's)* bälte *nt*; *(woman's)* skärp *nt* 117
bend *(road)* kurva *c* 79
berth bädd *c* 69, 71; sovplats *c* 69, 70
better bättre 14, 25, 101
between mellan 15
bicycle cykel *c* 74
bidet bidé *c* 28
big stor 14, 25, 101, 118
bilberry blåbär *nt* 54
bill nota *c* 61; räkning *c* 31, 102; *(banknote)* sedel *c* 130
billion *(Am.)* miljard *c* 148
binoculars kikare *c* 123
bird fågel *c* 85
birthday födelsedag *c* 151, 152
biscuit *(Br.)* kex *nt* 64
bitter besk 60
black svart 113
black and white svart-vit 124, 125
blackberry björnbär *nt* 54
bladder urinblåsa *c* 138
blanket filt *c* 27
bleed, to blöda 139, 145
blind *(window)* rullgardin *c* 29
blister blåsa *c* 139
blood blod *nt* 142
blood pressure blodtryck *nt* 141, 142
blood transfusion blodtransfusion *c* 144
blouse blus *c* 116
blow-dry, to föna 30
blue blå 113
blueberry blåbär *nt* 54
blusher rouge *nt* 110
boat båt *c* 73, 74
bobby pin hårklämma *c* 111
body kropp *c* 138
boil böld *c* 139
boiled kokt 49, 51, 52
bone ben *nt* 138
book bok *c* 12, 104
booking office biljettexpedition *c* 67; biljettkassa *c* 19
booklet *(of tickets)* biljetthäfte *nt* 72
bookshop bokhandel *c* 98, 104
boot stövel *c* 118
born född 149
botanical gardens botanisk trädgård *c* 81
botany botanik *c* 83
bottle flaska *c* 17, 57
bottle-opener flasköppnare *c* 106
bowel tarm *c* 138
bow tie fluga *c* 116
bowl skål *c* 127
box ask *c* 120
boy pojke *c* 112, 128
boyfriend pojkvän *c* 93
bra behå *c* 116
bracelet armband *nt* 121
braces *(suspenders)* hängslen *nt/pl* 116
braised bräserad 49
brake broms *c* 78
brake fluid bromsvätska *c* 75
brandy cognac *c* 58
bread bröd *nt* 36, 38, 64, 120
break, to bryta 139; gå sönder 123
break down, to gå sönder 78
breakdown motorstopp *nt* 78
breakdown van bärgningsbil *c* 78
breakfast frukost *c* 24, 34, 38
breast bröst *nt* 138
breathe, to andas 141, 142
bridge bro *c* 81, 85
bring, to ge 13; ta med 95
bring down, to ta ner 31
British britt *c* 93
broiled grillad 49
broken trasig 29; gått sönder 119; bruten 140
brooch brosch *c* 121
brother bror *c* 93
brown brun 113
bruise blåmärke *nt* 139
brush borste *c* 111
Brussels sprouts brysselkål *c/pl* 51
bubble bath skumbad *nt* 110
bucket hink *c* 106, 128
buckle spänne *nt* 117
buffet car cafévagn *c* 71
build, to bygga 83
building byggnad *c* 81, 83
building blocks/bricks byggklotsar *c/pl* 128
bulb glödlampa *c* 28, 75, 119
bump bula *c* 139
bun bulle *c* 63

burn brännsår *nt* 139
burned out *(bulb)* trasig 28
bus buss *c* 18, 19, 65, 66, 72, 80
business affär *c* 16, 131
business district affärskvarter *nt* 81
business trip affärsresa *c* 93
bus stop busshållplats *c* 72
busy upptagen 96
butane gas butangas *c* 32, 106
butcher's slaktare *c*, charkuteri *nt* 98
butter smör *nt* 36, 38, 64
button knapp *c* 29, 117
buy, to köpa 100, 104, 123, 163

C

cabana badhytt *c* 91
cabbage kål *c* 51
cabin *(ship)* hytt *c* 74
cable telegram *nt* 133
cable car linbana *c* 74
cable release trådutlösare *c* 125
café kafé *nt* 33
cake kaka *c* 55, 63
cake shop konditori *nt* 98
calculator räknare *c* 105
calendar kalender *c* 104
call *(phone)* samtal *nt* 134, 135, 136
call, to *(give name)* heta 11; *(phone)* ringa 78, 79, 134, 136, 156
camera kamera *c* 124, 125
camera case kamerafodral *nt* 125
camera shop fotoaffär *c* 98
camp, to campa 32
campbed tältsäng *c* 106
camping camping *c* 32
camping equipment camping utrustning *c* 106
camp site campingplats *c* 32
can *(of peaches)* burk *c* 120
can *(to be able)* kunna 12, 162
Canada Kanada *(nt)* 146
Canadian kanadensare *c* 93
cancel, to annullera, avbeställa 65
candle ljus *nt* 106
candlestick ljusstake *c* 127
candy godis *nt* 126
canoe kanot *c* 74
can opener konservöppnare *c* 106
cap mössa *c* 116
capital *(finance)* kapital *nt* 131
car bil *c* 19, 20, 32, 75, 76, 78; *(train)* vagn *c* 70, 71
carafe karaff *c* 57
carat karat *c* 121
caravan husvagn *c* 32
carbon paper karbonpapper *nt* 104
carbonated med kolsyra 59
carburettor förgasare *c* 78
card kort *nt* 93, 131
card game kortspel *nt* 128
cardamom kardemumma *c* 53
car hire biluthyrning *c* 20
car park parkering *c* 77
car racing biltävling *c* 89
car radio bilradio *c* 119
car rental biluthyrning *c* 20
carrot morot *c* 51
carry, to bära 21
cart kärra *c* 18, 71
carton *(of cigarettes)* limpa *c* 17, 126
cartridge *(camera)* kassett *c* 124
case fodral *nt* 123, 125; *(cigarettes)* étui *nt* 121, 126
cash, to lösa in 130, 133
cash desk kassa *c* 103, 155
cassette kassett *c* 119, 127
castle slott *nt* 81
catalogue katalog *c* 82
cathedral domkyrka *c* 81
Catholic katolsk 84
cauliflower blomkål *c* 51
caution varning *c* 155
cave grotta *c* 81
cemetery kyrkogård *c* 81
centimetre centimeter *c* 112
centre centrum *nt* 19, 21, 76, 81
century århundrade *nt* 149
ceramics keramik *c* 83, 127
cereal flingor *c/pl* 38
chain *(jewellery)* kedja *c* 121
chain bracelet armlänk *c* 121
chair stol *c* 106
change *(money)* växel *c* 61, 77, 130
change, to ändra 65; *(replace, train)* byta 60, 68, 69, 73, 75, 123; *(money)* växla 18, 130
chapel kapell *nt* 81
charcoal träkol *c* 106
charcoal tablets koltabletter *c/pl* 109
charge avgift *c* 77, 136; kostnad *c* 20, 40;
charge, to kosta 20, 24, 32, 89
charm *(trinket)* berlock *c* 121

charm bracelet berlockarmband *nt* 121
cheap billig 14, 24, 25, 101
check check *c* 130; *(restaurant)* nota *c* 62
check, to kontrollera 75, 123; *(luggage)* pollettera 71
checkbook checkhäfte *nt* 131
check-in *(airport)* incheckning *c* 65
check in, to *(airport)* checka in 65
check out, to checka ut 31
check-up *(medical)* hälsokontroll *c* 142
cheers! skål! 58
cheese ost *c* 38, 53, 62, 64, 120
chef kökschef *c* 40
chemist's apotek *nt* 98, 108
cheque check *c* 130
cheque book checkhäfte *nt* 131
cherry körsbär *nt* 54
chess schack *nt* 93
chess set schackspel *nt* 128
chest bröstkorg *c* 138; bröst *nt* 141
chewing gum tuggummi *nt* 126
chewing tobacco tuggtobak *c* 126
chicken kyckling *c* 50
child barn *nt* 24, 60, 82, 93, 139, 150
children's doctor barnläkare *c* 137
chilled kyld 58
China Kina *(nt)* 146
china porslin *nt* 98
chips pommes frites *c/pl* 52, 62; *(Am.)* chips *c/pl* 64
chives gräslök *c* 53
chocolate choklad *c* 38, 55, 59, 120
chocolate bar chokladkaka *c* 64, 126
choice val *nt* 40
chop kotlett *c* 48
Christmas jul *c* 151, 152
church kyrka *c* 81, 84
cigar cigarr *c* 126
cigarette cigarrett *c* 17, 95, 126
cigarette case cigarrettetui *nt* 121, 126
cigarette holder cigarrettmunstycke *nt* 126
cigarette lighter cigarrettändare *c* 121
cine camera filmkamera *c* 124
cinema bio *c* 86, 96
cinnamon kanel *c* 53
circle *(theatre)* första raden 87
citizen medborgare *c* 25
city stad *c* 81
city hall stadshus *nt* 81
classical klassisk 128
clean ren 61
clean, to tvätta 29; *(wipe)* torka av 76
cleansing cream rengöringskräm *c* 110
cliff klippa *c* 85
cloakroom garderob *c* 87
clock klocka *c* 121, 153
clock-radio klockradio *c* 119
clog träsko *c* 127
close *(near)* nära 78, 132
close, to stänga 11, 82, 108, 132
closed stängt 155
cloth tyg *nt* 118
clothes kläder *pl* 29, 116
clothes peg klädnypa *c* 106
clothing kläder *pl* 112
cloud moln *nt* 94
coach *(bus)* expressbuss *c* 66
coach station busstation *c* 67
coat *(man's)* rock *c* 116; *(woman's)* kappa *c* 116
cod torsk *c* 46
coffee kaffe *nt* 38, 59, 64
coin mynt *nt* 83
cold kall 14, 25, 61, 94, 155
cold *(illness)* förkylning *c* 108, 141
collar krage *c* 117
collect call Ba-samtal *nt* 135
colour färg *c* 103, 112, 124, 125
colour chart färgkarta *c* 30
colourfast färgäkta 114
colour rinse färgsköljning *c* 30
colour shampoo tonande shampo *nt* 111
colour slide färgdiapositiv *nt* 124
comb kam *c* 111
come, to komma 36, 92, 95, 137, 146
comedy komedi *c* 86
commission expeditionsavgift *c* 130
compact disc CD-skiva *c* 127
company kompani *nt* 154
compartment kupé *c* 70
compass kompass *c* 106
complaint klagomål *nt* 60
concert konsert *c* 88
concert hall konserthus *nt* 81, 88

condom kondom *c* 109
conductor *(orchestra)* dirigent *c* 88
conference room konferensrum *nt* 23
confirm, to bekräfta 65
confirmation bekräftelse *c* 23
congratulation gratulation *c* 151
connection *(train)* anslutning *c* 65, 68
consommé buljong *c* 44
constipation förstoppning *c* 140
consulate konsulat *nt* 156
contact lens kontaktlins *c* 123
contagious, to be smitta 142
contain, to innehålla 37
contraceptive preventivmedel *nt* 109
contract kontrakt *nt* 131
control kontroll *c* 16
conversion omvandling *c* 157
cookie kex *nt* 64
cool bag kylväska *c* 106
cool box kylbox *c* 106
copper koppar *c* 122
corduroy manchester *c* 114
corkscrew korkskruv *c* 106
corn *(Am.)* majs *c* 50; *(foot)* liktorn *c* 109
corner hörn *nt* 36; *(street)* gathörn *nt* 21, 77
corn plaster liktornsplåster *nt* 109
cost kostnad *c* 131
cost, to kosta 11, 24, 80, 133, 136
cot barnsäng *c* 24
cotton bomull *c* 114
cotton wool bomull *c* 109
cough hosta *c* 108, 141
cough, to hosta 142
cough drops halstabletter *c/pl* 109
counter lucka *c* 133
country land *nt* 92
countryside land *nt* 85
court house tingshus *nt* 81
cousin kusin *c* 93
crab krabba *c* 43, 46, 47
cramp kramp *c* 141
cranberry lingon *nt* 54
crayfish *(freshwater)* kräfta *c* 46
crayon färgkrita *c* 104
cream grädde *c* 38, 55, 59; *(toiletry)* kräm (crème) *c* 110; *(pharmaceutical)* salva *c* 109
crease resistant skrynkelfri 114
credit card kreditkort *nt* 20, 31, 61, 102, 130
cress krasse *c* 53
crispbread knäckebröd *nt* 38; hårt bröd *nt* 120
crisps chips *nt/pl* 64
crockery porslin *nt/pl* 106, 107
cross kors *nt* 121
cross-country skiing längdåkning *c* 91
crossing *(by sea)* överfart *c* 74
crossroads korsning *c* 77
crown *(money)* krona *c* 18, 101, 129
cruise kryssning *c* 74
crystal kristall *c* 122, 127
cucumber gurka *c* 51
cuff link manschettknapp *c* 121
cuisine kök *nt* 35
cup kopp *c* 36, 59, 107
curler papiljott *c* 111
currant vinbär *nt* 54
currency valuta *c* 129
currency exchange office växelkontor *nt* 18, 67, 129
current ström *c* 90
curtain gardin *c* 28
curve kurva *c* 79
customs tull *c* 16, 102
cut *(wound)* skärsår *nt* 139
cut, to *(scissors)* klippa 30
cut off, to avbryta 136
cut glass slipat glas *nt* 122
cuticle remover nagelbandsvatten *nt* 110
cutlery bestick *nt/pl* 106, 107, 121
cycle path cykelbana *c* 79
cycling cykel *c* 89
cystitis urinvägsinfektion *c* 142

D

dairy ostaffär *c* 98
dance, to dansa 88, 96
danger fara *c* 155, 156
dangerous farlig 79, 90
Danish pastry wienerbröd *nt* 63
dark mörk 25, 101, 112, 113
date *(day)* datum *nt* 25, 151; *(appointment)* träff *c* 95; *(fruit)* dadel *c* 54
daughter dotter *c* 93
day dag *c* 16, 20, 24, 32, 80, 150, 151

daylight dagsljus *nt* 124
day off ledig dag *c* 151
decade årtionde *nt* 149
decaffeinated koffeinfri 38, 59
December december *(c)* 150
decision beslut *nt* 25, 102
deck *(ship)* däck *nt* 74
deck chair solstol *c* 91, 106
declare, to *(customs)* förtulla 17
deep djup 90, 142
deep fried friterad 46
deer hjort *c* 50
delicatessen delikatessaffär *c* 98
deliver, to leverera 102
delicious utsökt 61
delivery leverans *c* 102
Denmark Danmark *(nt)* 146
dentist tandläkare *c* 98, 145
denture tandprotes *c* 145
deodorant deodorant *c* 110
department avdelning *c* 83, 100
department store varuhus *nt* 98
departure avgång *c* 65
deposit *(car hire)* deponeringsavgift *c* 20; *(bank)* insättning *c* 130
dessert efterrätt *c* 37, 55
detour *(traffic)* trafikomläggning *c* 79
diabetic diabetiker *c* 37, 141
dialling code riktnummer *nt* 134
diamond diamant *c* 122
diaper blöja *c* 111
diarrhoea diarré *c* 140
dictionary ordbok *c* 104
diesel diesel 75
diet diet *c* 37
difficult svår 14
difficulty svårighet *c* 28; problem *nt* 102
digital digital 122
dill dill *c* 53
dining car restaurangvagn *c* 68, 71
dining room matsal *c* 27
dinner middag *c* 34, 94
direct direkt 65
direct, to visa vägen 13
direction riktning *c* 76
director *(theatre)* regissör *c* 86
directory *(phone)* telefonkatalog *c* 134
disabled handikappad *c* 82
disc skiva *c* 127
discotheque diskotek *nt* 88, 96
discount rabatt *c* 131
disease sjukdom *c* 142
dish rätt *c* 37
dish of the day dagens rätt *c* 40
disinfectant desinfektionsmedel *nt* 109
dislocated ur led 140
display case monter *c* 100
dissatisfied missnöjd 103
district *(town)* kvarter *nt* 81
disturb, to störa 155
dive dyka 90
diversion *(traffic)* trafikomläggning *c* 79
dizzy yr 140
do, to göra 163
doctor läkare *c* 79, 137, 156; doktor *c* 98, 137, 144
doctor's office läkarmottagning *c* 137
dog hund *c* 155
doll docka *c* 128
dollar dollar *c* 18, 102, 130
door dörr *c* 155
double dubbel 74
double bed dubbelsäng *c* 23
double room dubbelrum *nt* 19, 23
down ner 15
downhill skiing utförsåkning *c* 91
downstairs där nere 15
downtown (stads)centrum *nt* 81
dozen dussin *nt* 148
draught beer fatöl *nt* 56
drawing pad ritblock *nt* 104
drawing pin häftstift *nt* 104
dress klänning *c* 116
dressing gown morgonrock *c* 116
drink dryck *c* 56, 58, 59; drink *c* 60, 95
drink, to dricka 35, 36, 37, 59
drinking water dricksvatten *nt* 32
drip, to droppa 28
drive, to köra 21, 76
driving licence körkort *nt* 20, 79
drop *(liquid)* droppe *c* 109
drugstore apotek *nt* 98, 108
dry torr 30, 58, 111
dry cleaner's kemtvätt *c* 29, 98
dry shampoo torrshampo *nt* 111
Dublin bay prawn havskräfta *c* 45
duck anka *c* 50
dummy napp *c* 111
during under 15, 149, 151
duty *(customs)* tull *c* 16, 17
duty-free shop taxfree-shop *c* 19
dye, to färga 30

E

each varje 125, 143, 149
ear öra *nt* 138
earache ont i örat 141
ear drops örondroppar *c/pl* 109
early tidig 14, 31
earring örhänge *nt* 121
east öster 77
Easter påsk *c* 152
easy lätt, enkel 14
eat, to äta 36, 37, 144
eat out, to äta ute 33
eel ål *c* 41, 42, 46
egg ägg *nt* 38, 42, 45, 62, 64
eggplant äggplanta *c* 51
eight åtta 147
eighteen arton 147
eighth åttonde 148
eighty åttio 147
elastic elastisk 109
elastic bandage elastisk binda *c* 109
Elastoplast plåster *nt* 109
electric(al) elektrisk 119
electrical appliance elektrisk artikel *c* 119
electrical goods shop elaffär *c* 98
electricity elektricitet *c* 32
electronic elektronisk 125, 128
elevator hiss *c* 27, 100, 155
eleven elva 147
elk älg *c* 50
embassy ambassad *c* 156
emergency nödsituation *c* 156
emergency exit nödutgång *c* 27, 155
emery board sandpappersfil *c* 110
empty tom 14
enamel emalj *c* 122
end slut *nt* 150
endive endiv *c* 51
engaged *(phone)* upptaget 136
engagement ring förlovningsring *c* 122
engine *(car)* motor *c* 78
England England *(nt)* 146
English engelsk 104, 126
English engelska *(c)* 12, 82, 84; *(person)* engelsman *c* 93
engrave gravera 121
enjoyable trevlig 31
enlarge, to förstora 125
enough tillräcklig 15
enquiry förfrågning *c* 68
entrance ingång *c* 67, 99, 155; infart *c* 79
entrance fee inträde *nt* 82
envelope kuvert *nt* 27, 104
equipment utrustning *c* 91, 106
eraser radergummi *nt* 104
escalator rulltrappa *c* 100
estimate *(cost)* uppskattning *c* 131
Europe Europa *(nt)* 146
evening kväll *c* 87, 95, 96, 151, 153
evening dress *(woman's)* aftonklänning *c* 116
everything allt 31
examine, to undersöka 137
exchange, to byta 103
exchange rate växelkurs *c* 18, 130
excursion rundtur *c* 80
excuse, to förlåta, ursäkta 11
exercise book skrivbok *c* 104
exhaust pipe avgasrör *nt* 78
exhibition utställning *c* 81
exit utgång *c* 67, 99, 155; utfart *c* 79
expect, to vänta 130
expenses omkostnad *c* 131
expensive dyr 14, 19, 24, 101
exposure *(photography)* bild *c* 124
exposure counter exponeringsmätare *c* 125
express express 133
expression uttryck *nt* 10
expressway motorväg *c* 76
extension *(phone)* anknytning *c* 135
extension cord/lead förlängningssladd *c* 119
extra extra 27, 40
eye öga *nt* 139
eyebrow pencil ögonbrynspenna *c* 110
eye drops ögondroppar *c/pl* 109
eye liner eyeliner *c* 110
eye shadow ögonskugga *c* 110
eyesight syn f 123
eye specialist ögonläkare *c* 137

F

fabric *(cloth)* tyg *nt* 113
face ansikte *nt* 138
face pack ansiktsmask *c* 30
face powder puder *nt* 110
factory fabrik *c* 81
fair mässa *c* 81
fall *(autumn)* höst *c* 150

fall, to ramla 139
family familj *c* 93
fan belt fläktrem *c* 75
far långt (bort) 11, 14, 100
farm bondgård *c* 85
fast snabb 124
fat *(meat)* fett *nt* 37
father far *c* 93
faucet kran *c* 28
February februari *(c)* 150
fee *(doctor)* arvode *nt* 144
feeding bottle nappflaska *c* 111
feel, to *(physical state)* känna sig 140, 142
felt filt *c* 114
felt-tip pen filtpenna *c* 104
fennel fänkål *c* 51
ferry färja *c* 74
fever feber *c* 140
few få 14; *(a)* några 14
field fält *nt* 85
fifteen femton 147
fifth femte 148
fifty femtio 147
fig fikon *nt* 54
file *(tool)* fil *c* 110
fill in, to fylla i 26, 144
filling *(tooth)* plomb *c* 145
filling station bensinstation *c* 75
film film *c* 86, 124, 125
film winder frammatning *c* 125
filter filter *nt* 125
filter-tipped med filter 126
find, to hitta 11, 12, 100
fine *(OK)* bra 11, 25
finger finger *nt* 138
finish, to sluta 87
Finland Finland *(nt)* 146
fire eld *c* 156
first första 68, 69, 148
first-aid kit förbandslåda *c* 106
first class första klass *c* 69
first name förnamn *nt* 25
fish fisk *c* 45
fish, to fiska 90
fishing permit fiskekort *nt* 90
fishing tackle fiskeutrustning *c* 106
fishmonger's fiskaffär *c* 98
fit, to passa 115
fitting room provrum *nt* 115
five fem 147
fix, to laga 75, 145
fizzy *(mineral water)* med kolsyra 59
flash *(photography)* blixt *c* 125
flash attachment blixtaggregat *nt* 125
flashlight ficklampa *c* 106
flat platt 118
flat *(appartment)* våning *c* 19
flat tyre punktering *c* 75, 78
flea market loppmarknad *c* 81
flight flyg *nt* 65
floor våning *c* 23, 27
floor show show *c* 88
florist's blomsteraffär *c* 98
flounder flundra *c* 45
flour mjöl *nt* 37
flower blomma *c* 85
flu influensa *c* 142
fluid vätska *c* 75, 123
fog dimma *c* 94
folding chair fällstol *c* 106
folding table fällbord *nt* 107
folk art allmogekonst *c* 83
folk music folkmusik *c* 128
follow, to följa 77
food mat *c* 37, 61
food box matlåda *c* 106
food poisoning matförgiftning *c* 142
foot fot *c* 138
football fotboll *c* 89
foot cream fotkräm *c* 110
footpath stig *c* 85
for för 15; *(time)* i 143, 151
forbid, to förbjuda 155
forest skog *c* 85
forget, to glömma 60
fork gaffel *c* 36, 60, 107
form *(document)* blankett *c* 25, 26, 133
fortnight fjorton dagar *c/pl* 151
fortress borg *c* 81
forty fyrtio 147
forwarding address eftersändningsadress *c* 31
foundation cream puderunderlag *nt* 110
fountain fontän *c* 81
fountain pen reservoarpenna *c* 105
four fyra 147
fourteen fjorton 147
fourth fjärde 148
fowl fågel *c* 50
frame *(glasses)* båge *c* 123
France Frankrike *(nt)* 146
free *(vacant)* ledig 14, 70, 96, 155

free (of charge) fri 155
French beans haricots verts *c/pl* 51
French fries pommes frites *c/pl* 52
fresh färsk 54, 60
Friday fredag *c* 150
fried stekt 46, 49
fried egg stekt ägg *nt* 38, 45
friend vän *c* 92, 93, 95
from från 15
frost frost *c* 94
fruit frukt *c* 54
fruit juice juice *c* 37, 38, 59
fruit salad fruktsallad *c* 54
frying pan stekpanna *c* 106
full full 14
full board helpension *c* 24
full insurance helförsäkring *c* 20
fur coat päls *c* 116
furniture möbler *c/pl* 83
furrier's körsnär *c* 98

G

gallery galleri *nt* 98
game spel *nt* 128; *(food)* vilt *nt* 50
gangway landgång *c* 74
garage *(parking)* garage *nt* 26; *(repairs)* verkstad *c* 78
garden(s) trädgård *c* 85
garlic vitlök *c* 52, 53
gas gas *c* 126, 156
gasoline bensin *c* 75, 78
gastritis magkatarr *c* 142
gauze gasbinda *c* 109
gem ädelsten *c* 121
general allmän 27, 100
general delivery poste restante 133
general practitioner allmänpraktiker *c* 137
genitals könsorgan *nt* 138
gentleman herre *c* 155
genuine äkta 118, 121
geology geologi *c* 83
Germany Tyskland *(nt)* 146
get, to få 108; *(fetch)* skaffa 21, 31, 137; *(find)* få tag på 11, 19, 21, 32
get off, to stiga av 72
get to, to komma till 19, 70, 76
get up, to stiga upp 144
gherkin ättiksgurka *c* 51, 64
gift present *c* 17
gin gin *c* 58
gin and tonic gin och tonic *c* 58
girdle höfthållare *c* 116
girl flicka *c* 112, 128
girlfriend flickvän *c* 93
give, to ge 13, 135
give way, to *(traffic)* lämna företräde 79
gland körtel *c* 138
glass glas *nt* 36, 57, 59, 60, 143
glasses glasögon *c/pl* 123
glassware glas *nt* 127
gloomy dyster 84
glove handske *c* 116
glue klister *nt* 105
go, to gå 96
go away! ge er i väg! 156
gold guld *nt* 121, 122
golden guldfärgad 113
gold plate gulddoublé *c* 122
golf golf *c* 89
golf course golfbana *c* 89
good bra 14, 101
good afternoon god middag 10
good-bye adjö 10
good evening god afton 10
Good Friday långfredag *c* 152
good morning god morgon 10
good night god natt 10
goods vara *c* 16
goose gås *c* 50
gooseberry krusbär *nt* 54
go out, to gå ut 96
gram gram *nt* 120
grammar book grammatik *c* 105
grape vindruva *c* 54
grapefruit grapefrukt *c* 54
grapefruit juice grapefruktjuice *c* 38, 59
gravy sky *c* 52
gray grå 113
graze skrubbsår *nt* 139
greasy fet 30, 111
Great Britain Storbritannien *(nt)* 146
green grön 113
green beans haricots verts *c/pl* 51
greengrocer's grönsaksaffär *c* 98
greeting hälsning *c* 151
grey grå 113
grilled grillad 46, 49
grocer's livsmedelsaffär *c* 98, 120
groundsheet fältunderlag *nt* 106
group grupp *c* 82
guest house pensionat *nt* 19, 22

guide guide *c* 80
guidebook guidebok *c* 82, 104, 105
gum *(teeth)* tandkött *nt* 145
gynaecologist gynekolog *c* 137

H

habit vana *c* 34
haddock kolja *c* 46
hair hår *nt* 30, 111
hairbrush hårborste *c* 111
haircut klippning *c* 30
hairdresser's frisersalong *c* 27, 30; frisör *c* 98
hair dryer hårtork *c* 119
hair dye hårfärgningsmedel *nt* 111
hair gel frisyrgelé *nt* 111
hairgrip hårklämma *c* 111
hair lotion hårvatten *nt* 111
hair pin hårnål *c* 111
hair slide hårspänne *nt* 111
hairspray (hår)spray *c* 30, 111
half halv 149
half halva *c* 149
half an hour halvtimme *c* 153
half board halvpension *c* 24
half price ticket halv biljett *c* 69
halibut hälleflundra *c* 46
hall porter portier *c* 26
hallo hej 10
ham skinka *c* 48, 62, 64
ham and eggs skinka och ägg 38
hamburger pannbiff *c* 48
hammer hammare *c* 106
hammock hängmatta *c* 106
hand hand *c* 138
handbag handväska *c* 116, 156
hand cream handkräm *c* 110
handicrafts konsthantverk *nt* 83; slöjd *c* 127
handkerchief näsduk *c* 116
handmade handgjord 113
hanger hängare *c* 27
hangover baksmälla *c* 108
happy glad 152
harbour hamn *c* 81
hard hård 123
hard-boiled hårdkokt 38
hardware store järnhandel *c* 98
hare hare *c* 50
hat hatt *c* 116
have, to ha 162
haversack ryggsäck *c* 106
hayfever hösnuva *c* 108, 141
hazelnut hasselnöt *c* 54
he han 162
head huvud *nt* 138, 139
headache huvudvärk *c* 141
headphones hörlurar *c/pl* 119
head waiter hovmästare *c* 61
health food shop hälsokostaffär *c* 98
health insurance sjukförsäkring *c* 144
health insurance form sjukförsäkringsblankett *c* 144
heart hjärta *nt* 138
heart attack hjärtattack *c* 141
heat, to värma upp 90
heating värme *c* 23, 28
heavy tung 14, 101
heel klack *c* 118
helicopter helikopter *c* 74
hello *(phone)* hallå 135
help hjälp *c* 156
help! hjälp! 156
help, to hjälpa 13, 21, 71, 100, 134; *(oneself)* ta själv 120
her hennes 162; sin, sitt (*pl* sina) 161
herb ört *c* 53
here här 13
herring sill *c* 41, 42, 43, 46, 47
hi hej 10
high hög 85, 141
high season högsäsong *c* 149
hill kulle *c* 85
hire uthyrning *c* 20, 74
hire, to hyra 19, 20, 74, 90, 91, 119, 155
his hans 162; sin, sitt (*pl* sina) 161
history historia *c* 83
hitchhike, to lifta 74
hold on! *(phone)* var god dröj! 136
hole hål *nt* 29
holiday helgdag *c* 151, 152
holidays semester *c* 16, 151, 152; *(school)* skollov *nt* 151
home address bostadsadress *c* 31
home town hemort *c* 25
honey honung *c* 38
hope, to hoppas 96
horse häst *c* 127
horseback riding ridning *c* 89
horse racing hästkapplöpning *c* 89
horseradish pepparrot *c* 49, 52
hospital sjukhus *nt* 99, 144
hot varm 14, 25, 38, 94, 155
hotel hotell *nt* 19, 21, 22
hotel guide hotellguide *c* 19

hotel reservation hotellreservation *c* 19
hot water varmvatten *nt* 23, 28
hot-water bottle varmvattensflaska *c* 27
hour timme *c* 80, 143, 153
house hus *nt* 83, 85
how hur 11
how far hur långt 11, 76, 85
how long hur länge 11, 24
how many hur många 11
how much hur mycket 11, 24
hundred hundra 147
hungry hungrig 13, 35
hunt, to jaga 89
hunting jakt *c* 89
hurry *(to be in a)* ha bråttom 21
hurt, to göra ont 139, 140, 145; *(oneself)* slå sig 139
husband man *c* 93
hydrofoil svävare *c* 74

I

I jag 162
ice is *c* 94
ice-cream glass *c* 55, 62
ice cube is *c* 27
iced tea iste *nt* 59
icehockey ishockey *c* 91
Iceland Island *(nt)* 146
ice pack frysklamp *c* 106
ill sjuk 140, 156
illness sjukdom *c* 140
important viktig 13
imported importerad 113
impressive imponerande 84
in i 15
include, to ingå 24, 80
included inräknad 20, 40, 61; inkluderad 31
India Indien *(nt)* 146
indigestion dålig matsmältning *c* 141
indoor inomhus 90
inexpensive billig 35, 124
infected infekterad 140
infection infektion *c* 141
inflammation inflammation *c* 142
inflation inflation *c* 131
influenza influensa *c* 142
information information *c* 67; upplysning *c* 155
injection injektion *c* 144; spruta *c* 142
injure, to skada 139
injured skadad 79, 139
injury skada *c* 139
ink bläck *nt* 105
inn värdshus *nt* 33
inquiry förfrågan *c* 68
insect bite insektsbett *nt* 108, 139
insect repellent insektsspray *c* 109
insect spray insektsspray *c* 109
inside inne 15
instant coffee snabbkaffe *nt* 64
instead i stället 37
insurance försäkring *c* 20, 144
insurance company försäkringsbolag *nt* 79
interest ränta *c* 131
interested, to be intresserad 83
interesting intressant 84
international internationell 133
international operator utlandstelefonist *c* 134
interpreter tolk *c* 131
intersection korsning *c* 77
introduce, to presentera 92
introduction *(social)* presentation 92
investment investering *c* 131
invitation inbjudan *c* 94
invite, to bjuda 94
invoice faktura *c* 131
iodine jod *c* 109
Ireland Irland *(nt)* 146
Irish irländare *c* 93
iron *(laundry)* strykjärn *nt* 119
iron, to stryka 29
ironmonger's järnhandel *c* 99
Israel Israel *(nt)* 146
its dess 162; sin, sitt (*pl* sina) 161

J

jacket kavaj *c* 116
jam sylt *c* 38, 63
jam, to fastna 28, 125
January januari *(c)* 150
Japan Japan *(nt)* 146
jar burk *c* 120
jaundice gulsot *c* 142
jaw käke *c* 138
jeans jeans *c/pl* 116
jersey jumper *c*, tröja *c* 116
jetty brygga *c* 74
jewel box smyckeskrin *nt* 121
jeweller's juvelerare *c*, guldsmedsaffär *c* 99, 121

jewellery smycke *nt* 127
joint led *c* 138
journey *(trip)* resa *c* 152
juice juice *c* 37, 38, 59
July juli *(c)* 150
June juni *(c)* 150
juniper berry enbär *nt* 53
just *(only)* bara 16, 37, 100

K

kale grönkål *c* 51
keep, to behålla 61
kerosene fotogen *c* 106
key nyckel *c* 27
kidney njure *c* 48, 138
kilo(gram) kilo(gram) *nt* 120
kilometre kilometer *c* 20
kind snäll 96
kind *(type)* slags *nt/c* 48, 140
knapsack ryggsäck *c* 106
knee knä *nt* 138
kneesocks knästrumpor *c/pl* 116
knife kniv *c* 36, 60, 107, 127
know, to veta 16, 24, 96; känna till 114

L

label etikett *c* 105
lace spets *c* 114
lady dam *c* 155
lake sjö *c* 81, 85, 90
lamb lamm *nt* 48
lamp lampa *c* 29, 106, 119
landmark landmärke *nt* 85
lantern lykta *c* 106
large stor 20, 101, 118, 130
last sista 14, 68; förra 149, 150, 151
late sen 14; försenad 69
later senare 135
laugh, to skratta 95
launderette snabbtvätt *c* 99
laundry *(place)* tvättinrättning *c* 99; *(clothes)* tvätt *c* 29
laundry service tvättservice *c* 23
laxative laxermedel *nt* 109
lead *(metal)* bly *nt* 75
leap year skottår *nt* 149
leather läder *nt* 114, 118; skinn *nt* 114
leave, to lämna 20, 26, 71, 156; *(go)* gå 95; åka 31; *(train)* (av)gå 68, 69, 74
leek purjolök *c* 51
left vänster 21, 62, 69, 77
left-luggage office effektförvaring *c* 67, 71
leg ben *nt* 138
lemon citron *c* 37, 38, 54, 59
lemonade läsk *c* 59
lens *(glasses)* glas *nt* 123; *(camera)* objektiv *nt* 125
lens cap linsskydd *nt* 125
less mindre 14
lesson lektion *c* 90
let, to *(hire out)* hyra 155
letter brev *nt* 28, 132
letter box brevlåda *c* 132
letter of credit remburs *c* 130
lettuce grönsallad *c* 44, 51
level crossing järnvägskorsning *c* 79
library bibliotek *nt* 81, 99
licence *(driving)* körkort *nt* 20, 79
lie down, to lägga sig 142
life belt livbälte *nt* 74
life boat livbåt *c* 74
lift hiss *c* 27, 100, 155
ligament ligament *nt* 140
light lätt 14, 55, 58, 101, 128; *(colour)* ljus 101, 112, 113
light ljus *nt* 28, 124; *(cigarette)* eld *c* 95
lighter tändare *c* 126
lighter fluid bensin till tändare *c* 126
lighter gas gas till tändare *c* 126
light meter ljusmätare *c* 125
lightning blixt *c* 94
like, to tycka om 25, 61, 92, 112; ha lust 96; *(want)* vilja 13, 20, 23; önska 103
line linje *c* 73
linen *(cloth)* linne *nt* 114
lip läpp *c* 138
lipbrush läppstiftpensel *c* 110
lipsalve cerat *nt* 110
lipstick läppstift *nt* 110
liqueur likör *c* 58
liquid vätska *c* 123
liquor store systembolag *nt* 99
listen, to lyssna 128
litre liter *c* 75, 120
little *(a)* lite 14
live, to leva 83; *(reside)* bo 83
liver lever *c* 48, 138
lobster hummer *c* 43, 46
local lokal 36
local train lokaltåg *nt* 65, 69

long lång 116; *(time)* lång tid 60, 62, 76, 116; länge 77, 92
long-sighted långsynt 123
look, to se 123; titta 100
look for, to leta efter 13
look out! se upp! 156
loose vid 145; stor 116
lose, to tappa 123, 156; förlora 156
loss förlust *c* 131
lost, to be inte hitta 13; gå vilse 156
lost and found office hittegodsexpedition *c* 67, 156
lost property office hittegodsexpedition *c* 67, 156
lot *(a)* mycket 14
loud *(voice)* hög 135
love, to älska 92
lovely underbar 94
low låg 141
lower under- 69, 70
low season lågsäsong *c* 149
luck lycka *c* 152
luggage bagage *nt* 18, 26, 31, 71; *(registered)* resgods *nt/pl* 71
luggage locker förvaringsbox *c* 18, 67, 71
luggage trolley bagagekärra *c* 18, 71
lump *(bump)* knöl *c* 139
lunch lunch *c* 34, 80, 94
lung lunga *c* 138

M

macaroni makaroner *c/pl* 52
machine maskin *c* 114
mackerel makrill *c* 46
magazine veckotidning *c* 105
magnificent storslagen 84
maid städerska *c* 26
mail post *c* 28, 133
mail, to posta 28
mailbox brevlåda *c* 132
make, to göra 131, 163
make up, to *(prepare)* göra i ordning 108
make-up bag sminkväska *c* 110
make-up remover pad make-up remover pad *c* 110
mallet träklubba *c* 106
man man *c* 156; herre *c* 115, 155
manager direktör *c* 26
manicure manikyr *c* 30
many många 11, 14
map karta *c* 76, 105
March mars *(c)* 150
marinated gravad 41, 43, 46; marinerad 46
market marknad *c* 99, torghandel *c* 99
marmalade apelsinmarmelad *c* 38
married gift 93
mashed potatoes potatismos *nt* 52, 62
mass *(church)* mässa *c* 84
match tändsticka *c* 106, 126; *(sport)* match *c* 89
match, to *(colour)* passa till 112
matinée matiné *c* 87
mattress madrass *c* 106
May maj *(c)* 150
may *(can)* kunna 12, 162
meadow äng *c* 85
meal måltid *c* 24, 143
mean, to betyda 11, 26
measles mässling *c* 142
measure, to ta mått 114
meat kött *nt* 48, 60
meatball köttbulle *c* 42, 48, 62
mechanic mekaniker *c* 78
mechanical pencil stiftpenna *c* 105, 121
medical certificate läkarintyg *nt* 144
medicine medicin *c* 83, 143
medium medium 49
meet, to träffa 92, 96; ses 96
melon melon *c* 54
memorial minnesmärke *nt* 81
mend, to laga 29, 75
menthol *(cigarettes)* mentol 126
menu meny *c* 37, 39; *(printed)* matsedel *c* 36, 39, 40
message meddelande *nt* 28, 136
methylated spirits rödsprit *c* 106
metre meter *c* 112
mezzanine *(theatre)* första raden 87
middle mitten 69, 87, 150; mellan 69
midnight midnatt *c* 153
midnight sun midnattssol *c* 94
mileage kilometerkostnad *c* 20
milk mjölk *c* 38, 59, 64
milkshake milkshake *c* 59
milliard milliard *c* 148
million million *c* 148

mineral water mineralvatten *nt* 59
minister *(religion)* protestantisk präst *c* 84
minute minut *c* 21, 153
mirror spegel *c* 115, 123
miscellaneous diverse 127
Miss fröken *c* 10
miss, to fattas 18, 29, 60
mistake fel *nt* 31, 61, 102; misstag *nt* 60
modified American plan halvpension *c* 24
moisturizing cream fuktighetsbevarande kräm *c* 110
moment ögonblick *nt* 12, 136
monastery kloster *nt* 81
Monday måndag *c* 150
money pengar *c/pl* 129, 130
money order postanvisning *c* 133
month månad *c* 16, 150
monument monument *nt* 81
moon måne *c* 94
moped moped *c* 74
more mer 14
morning morgon *c* 31, 151, 153
mortgage hypotek *nt* 131
mosque moské *c* 84
mosquito net myggnät *nt* 106
motel motell *nt* 22
mother mor *c* 93
motorbike motorcykel *c* 74
motorboat motorbåt *c* 91
motorway motorväg *c* 76
mountain berg *nt* 85
moustache mustasch *c* 31
mouth mun *c* 138, 142
mouthwash munvatten *nt* 109
move, to röra 139
movie film *c* 86
movie camera filmkamera *c* 124
movies bio *c* 86, 96
Mr. herr *c* 10
Mrs. fru *c* 10
much mycket 11, 14
mug mugg *c* 107
muscle muskel *c* 138
museum museum *nt* 81
mushroom svamp *c* 51
music musik *c* 83, 128
musical musical *c* 86
music box speldosa *c* 121
mussel mussla *c* 43
must *(have to)* måste 23, 31, 95
mustard senap *c* 64
my min, mitt (*pl* mina) 161

N

nail *(human)* nagel *c* 110
nail brush nagelborste *c* 110
nail clippers nageltång *c* 110
nail file nagelfil *c* 110
nail polish nagellack *nt* 110
nail polish remover nagellacks-borttagningsmedel *nt* 110
nail scissors nagelsax *c* 110
name namn *nt* 23, 79, 133; *(surname)* efternamn *nt* 25
napkin servett *c* 36, 105, 106
nappy blöja *c* 111
narrow trång 118
nationality nationalitet *c* 92
natural history naturhistoria *c* 83
near nära 14
nearby i närheten 77
nearest närmaste 73, 75, 78, 132
neat *(drink)* ren 58
neck nacke *c* 30, 138
necklace halsband *nt* 121
need, to behöva 29, 118, 137
needle nål *c* 27
negative negativ *nt* 124, 125
nerve nerv *c* 138
nervous system nervsystem *nt* 138
Netherlands Nederländerna *(nt/pl)*, Holland *(nt)* 146
never aldrig 15
new ny 14, 149
newspaper tidning *c* 104, 105
newsstand tidningskiosk *c* 19, 67, 99, 104
New Year nyår *nt* 152
New Zealand Nya Zeeland *(nt)* 146
next nästa 14, 65, 68, 73, 76, 149, 150, 151
next time nästa gång 95
next to bredvid 15, 77
nice *(beautiful)* vacker 94
night natt *c* 10, 24, 151; kväll *c* 88, 96
night club nattklubb *c* 88
night cream nattkräm *c* 110
nightdress nattlinne *nt* 116
nine nio 147
nineteen nitton 147
ninety nittio 147
ninth nionde 148
no nej 10
nonalcoholic alkoholfri 59
none ingen 15
nonsmoker icke rökare *c* 70, 155

noon klockan tolv (på dagen) 153
normal normal 30
north norr 77
North America Nordamerika *(nt)* 146
Norway Norge *(nt)* 146
nose näsa *c* 138
nosebleed näsblod *nt* 141
nose drops näsdroppar *c/pl* 109
not inte 15, 163
note *(banknote)* sedel *c* 130
notebook anteckningsbok *c* 105
note paper brevpapper *nt* 105
nothing ingenting 15; inget 16, 17
notice *(sign)* anslag *nt* 155
notify, to underrätta 144
November november *(c)* 150
now nu 15
number nummer *nt* 25, 135, 136; räkneord *nt* 147
nurse sköterska *c* 144

O

observatory observatorium *nt* 81
occupation yrke *nt* 25
occupied upptagen 14, 155
o'clock klockan *c* 154
October oktober *(c)* 150
octopus bläckfisk *c* 45
office kontor *nt* 132
oil olja *c* 37, 75, 111
oily *(greasy)* fet 30, 111
old gammal 14, 149
old town gamla stan *c* 81
omelet omelett *c* 45
on på 15
once en gång 148
one ett 147
one-way *(ticket)* enkel (biljett *c*) 65, 69
on foot till fots 76
onion lök *c* 51
only bara 15, 24, 80
on time i tid 68
open öppen 14, 82, 155
open, to öppna 11, 17, 82, 108, 130, 132, 142
opening hours öppettider *c/pl* 155
opera opera *c* 88
opera house opera *c* 81, 88
operation operation *c* 144
operetta operett *c* 88
opposite mitt emot 77
optician optiker *c* 99, 123
or eller 15
orange orange 113
orange apelsin *c* 54
orange juice apelsinjuice *c* 38, 59
orchestra orkester *c* 88; *(seats)* parkett *c* 87
order beställning *c* 40, 102
order, to beställa 36, 60, 102, 103
ornithology ornitologi *c* 83
other andra 58, 74
our vår, vårt *(pl* våra) 161
out of order trasig 136; ur funktion 155
out of stock slut på lagret 103
outlet *(electric)* uttag *nt* 27
outside ute 15, 36
oval oval 101
overalls overall *c* 116
overdone för mycket stekt 60
overheat, to *(engine)* gå varm 78
overnight *(stay)* över natt 24
overtake, to köra om 79
owe, to vara skyldig 144
oyster ostron *nt* 43

P

pacifier napp *c* 111
packet paket *nt* 120, 126
page *(hotel)* pickolo *c* 26
pail hink *c* 106, 128
pain smärta *c* 140, 143
paint, to måla 83
paintbox färglåda *c* 105
painter konstnär *c* 83
painting måleri *nt* 83
pair par *nt* 116, 118, 148
pajamas pyjamas *c* 117
palace slott *nt* 81
palpitation hjärtklappning *c* 141
pancake pannkaka *c* 45; *(small)* plätt *c* 55
panties trosor *c/pl* 116
pants *(trousers)* (lång)byxor *c/pl* 116
panty girdle byxgördel *c* 116
panty hose strumpbyxor *c/pl* 117
paper papper *nt* 105
paperback pocketbok *c* 105
paperclip gem *nt* 105
paper napkin pappersservett *c* 105, 106
paraffin *(fuel)* fotogen *c* 106
parcel paket *nt* 132

DICTIONARY Ordlista

pardon förlåt 11
parents föräldrar *c/pl* 93
park park *c* 81
park, to parkera 26, 77
parka anorak *c* 117
parking parkering *c* 77, 79
parking meter parkeringsautomat *c* 77
parliament riksdag *c* 81
parliament building riksdagshus *nt* 81
parsley persilja *c* 53
part del *c* 138
party *(social gathering)* fest *c* 95
pass, to *(overtake)* köra om 79
passport pass *nt* 16, 17, 25, 26, 156
passport photo passfoto *nt* 124
pass through, to vara på genomresa 16
paste *(glue)* klister *nt* 105
pastry bakverk *nt* 63
pastry shop konditori *nt* 99
path stig *c* 85
patient patient *c* 144
pattern mönster *nt* 112
pay, to betala 31, 61, 100, 102
payment betalning *c* 102, 131
pea ärta *c* 51
peach persika *c* 54
peak topp *c* 85
pear päron *nt* 54
pearl pärla *c* 122
peg *(tent)* pinne *c* 107
pen bläckpenna *c* 105
pencil blyertspenna *c* 105
pencil sharpener pennvässare *c* 105
pendant hängsmycke *nt* 121
penicilline penicillin *nt* 143
penknife pennkniv *c* 106
pensioner pensionär *c* 82
people människor *c/pl* 92
pepper peppar *c* 37, 38, 53
per cent procent *c* 148
percentage procentsats *c* 131
perch abborre *c* 45, 47
per day per dag 20, 32, 89
perfume parfym *c* 110
perfume shop parfymeri *nt* 99
perhaps kanske 15
per hour per timme 77, 89
period *(monthly)* mens(truation) *c* 141
period pains mens(truations)-smärtor *c/pl* 141
permanent wave permanent *c* 30
per night per natt 24
per person per person 32
person person *c* 32
personal personlig 17
personal call personligt samtal *nt* 134
person-to-person call personligt samtal *nt* 134
per week per vecka 20, 24
petrol bensin *c* 75, 78
pewter tenn *nt* 122
pheasant fasan *c* 50
photo foto *nt* 124; kort *nt* 125
photocopy fotokopia *c* 131
photograph, to fotografera 82
photographer fotograf *c* 99
photography fotografering *c* 124
phrase uttryck *nt* 12
pick up, to *(person)* hämta 80, 96
pickled gherkin ättiksgurka *c* 51, 64
picnic picknick *c* 64
picture *(painting)* tavla *c* 83; *(photo)* bild *nt* 105
picture-book bilderbok *c* 105
piece bit *c* 63, 120
pier pir *c* 74
pill tablett *c* 109, 143; *(contraceptive)* p-piller *nt* 141
pillow kudde *c* 27
pin nål *c* 110, 111, 122
pineapple ananas *c* 54
pink rosa 113
pipe pipa *c* 126
pipe cleaner piprensare *c* 126
pipe tool pipverktyg *nt* 126
place ort *c* 25; plats *c* 76
place of birth födelseort *c* 25
plaice rödspätta *c* 46
plane flyg *nt* 65
planetarium planetarium *nt* 81
plaster, to *(cast)* gipsa 140
plastic plast *c* 107
plastic bag plastpåse *c* 107
plate tallrik *c* 36, 60, 107
platform *(station)* perrong *c* 67, 68, 69, 70
platinum platina *c* 122
play *(theatre)* pjäs *c* 86
play, to spela 86, 88, 89, 93
playground lekplats *c* 32
playing card spelkort *nt* 105
please var snäll och ... 10; tack 10
plimsoll tennissko *c* 118
plug *(electric)* stickkontakt *c* 29, 119
plum plommon *nt* 54
pneumonia lunginflammation *c* 142

poached pocherad 46; *(egg)* förlorat 45
pocket ficka *c* 117
pocket calculator fickräknare *c* 105
pocket dictionary fickordbok *c* 104
pocket watch fickur *nt* 121
point, to peka 12
poison gift *nt* 109, 156
poisoning förgiftning *c* 142
Poland Polen *(nt)* 146
pole *(ski)* stav *c* 91; *(tent)* stång *c* 107
police polis *c* 78, 156
police station polisstation *c* 99, 156
pond damm *c* 85
pork fläskkött *nt* 48
port hamn *c* 74; *(wine)* portvin *nt* 58
portable bärbar 119
porter bärare *c* 18, 26, 71
portion portion *c* 37, 60
possible möjlig 137
post *(mail)* post *c* 133; brev *nt* 28
post, to posta 28
postage porto *nt* 132
postage stamp frimärke *nt* 28, 126, 132
postcard vykort *nt* 105, 126, 132
poste restante poste restante 133
post office postkontor *nt* 99, 132; post *c* 132
pot kanna *c* 59
potato potatis *c* 51
pottery lergods *nt* 83
poultry fågel *c* 50
pound *(money)* pund *nt* 18, 102, 130; *(weight)* halvt kilo *nt* 120
powder puder *nt* 110
powder compact puderdosa *c* 122
prawn räka *c* 43, 46
prefere, to föredra 101
pregnant gravid 141
premium *(gasoline)* högoktanig 75
prescribe, to skriva ut 143
prescription recept *nt* 108, 143; ordination *c* 143
present present *c* 17, 121
press, to *(iron)* pressa 29
press stud tryckknapp *c* 117
pressure tryck *nt* 75, 141
pretty söt 84
price pris *nt* 24
priest katolsk präst *c* 84
print *(photo)* kopia *c* 125
private privat 79, 80, 155
processing *(photo)* framkallning *c* 124, 125
profession yrke *nt* 25
profit vinst *c* 131
programme program *nt* 87
prohibit, to förbjuda 79
pronunciation uttal *nt* 6
propelling pencil stiftpenna *c* 105, 122
propose, to rekommendera 40
Protestant protestantisk 84
provide, to skaffa 131
prune katrinplommon *nt* 54, 55
public holiday allmän helgdag *c* 152
pull, to dra 155
pullover jumper *c*, tröja *c* 117
puncture punktering *c* 75
purchase köp *nt* 131
pure ren 114
push, to *(button)* trycka 155
put, to ställa 24
pyjamas pyjamas *c* 117

Q

quality kvalitet *c* 103, 113
quantity kvantitet *c* 14
quarter fjärdedel *c* 148; *(part of town)* kvarter *nt* 81
quarter of an hour kvart *c* 153
quartz quartz 122
question fråga *c* 11
quick snabb 14
quickly fort 79, 137, 156
quiet tyst 23, 25

R

rabbi rabbin *c* 84
race tävling *c* 89
race course/track hästkapplöpningsbana *c* 90
racket *(sport)* racket *c* 90
radiator *(car)* kylare *c* 78
radio *(set)* radio *c* 23, 28, 119
radish rädisa *c* 51
railway järnväg *c* 154
railroad crossing järnvägskorsning *c* 79
railway station järnvägsstation *c* 19, 21, 67
rain regn *nt* 94
rain, to regna 94
raincoat *(man's)* regnrock *c* 117; *(woman's)* regnkappa *c* 117

raisin russin *nt* 54
rangefinder ljusmätare *c* 125
rare *(meat)* blodig 49, 60
rash utslag *nt* 139
raspberry hallon *nt* 54
rate *(price)* pris *nt* 20; *(exchange)* kurs *c* 18, 130
razor rakhyvel *c* 110
razor blade rakblad *nt* 110
reading-lamp läslampa *c* 27
ready klar 29, 31, 118, 123, 125, 145
real *(genuine)* äkta 118, 121
rear bak 75
receipt kvitto *nt* 103, 144
reception reception *c* 23
receptionist receptionist *c* 26
recommend, to rekommendera 35, 36, 88, 137, 145; *(suggest)* föreslå 35, 44, 80
record *(disc)* skiva *c* 127, 128
record player skivspelare *c* 119
rectangular rektangulär 101
red röd 58, 113
reduction rabatt *c* 24, 82
refill *(pen)* refill *c* 105
refund, to get a få pengarna tillbaka 103
regards hälsningar *c/pl* 152
register, to *(luggage)* pollettera 71
registered mail rekommenderat 133
registration incheckning *c* 25
registration form inskrivningsblankett *c* 25
regular *(petrol)* lågoktanig 75
reindeer ren *c* 42, 50
religion religion *c* 83
religious service gudstjänst *c* 84
rent, to hyra 19, 20, 74, 90, 91, 119, 155
rental uthyrning *c* 20, 74
repair reparation *c* 125
repair, to laga 29, 118, 119, 121, 123, 125, 145
repeat, to upprepa 12
report, to *(a theft)* anmäla 156
reservation reservation *c* 19, 65; beställning *c* 69
reservations office biljettkontor *nt* 19, 67
reserve, to beställa 19, 23, 36, 87; reservera 69, 155
restaurant restaurang *c* 19, 32, 33, 35, 67
return *(ticket)* tur och retur 65, 69
return, to *(come back)* vara tillbaka 21, 80; *(give back)* lämna tillbaka 103
reverse-charge call Ba-samtal *nt* 135
revue revy *c* 86
rheumatism reumatism *c* 141
rhubarb rabarber *c* 54
rib revben *nt* 138
ribbon band *nt* 105
rice ris *nt* 51
right höger 21, 62, 69, 77; *(correct)* rätt 14, 70
ring *(on finger)* ring *c* 122
ring, to ringa 134, 155
river flod *c* 85, 90
road väg *c* 76, 77, 85
road assistance hjälp på vägen *c* 78
road map vägkarta *c* 105
road sign vägmärke *nt* 79
roasted stekt 49
roast beef rostbiff *c* 48
roll *(bread)* småfranska *nt* 38; bröd *nt* 62
roller skates rullskridskor *c/pl* 128
roll film filmrulle *c* 124
romantic romantisk 84
room rum *nt* 19, 23, 24, 25; *(space)* plats *c* 32
room number rumsnummer *nt* 26
room service rumsbetjäning *c* 23
rope rep *nt* 107
rosé rosé 58
rouge rouge *nt* 110
round rund 101
round *(golf)* runda *c* 89
round-neck rundringad 117
round trip *(ticket)* tur och retur 65, 69
route väg *c* 85
rowing boat roddbåt *c* 74, 91
royal kunglig 82
rubber *(material)* gummi *nt* 118; *(eraser)* radergummi *nt* 105
rubber band gummisnodd *c* 105
rucksack ryggsäck *c* 107
ruin ruin *c* 81
ruler *(for measuring)* linjal *c* 105
rum rom *c* 58
running water rinnande vatten *nt* 23

S

safe *(not dangerous)* riskfri 90
safe kassaskåp *nt* 26
safety pin säkerhetsnål *c* 110
sailing boat segelbåt *c* 74, 91
salad sallad *c* 44, 51
sale försäljning *c* 131; *(bargains)* rea(lisation) *c* 100, 155
sales tax moms *c* 24, 102
salmon lax *c* 42, 43, 46, 47
salmon trout laxöring *c* 46
salt salt *nt* 37, 38, 53,
salty salt 60
sand sand *c* 90
sandal sandal *c* 118
sandwich sandwich *c* 43; smörgås *c* 62
sanitary towel/napkin dambinda *c* 109
sardine sardin *c* 46
satin satin *c* 114
Saturday lördag *c* 150
sauce sås *c* 52
saucepan kastrull *c* 107
saucer tefat *nt* 107
sauna bastu *c* 23, 32
sausage korv *c* 48, 64
scarf scarf *c* 117
school skola *c* 79
school holidays skollov *nt* 151
scissors sax *c* 107, 110
scooter skoter *c* 74
Scotland Skottland *(nt)* 146
scrambled egg äggröra *c* 38, 45
screwdriver skruvmejsel *c* 107
sculptor skulptör *c* 83
sculpture skulptur *c* 83
sea hav *nt* 85, 90
seafood skaldjur *nt/pl* 45
season årstid *c* 149
seasoning krydda *c* 37
seat plats *c* 69, 70, 87
seat belt bilbälte *nt* 75
second andra 153
second sekund *c* 153
second class andra klass *c* 69
second hand sekundvisare *c* 122
second-hand (*book*) antikvarisk 104
second-hand shop andrahandsaffär *c* 99
secretary sekreterare *c* 27, 131
see, to se 12, 89; *(examine)* undersöka 137
sell, to sälja 100
send, to skicka 78, 102, 103, 132, 133
send up, to skicka upp 26
sentence mening *c* 12
September september *(c)* 150
serve, to servera 41
service (charge) betjäningsavgift *c* 24; serveringsavgift *c* 61; *(religion)* gudstjänst *c* 84
serviette servett *c* 36
set menu meny *c* 36, 40
setting lotion läggningsvätska *c* 30, 111
seven sju 147
seventeen sjutton 147
seventh sjunde 148
seventy sjuttio 147
sew, to sy 29
shade *(colour)* nyans *c* 112
shallow långgrunt 90
shampoo shampo *nt* 30, 111
shampoo and set tvättning och läggning *c* 30
shape form *c* 103
share *(finance)* aktie *c* 131
shave rakning *c* 31
shaver rakapparat *c* 27, 119
shaving brush rakborste *c* 111
shaving cream rakkräm *c* 111
she hon 162
sherry sherry *c* 58
ship fartyg *nt* 74
shirt skjorta *c* 117
shoe sko *c* 118
shoelace skosnöre *nt* 118
shoemaker's skomakare *c* 99
shoe polish skokräm *c* 118
shoe shop skoaffär *c* 99
shop affär *c* 98
shopping shopping *c* 97
shopping area affärscentrum *nt* 81, 100
shopping centre shoppingcenter *nt* 99
shop window (skylt)fönster *nt* 100, 112
short kort 30, 116
shorts shorts *c/pl* 117
short-sighted närsynt 123
shoulder axel *c* 138
shovel spade *c* 128
show show *c* 88; *(theatre)* föreställning *c* 87
show, to visa 12, 13, 76, 100, 101, 119, 124

shower dusch *c* 23, 32
shrimp räka *c* 43, 46, 62
shrink, to krympa 114
shut stängd 14
shutter *(camera)* slutare *c* 125
sick *(ill)* sjuk 140, 156
sickness *(illness)* sjukdom *c* 140
side sida *c* 30
sideboards/burns polisonger *c/pl* 31
sightseeing sightseeing *c* 80
sightseeing tour sightseeingtur *c* 80
sign *(notice)* skylt *c* 79, 155
sign, to skriva under 26, 130
signature underskrift *c* 25
signet ring signetring *c* 122
silk siden *nt*, silke *nt* 114
silver *(colour)* silverfärgad 113
silver silver *nt* 121, 122
silver plate nysilver *nt* 122
silversmith silversmed *c* 99
simple enkel 124
since sedan 15, 150
sing, to sjunga 88
single *(not married)* ogift 93; *(ticket)* enkel 65, 69
single room enkelrum *nt* 19, 23
sister syster *c* 93
sit down, to sätta sig 95
six sex 147
sixteen sexton 147
sixth sjätte 148
sixty sextio 147
size format *nt* 124; *(clothes)* storlek *c* 114, 115, 118
skate skridsko *c* 91
skating rink skridskobana *c* 91
ski skida *c* 91
ski, to åka skidor 91
ski boot pjäxa *c* 91
skiing skidåkning *c* 89
ski lift skidlift *c* 91
skin hud *c* 138
skirt kjol *c* 117
ski run (skid)backe *c* 91
sky himmel *c* 94
sleep, to sova 144
sleeping bag sovsäck *c* 107
sleeping car sovvagn *c* 68, 69, 70
sleeping pill sömntablett *c* 143
sleeve ärm *c* 117
slice skiva *c* 120
slide *(photo)* diapositiv *nt* 124
slip underklänning *c* 117
slipper toffel *c* 118
slow långsam 14
slow down, to köra sakta 79
slowly långsamt 12, 21, 135
small liten 14, 20, 25, 101, 118
smoke, to röka 95
smoked rökt 42, 43, 46, 49
smoker rökare *c* 70, 155
snack mellanmål *nt* 63
snack bar snackbar *c* 67
snail snigel *c* 43
snap fastener tryckknapp *c* 117
sneakers tennisskor *c/pl* 118
snorkel snorkel *c* 128
snow snö *c* 94
snow, to snöa 94
snuff snus *nt* 126
soap tvål *c* 27, 111
soccer fotboll *c* 89
sock socka *c* 117
socket *(outlet)* uttag *nt* 27
soda water sodavatten *nt* 58
soft mjuk 123
soft-boiled *(egg)* löskokt 38
soft drink juice *c*, läsk *c* 59
sold out *(theatre)* utsålt 87, 155
sole sula *c* 118; *(fish)* sjötunga *c* 46
soloist solist *c* 88
some några 15
someone någon 31, 95
something något 29, 36, 108, 112, 125, 139; någonting 55,113
somewhere någonstans 87
son son *c* 93
song sång *c* 128
soon snart 15, 137
sore *(painful)* öm 145
sore throat ont i halsen 141
sorry *(I'm)* förlåt 11, 16; jag är ledsen 103
sort *(kind)* slag *nt* 86; sort *c* 120
soup soppa *c* 44
sour cream gräddfil *c* 52
south söder 77
South Africa Sydafrika *(nt)* 146
South America Sydamerika *(nt)* 146
souvenir souvenir *c* 127
souvenir shop souveniraffär *c* 99
Soviet Union Sovjetunionen *(nt)* 146
spade spade *c* 128
Spain Spanien *(nt)* 146
sparerib revbensspjäll *nt* 42, 48
spare tyre reservdäck *nt* 75
spark(ing) plug tändstift *nt* 75
sparkling *(wine)* mousserande 58
speak, to tala 12, 135

speaker *(loudspeaker)* högtalare *c* 119
special special- 20, 37
special delivery express 133
specialist specialist *c* 142
speciality specialitet *c* 36
specimen *(medical)* prov *nt* 142
spectacle case glasögonfordral *nt* 123
spell, to bokstavera 12
spend, to lägga ut 101
spice krydda *c* 50
spinach spenat *c* 51
spine ryggrad *c* 138
sponge tvättsvamp *c* 111
sponge bag necessär *c* 111
spoon sked *c* 36, 60, 107
sport sport *c* 89
sporting goods shop sportaffär *c* 99
sprain, to vricka 140
sprat skarpsill *c* 46
spring *(season)* vår *c* 149; *(water)* källa *c* 85
square kvadratisk 101
square torg *nt* 82
stadium stadion *nt* 82
staff personal *c* 26
stain fläck *c* 29
stainless steel rostfritt stål *nt* 107, 122
stalls *(theatre)* parkett *c* 87
stamp *(postage)* frimärke *nt* 28, 126, 132, 133
stapler häftapparat *c* 105
staple häftklammer *c* 105
star stjärna *c* 94
start, to börja 87, 88; starta 80; *(car)* starta 78
starter *(appetizer)* förrätt *c* 43
station *(railway)* (järnvägs)station *c* 19, 21, 67, 70; *(underground, subway)* tunnelbanestation *c* 73
stationer's pappershandel *c* 99, 104
statue staty *c* 82
stay vistelse *c* 31
stay, to stanna 16, 24, 26; *(reside)* bo 93
steak tartare råbiff *c* 48
steal, to stjäla 156
steamed ångkokt 46
steamer ångbåt *c* 74
stew pot gryta *c* 107
stewed stuvad 49
stiff neck stel nacke *c* 141
still *(mineral water)* utan kolsyra 59
sting stick *nt* 139
sting, to bita 139
stitch, to *(clothes)* sy ihop 29, 118
stock *(in shop)* lager *nt* 103
stock exchange (fond)börs *c* 82
stocking strumpa *c* 117
stomach mage *c* 138
stomach ache ont i magen 141
stools avföring *c* 142
stop *(bus)* (buss)hållplats *c* 72
stop, to stanna 21, 68, 70, 72
stop thief! stoppa tjuven! 156
store *(shop)* affär *c* 98
straight *(drink)* ren 58
straight ahead rakt fram 21, 77
strange underlig 84
strawberry jordgubbe *c* 54, 55
street gata *c* 25
streetcar spårvagn *c* 72
street map karta *c* 19, 105
string snöre *nt* 105
strong stark 126, 143
student studerande *c* 82
study, to studera 93
stuffed fylld 51
sturdy kraftig 101
subway *(railway)* tunnelbana *c* 73
suede mocka *c* 114, 118
sugar socker *nt* 37, 64
suit *(man's)* kostym *c* 117; *(woman's)* dräkt *c* 117
suitcase väska *c* 18
summer sommar *c* 149
sun sol *c* 94
sunburn solsveda *c* 108
Sunday söndag *c* 150
sunglasses solglasögon *c/pl* 123
sunshade *(beach)* parasoll *nt* 91
sunstroke solsting *nt* 141
sun-tan cream solkräm *c* 110
sun-tan oil sololja *c* 111
super *(petrol)* högoktanig 75
superb utomordentlig 84
supermarket snabbköp *nt* 99
suppository stolpiller *nt* 109
surcharge extra kostnad *c* 40
surgery *(consulting room)* läkarmottagning *c* 137
surname efternamn *nt* 25
suspenders *(Am.)* hängslen *nt/pl* 117
swallow, to svälja 143
sweater tröja *c* 117
sweatshirt sweatshirt *c* 117

Sweden Sverige *(nt)* 146
Swedish svensk 18, 114
Swedish svenska *c* 11, 12, 98
sweet söt 54, 58, 60
sweet *(candy)* godis *c* 126
sweet corn majs *c* 50
sweetener sötningsmedel *nt* 37
sweet pepper paprika *c* 51
sweet shop godisaffär *c* 99
swell, to svullna 139
swelling svullnad *c* 139
swim, to simma, bada 90
swimming simning *c* 89; badning *c* 91
swimming pool simbassäng *c* 23, 32, 90
swimming trunks badbyxor *c/pl* 117
swimsuit baddräkt *c* 117
switch *(light)* strömbrytare *c* 29
switchboard operator telefonist *c* 26
swollen svullen 139
synagogue synagoga *c* 84
synthetic syntetisk 114
system system *nt* 138

T

table bord *nt* 36, 107; *(list)* tabell *c* 157
table tennis bordtennis *c* 89
tablet tablett *c* 109
tailor's skräddare *c* 99
take, to ta 18, 25, 60, 73, 76, 102
take away, to *(carry)* ta med 62, 102
talcum powder talkpuder *nt* 111
tampon tampong *c* 109
tap *(water)* kran *c* 28
tape recorder bandspelare *c* 119
tarragon dragon *c* 53
taste, to smaka 60
taxi taxi *c* 18, 19, 21, 31, 67
tea te *nt* 38, 59, 64
team lag *nt* 89
tear, to *(ligament)* slita av 140
teaspoon tesked *c* 107, 143
telegram telegram *nt* 133
telegraph office telegraf *c* 99, 133; telebutik *c* 134
telephone telefon *c* 27, 28, 78, 134
telephone, to ringa 134, 136
telephone booth telefonkiosk *c* 134
telephone call (telefon)samtal *nt* 136; telefon *c* 136
telephone directory telefonkatalog *c* 134
telephone number (telefon)nummer *nt* 134, 135, 136
telephoto lens teleobjektiv *nt* 125
television *(set)* TV *c* 23, 28, 119
telex telex *nt* 133
telex, to skicka ett telex 130
tell, to säga 13, 72, 76, 153; tala om 76, 136
temperature temperatur *c* 142; *(fever)* feber *c* 140
temporary provisorisk 145
ten tio 147
tendon sena *c* 138
tennis tennis *c* 89
tennis court tennisbana *c* 89
tennis racket tennisracket *nt* 90
tent tält *nt* 32, 107
tenth tionde 148
tent peg tältpinne *c* 107
tent pole tältstång *c* 107
terrible hemsk 84
tetanus stelkramp *c* 140
than än 14
thank you tack 10, 95, 96
that den där 160; det där 11, 100, 160
theatre teater *c* 82, 86
theft stöld *c* 156
their deras 161
then då, sedan 15
there där 13
thermometer termometer *c* 109, 144
these de här 62, 160
they de, dem 162
thief tjuv *c* 156
thigh lår *nt* 138
thin tunn 113
think, to *(believe)* tro 31, 94
third tredje 148
third tredjedel *c* 148
thirsty törstig 13, 35
thirteen tretton 147
thirty trettio 147
this den här 160; det här 11, 100, 160
those de där 62, 120, 160
thousand tusen 148
thread tråd *c* 27
three tre 147
throat hals *c* 138, 141
throat lozenge halstablett *c* 109
through genom 15

through train direktgående tåg *nt* 68, 69
thumb tumme *c* 138
thumbtack häftstift *nt* 105
thunder åska *c* 94
thunderstorm åskväder *nt* 94
Thursday torsdag *c* 150
ticket biljett *c* 65, 69, 72, 87, 89
ticket office biljettluckan *c* 67
tie slips *c* 117
tie clip slipshållare *c* 122
tie pin kravattnål *c* 122
tight *(clothes)* trång 116
tights strumpbyxor *c/pl* 117
time tid *c* 80; *(occasion)* gång *c* 95, 148
timetable tidtabell *c* 68
tin *(can)* burk *c* 120
tinfoil aluminiumfolie *c* 107
tin opener konservöppnare *c* 107
tint toningsmedel *nt* 111
tint, to tona 30
tinted färgad 123
tire däck *nt* 75
tired trött 13
tissue *(handkerchief)* pappersnäsduk *c* 111
tissue paper silkespapper *nt* 105
to till 15
toast rostat bröd *nt* 38
tobacco tobak *c* 126
tobacconist's tobaksaffär *c* 99, 126
today idag 29, 150, 151
toe tå *c* 138
toilet paper toalettpapper *nt* 111
toiletry toilettartikel *c* 110
toilets toalett *c* 27, 32, 37, 67
toilet water eau de toilette *c* 111
tomato tomat *c* 51
tomato juice tomatjuice *c* 59
tomb grav *c* 82
tomorrow i morgon 29, 96, 151
tongs tång *c* 107
tongue tunga *c* 48, 138
tonic water tonic *c* 59
tonight i kväll 29, 86, 87, 96
tonsils mandlar *c/pl* 138
too för 15; *(also)* också 15
tooth tand *c* 145
toothache tandvärk *c* 145
toothbrush tandborste *c* 111, 119
toothpaste tandkräm *c* 111
torch *(flashlight)* ficklampa *c* 107
torn *(ligament)* avsliten 140
touch, to (vid)röra 155
tough *(meat)* seg 60
tour tur *c* 80
tourist office turistbyrå *c* 22, 80
towards mot 15
towel handduk *c* 111
tower torn *nt* 82
town stad *c* 19, 88
town hall rådhus *nt* 82
tow truck bärgningsbil *c* 78
toy leksak *c* 128
toy shop leksaksaffär *c* 99
track *(station)* spår *nt* 67, 68, 69
tracksuit träningsoverall *c* 117
traffic trafik *c* 76
traffic light trafikljus *nt* 77
trailer husvagn *c* 32
train tåg *nt* 66, 67, 68, 69, 70
tram spårvagn *c* 72
tranquillizer något nervlugnande 143
transfer *(bank)* överföring *c* 131
transformer transformator *c* 119
translate, to översätta 12
transport transport *c* 74
travel, to resa 92
travel agency resebyrå *c* 99
travel guide reseguide *c* 105
traveller's cheque resecheck *c* 18, 61, 102, 130
travelling bag bag *c* 18
travel sickness åksjuka *c* 108
treatment behandling *c* 143
tree träd *nt* 85
tremendous förfärlig 84
trim, to *(beard)* putsa 31
trip resa *c* 93, 152; tur *c* 73
trolley kärra *c* 18, 71
trousers (lång)byxor *nt/pl* 117
trout forell *c* 45
try, to försöka 135; *(try on)* prova 115; *(sample)* smaka 63, 64
T-shirt T-shirt *c* 117
tube tub *c* 120
Tuesday tisdag *c* 150
tumbler dricksglas *nt* 107
tuna/tunny tonfisk *c* 44, 46
turbot piggvar *c* 46
turkey kalkon *c* 50
turn, to *(change direction)* svänga 21, 77
turquoise turkos 113
turquoise turkos *c* 122
turtleneck polokrage *c* 117

tweezers pincett *c* 111
twelve tolv 147
twenty tjugo 147
twice två gånger 148
twin beds två sängar *c/pl* 23
two två 147
typewriter skrivmaskin *c* 27
typewriter ribbon skrivmaskinsband *nt* 105
typically typisk 127
typing paper skrivmaskinspapper *nt* 105
tyre däck *nt* 75, 76

U

ugly ful 14, 84
umbrella paraply *nt* 117; *(beach)* parasoll *nt* 91
uncle farbror *c*, morbror *c* 93
unconscious medvetslös 139
under under 15
underdone *(meat)* blodig 49, 61
underground *(railway)* tunnelbana *c* 73
underpants kalsonger *c/pl* 117
undershirt undertröja *c* 117
understand, to förstå 12, 16
undress, to klä av sig 142
United States USA *(nt)* 146
university universitet *nt* 82
unleaded blyfri 75
until till 15, 150
up upp 15
upper över- 69
upset stomach orolig mage *c* 108
upstairs där uppe 15; uppför trappan 69
urgent brådskande 13
urine urin *c* 142
use bruk *nt* 17, 109
useful användbar 15
usual vanlig 143

V

vacancy ledigt rum *nt* 23
vacant ledig 14
vacation semester *c* 157
vaccinate, to vaccinera 140
vacuum flask termos *c* 107
vaginal infection underlivsinfektion *c* 141
valley dal *c* 85
value värde *nt* 131
value-added tax moms *c* 24, 102, 154
vanilla vanilj *c* 55
vase vas *c* 127
VAT *(sales tax)* moms *c* 24, 102, 154
veal kalv *c* 48, 49
vegetable grönsak *c* 40, 51
vegetable store grönsaksaffär *c* 99
vegetarian vegetarisk 37
vein ven *c*, åder *c* 138
velvet sammet *c* 114
velveteen bomullssammet *c* 114
venereal disease könssjukdom *c* 142
venetian blind persienn *c* 29
venison rådjur *nt* 50
vermouth vermouth *c* 58
very mycket 15
vest undertröja *c* 117; *(Am.)* väst *c* 117
veterinarian veterinär *c* 99
video cassette videokassett *c* 119, 127
video recorder videobandspelare *c* 119
view utsikt *c* 23, 25
village samhälle *nt* 76; by *c* 85
vinegar vinäger *c* 37
visit, to *(a person)* hälsa på 95; *(a place)* titta på 84
visit besök *nt* 92
visiting hours besökstid *c* 144
vitamin pill vitamintablett *c* 109
V-neck V-ringad 117
vodka vodka *c* 58
voltage spänning *c* 27
vomit, to kräkas 140

W

waistcoat väst *c* 117
wait, to vänta 21, 95, 108, 155
waiter kypare *c*, servitör *c* 26
waiting room väntsal *c* 67
waitress servitris *c* 26
wake, to väcka 27, 71
Wales Wales *(nt)* 146
walk, to gå 74, 85
wall mur *c* 85
wallet plånbok *c* 156
walnut valnöt *c* 54
want, to vilja, *(wish)* önska 13
warm varm 94
wash to tvätta 29, 114
wash basin handfat *nt* 28

washing powder tvättmedel *nt* 107
washing-up liquid diskmedel *nt* 107
watch klocka *c* 121, 122
watchmaker's urmakare *c* 99, 121
watchstrap klockarmband *nt* 122
water vatten *nt* 23, 28, 32, 38, 75, 90
waterfall vattenfall *nt* 85
water flask fältflaska *c* 107
watermelon vattenmelon *c* 54
waterproof vattentät 122
water ski vattenskida *c* 91
way väg *c* 76, 77
we vi 162
weather väder *nt* 94
weather forecast väderleksutsikt *c* 94
wedding ring vigselring *c* 122
Wednesday onsdag *c* 150
week vecka *c* 16, 20, 24, 80, 151
weekend weekend *c* 151
well bra 10, 140
well källa *c* 85
well-done *(meat)* genomstekt 49
west väster 77
wet paint nymålat 155
what vad 11
wheel hjul *nt* 78
when när 11
where var 11
which vilken 11
whipped cream vispgrädde *c* 55
whisky whisky *c* 17, 58
white vit 58, 113
Whit Sunday Pingstdagen *c* 152
who vem 11
why varför 11
wick veke *c* 126
wide bred 118
wide-angle lens vidvinkelobjektiv *nt* 125
wife fru *c* 93
wig peruk *c* 111
wild duck vildand *c* 50
wind vind *c* 94
window fönster *nt* 28, 36; *(shop)* skyltfönster *nt* 100, 112
window seat plats vid fönstret *c* 65; fönsterplats *c* 69
windscreen/shield vindruta *c* 76
wine vin *nt* 57, 60
wine list vinlista *c* 59
wine merchant's systembolag *nt* 99
winter vinter *c* 149
winter sports vintersport *c* 91
wiper vindrutetorkare *c* 75
wish gratulation *c* 151; välgångsönskning *c* 152
with med 15
withdraw, to *(bank)* ta ut 131
without utan 15
woman kvinna *c* 156; dam *c* 115
wonderful underbar 96
wood *(material)* trä *nt* 127; *(forest)* skog *c* 85
wood alcohol rödsprit *c* 107
wool ull *c*, ylle *nt* 114
word ord *nt* 12, 15, 133
work arbete *nt* 79
work, to arbeta 79; *(function)* fungera 28, 119
working day arbetsdag *c* 151
worse sämre 14
wound sår *nt* 139
wrap, to slå in 103
wrapping paper omslagspapper *nt* 105
wrinkle resistant skrynkelfri 114
wristwatch armbandsur *nt* 122
write, to skriva 12, 101
writing pad skrivblock *nt* 105
writing-paper brevpapper *nt* 27
wrong fel 14, 135

X

X-ray *(photo)* röntgenbild *c* 140

Y

year år *nt* 149
yellow gul 113
yes ja 10
yesterday igår 151
yet än 15, 16
yield, to *(traffic)* lämna företräde 79
yoghurt yoghurt *c* 38, 64
you du, ni 10, 162
young ung 14, 149
your din, ditt (*pl* dina) 161; er, ert (*pl* era) 161
youth hostel vandrarhem *nt* 22, 32

Z

zero noll 147
zip(per) blixtlås *nt* 117
zoo djurpark *c* 82
zoology zoologi *c* 83

Svenskt register

N
ATLANTIC OCEAN
Kiruna
Gällivare
Arjeplog
Luleå
Vilhelmina
Umeå
Östersund
SWEDEN
Sundsvall
GULF OF BOTHNIA
FINLAND
Mora
Gävle
NORWAY
OSLO
HELSINKI
Uppsala
Västerås
Mälaren
GULF OF FINLAN
Strömstad
Vänern
STOCKHOLM
SKAGERRAK
Linköping
Vättern
Göteborg
Västervik
Visby
KATTEGAT
Jönköping
Gotland
Halmstad
USS
NORTH SEA
DENMARK
Helsingborg
Öland
BALTIC SEA
Karlskrona
Lund
COPENHAGEN
Malmö